"Don't Be This Girl"

BY

CYNDI GALLEY & IVETTE P. OSBORNE

Don't Be This Girl!
by Cyndi Galley & Ivette P. Osborne
First Edition, November 2023

Published by New Gal Publishing in partnership with Holland Robinson Publishing

ISBN: 978-1-961074-05-7
Cover design by: Cyndi Galley
Interior layout by: Kalo Creative
Printed in the United States of America

To Evelyn, Olivia, Parker, Samantha ...

May the words of love in this book be a gift of wisdom to you and women in the generations to come.

CONTENTS

Acknowledgements

From Cyndi:

To my mom and my dads, thank you for supporting the dreams in my heart—even when I've felt like quitting or giving up. The words of life you've given continue to speak to my heart. The prayers you've prayed continue to lead and strengthen me to do what I know in my heart, needs to be done. And thank you for the life we've lived, with moments and memories shared, giving me the stories and life experiences to include in this book.

I am thankful for my pastors, Jerry & Kimberly Dirmann, and for every mentor, teacher and pastor who has poured into me, teaching me the word, which without it, I would be even more of the hot mess I already am (can you imagine that?!).

To my team at New Gal Global, I thank you for releasing me to write this book. If it wasn't for each one of you selflessly carrying your part in our media & ministry, I wouldn't have been able to write this book. I wouldn't have had the time. Thank you!

A huge shout out to Dyanna Hoage, for your faithfulness in proofing for New Gal ... and a huge shout of thanks to Michelle Robinson for picking this book up and publishing it, so that you could read what is in your hand now.

To my Lord & Savior, Jesus, I am forever thankful for your unconditional and unrelenting love that has picked me up as a single daughter of the King, time and time again. I wouldn't be living the life I live, with the joy I've been given, had it not been for You.

From Ivette:

To Kyle, my best friend, husband and partner in life. Thank you for always believing in me and supporting me through this and so many other projects. Thank you for the countless meals, cups of coffee and for enduring some of these films with me over and over again. I couldn't have done it without you by my side and I am forever grateful for you. Without you, I could not be as confident in sharing my stories within these pages for those seeking what I found with you. You are my reward and I love you more than you know.

To my dad aka Pop, thank you for being my inspiration. You are the most loyal person I know. Thank you for never stopping to work for our family and showing us that, you are never too old to start over. Te quiero mucho, Your little monster

To my son Elijah, my one and only, you are the reason why I've made changes in my life. Not just becoming a mom, but one that you, can be proud of. You are the reason I'm stronger and the reason I continue to reach for more. I could never imagine my life without you, I'm so proud of you and Emily and the family you have made.

Introduction

Have you ever watched a movie and thought, "Why is this girl doing that?" or "I'm so embarrassed for her...I never want to be this girl!"? Even worse, you're watching a movie, recognizing you have done some of those very same things, without even realizing it ... until now. If you're anything like us, you enjoy "romcoms" (romantic comedies) — overlooking the messiness of the characters portrayed, because you're a romantic at-heart. The movies leave us hopeful, and in many cases, in love with love. And yet, even though we've watched some of the most painful scenes of movies time after time, we somehow get the notion when we're personally living out in real life, things might turn out the way it did for the flawed characters we've grown to love, longing for our own romantic happily-ever-after. The problem with that is that for the most part, our lives *don't* end up the way we see them panning out on the big screen and it is for that exact reason—it's a movie. It's scripted, and therefore is written to end that way. Meanwhile, we romanticize about the what-could-be in our own lives, based on films that've taught us how to obtain love in the worst ways possible. What becomes of us when we set out to find love the way we see it played out on-screen? Our hearts our broken, we're devastated, and we're not quite sure how to pick up the pieces of our heart because most on-screen romances don't show *that* part of her story.

We've idolized these movies, and in many cases, the leading ladies, hopeful that the romance in our own lives will somehow end up the same as what we've seen played out on-screen—with love. Now, we realize that all women are not Romcom fiends, but like the many all around the world who are, we've been shaped by the movies we've watched, and this is especially true of Romantic Comedies which we both have been watching since we were way too young to know what we were doing or what we thought a fairy-tale love looked like (we thank Disney for that!). There were so many movies on our list, but we had to bring it in! Every good story has that constant tension that makes so many of us watch it to the very end, but we've all done it. We bet you can quickly recount more than a dozen on-screen romantic comedies or TV shows where you've just CRINGED watching the leading lady doing something that is *beyond* painful to watch. But, like a bad accident, even though you're embarrassed for her, you can't seem to look away. Whether she's being manipulative or throwing herself at a man who has no interest in her whatsoever, or she's sabotaging a potential love-interest because she doesn't know who she is, you're wincing, thinking you don't ever want to be her.

Sometimes it's a conversation, a song, a holiday, a fragrance, or a scene that touches us at our core, making us want to be in a romantic relationship. Oh, how the senses so strongly pull at the heartstrings. The good news is that we were meant to enjoy all these beautiful facets of life. The bad news is that somehow, it's the on-screen scenes—and their playbacks of certain characters—that have conformed us as women, sowing in our hearts little tiny seeds to the degree that many of us have come to believe that it's okay to *be* her, forgetting the cringey parts of even our favorite movies. Whether it's a movie like "When Harry Met Sally," or TV shows like Golden Girls, The Gilmore Girls, or The Mindy Project, most of us can clearly call out the embarrassing behavior of the gals on-screen. And yet, even though we know better, many of us have continued carrying on as though this is the way we should be acting and carrying on in the name of love. Furthermore, while we don't like to admit it, many of us have unfortunately enabled men to treat us the way they have and do. So, who ends up paying the price? We do.

Now before you get all comfy cozy in reading this book, know that some toes may get stepped on, stumbling onto an occasional "ouch" or two. How do we know? Because we've not only experienced them, but we've been these girls ourselves in our younger years. We only wished we had a big sis or someone who was honest enough with us at the time to steer us in a different direction. That being said, this book is so that you can live a life of freedom, with your head held high and knowing your worth—even if you've made any of the same mistakes you'll be reading about from our colorful, on-screen characters.

We know that being a single woman comes with its share of pressures and opinions. Besides being "personal experts," of relationship woes, Ivette is a married Health & Lifestyle Coach, and Cyndi (never married, *still* single in her fifties and loving life to the fullest), is a pastor, the Founder of "She is Single, She is Strong," a community created to strengthening single women. In our forty-plus years of life (or "living"), what we've seen as a recurring stumbling block is when we succumb to behaving or acting in a way that—if we're honest—we know is less than who we really are. The result? A broken heart. Both having lost a dear friend to suicide that was very much connected to rejection and a devastated heart, our hope is to give you the courage, strength, and wisdom in our commentary as we talk through movies that have helped shape us into who we are and how we behave as women in today's culture. In our imperfections and years of making our fair share of mistakes, we're certainly not ones to judge, but are most definitely here to help. The truth of the matter? If we try and live our lives like some of the ladies we see on-screen, we'll end up in a heap of trouble. If it's true love we're after, ladies, we can't mimic behavior that's manipulative, desperate, self-degrading, lying, cheating, deceiving or even pursuing men (shall we continue?), and think that we are laying a solid foundation for love and bearing all fruit that is good.

Aware that some of these chapters (and themes) can be a bit heavy (we, too, were confronted with some of the embarrassing scenes we're about to embark on, having experienced some of these in our own personal lives over the years), we're turning to some of the actual Romcoms that have shown us that these behaviors are acceptable when it comes to finding true love (or say, "matters of the heart."). As we tackle the worst characteristics of our on-screen leading ladies chapter by chapter—each from a different movie or TV show—our hope is to undo and call out some of the modeling that may have unfortunately influenced many of us who have hopelessly watched these movies and TV shows, embedding some of the on-screen memories in our minds that have undoubtedly replayed from time to time. While there were many movies to choose from, we decided to lean on some of the cinematic gems we both loved throughout the years. Also loving books, we want this to be something you enjoy reading, and therefore have written this in a lighthearted tone for you to enjoy, reflect, engage, and apply. Single, married, separated, or divorced, may the insight shared in each chapter help heal, strengthen, and give you the courage to be the girl you were always meant to be.

We love you and are excited for the beautiful life that awaits you!

Cyndi & Ivette

P.S. Please note that while we are breaking down characters from specific movies and TV shows, if you haven't yet, we are not endorsing or encouraging you to watch them. The one TV show we write about is rated MA, more than a handful of these movies are PG-13, and three of the 11 have an R rating. Some of these movies you may be well-acquainted with already, having watched many of these same flicks or shows in your lifetime. However, in the event you feel you must, we strongly advise watching either the broadcast TV version, with Clearplay or VidAngel, or skipping over and muting scenes and language to not subject yourself to anything lude, offensive, or inappropriate.

"These years that I have been in love have been the darkest days of my life…all because I've been cursed by being in love with a man who does not and will not love me back."

Iris Simpkins,
The Holiday

Iris Simpkins, A Romantic Illusionist

The Holiday

There should be zero tolerance for loving someone who doesn't love you back, and yet, this is exactly where we find Iris, one of the two leading ladies in The Holiday. As jolly and Christmas-y as this movie is, nothing merry or more heartbreaking than when we lay our eyes on Kate Winslet's character, Iris Simpkins, who is desperately in love with the overly confident and stringing-her-along-for-as-long-as-she'll-let-him, Jasper. From the get-go, Iris' voiceover acknowledges that she is the victim of "unrequited love," a love that is merely one-sided. SO really, is it even love at all? This camp throws out a solid, "no." This is NOT love at all, and yet, as women, so many of us have sat in the same seat as Iris, pining for someone who does not at all have the same feelings for us, hoping that someday he'll change. But here's the thing—he won't. And you won't be the one girl who changes him. So please stop thinking that you will. You won't. What he needs in order to grow up or change, is not *yours* to give him.

Isn't it almost always easier to detect or call something or someone out when you're on the outside looking in? It's true. While watching this film, it was easy to get so infuriated with how smitten she was with a man whose only interest was using her, for whatever she was willing to give. Does this sound familiar? Not only is this a bad start off to a relationship, but here is the newsflash: if this is all your relationship with your person consists of, it's not a relationship.

What is it that makes us do the same? Is it low self-esteem? Is there a sense of excitement reaching for the wind? Is there something about this idea of unreturned love that is exhilarating? We hope—for those who are answering these questions out loud, that regardless of how much you love the late Olivia Newton John's "Hopelessly Devoted to You," —that the answer is, "no." And it should be. For some it's the whole idea of taking care of him. "But he needs me to help him." Here's another thing to note, sister—you're not his savior. You're not his mom, his keeper, or his sitter. How can you take care of him when you can't even take care of *yourself*? You need to invest in yourself a bit–even if it's just taking the time to learn about who you are, so you can (re)build your *own* self-confidence and worth. Okay, so we know this is a little harsh, so we're going to give this a little break and talk about love.

When it comes to love—true love—you will find that each puts the needs of the other before their own. There is protection, oneness, respect, honor, and it doesn't fail. In other words, when the going gets tough, the tough stay. How many weddings have you attended to know what love is based on the readings out of 1 Corinthians 13, for we've heard it time and time again at many a wedding:

> *Love is patient, love is kind. It does not envy, it does not boast, it is not proud. It does not dishonor others, it is not self-seeking, it is not easily angered, it keeps no record of wrongs. Love does not delight in evil but rejoices with the truth. It always protects, always trusts, always hopes, always perseveres. Love never fails.*
>
> *(vv. 4-8, NIV)*

So, basically what we just read above is what real love is. Anything outside of what we read isn't love. It might be lust, having nothing to do with love at all. Or maybe there is love, say with a best guy friend, mixed in with a little bit (or a lotta bit) of infatuation. To one or the other we can both relate.

Cyndi: I can remember singing Vanessa Williams "Save the Best for Last," which I always thought was sung by Natalie Cole until writing this book (don't judge). Sorry, Vanessa! The thing is, I would get teary-eyed every time I belted out, "Cause how could you give your love to someone else and share your dreams with me? Sometimes the very thing you're looking for is the one thing you can't see." Scratch that. Not only would I get teary-eyed, I would get a huge lump in my throat for at that ripe age of 20 (maybe even 21), I was singing about my best friend, who was a beautiful being. He was a light-skinned brotha with a more-than-charismatic personality. He was charming, fit, and could make me laugh like no one else in the world, plus he was mixed—like me. We worked together, and as soon as work was done, we did life together. We double-dated a couple of times, we'd hang out after work, we'd go to parties together, he'd look out for me, and though he loved me dearly, the biggest red flag for me is that he was a player. Play-yah. He told me everything about every girl who was hot after him, and the sad thing was, as much as they chased him, he wasn't interested. They'd page him. He called back. They flirted. He responded. Yes, there'd be a hookup later that night, but to him, they weren't more than a booty-call. Sad, but true. This was his pattern for every girl who hunted him down. If they could only hear what he said about them once he hung up the phone. It was just plain old sad. So sad, that even though I was in love with him, I never said a word. I didn't want to get played that way, and most certainly not by him. It's interesting, because we kissed years later after wondering if we missed out on the "us" we each—at different times in our lives—thought could one day be. The answer was a hard "no." (Lol) The good news is, though my heart was stomped on for a while in the witnessing and personally hearing all his accounts with the many women that came in and out of his life faster than the fastest planet Jupiter makes a full rotation (which is roughly about ten hours), I wasn't foolish enough to take matters into my own hands. I was a little naive, and also a little smart.

Ivette: For a second there, I was asking myself those questions and thinking," I got nothing," and then it came to me. I did have that one person that I thought I wanted to be with, but he ended up breaking me. Not breaking my heart but my soul. But I'll explain how that became my "pull up your big girl pants" and move-on-in-life moment. See when we met, he was very interested in getting to know me, or so I thought. We were introduced at a bar, where he had been out with some friends. This was just before a dinner party at a nearby restaurant that my friends and I were going to. He quickly left his friends in the dust and came over to talk with me. I thought it was cute and didn't think much about it, as I was there with a guy friend (really just a friend) and didn't want to be rude. But my friends were excited for me as they knew him and thought he was a catch. So, we exchanged numbers and met up again on our own a few times. I was enjoying his company and thought he was a great guy. We would hang out a handful of times, enough to make me think that there may be something worthwhile growing. But we do that, right? We think that there are things happening in a man's heart, just because we are such emotional beings and it's happening in our hearts. So, after a few months of seeing each other, then a few months not seeing each other due to kids, work, and life in general, we met up one last time, and I made the mistake of saying to him, "I miss you" to which he returned with, "I don't miss you, but I do miss this."

Did you FEEL that? Yes, the biggest blow I never imagined just hit me straight in my soul! See, I was always the one that ended a relationship, so this caught me completely off guard. I did have a little touch of low self-esteem because I was heavier than I would have liked to have been at that time. But this—this sealed the deal for me and my self-esteem, which was the lowest it had ever been. And at that moment, something came over me. I gathered my things and never looked back. I would never allow anyone to make me feel so low again. Thanks, dude!

Quit playing games with my heart

Okay, so speaking of smart, what's so interesting about Iris is that she really is a very smart girl. Not only is she an excellent writer, but she is obviously aware that Jasper causes her great pain, admitting to the three years "with him" (he thought they were only dating), were, "The absolute worst years of my life. The worst Christmases…the worst birthdays…tears and Valium…These years that I have been in love have been the darkest days of my life… all because I've been cursed by being in love with a man who does not and will not love me back." Ugh, we hate that! She clearly is quite aware that she is under some sort of spell by the man who makes her heart pound so heavily, though it has been the reason she's had the three worst years of her life. We're coming to a screeching halt on this one. Stop right there, please. Ladies, is this you? Has this ever been you? Is this still you? If so, what can we do NOW to fix this? Because this should *not* be you.

There is no reason that any of us should put ourselves through this kind of pain, but let's be real—we do. It's time for the punishment we deserve, though for whatever reason, we don't know why we "deserve it" but we do. Right? WRONG.

Cyndi: Iris makes me think of a love I had in my late teens. He was very charismatic, handsome (to me, anyways) and unlike any man I had ever known or met. We met in junior community college, and if I've ever only loved two men, even perhaps three, I absolutely adored him. Though we were the same age, he was more experienced in life and in love. And even though I had boyfriends ever since I can remember in Junior High (yep, I started young), this relationship was so very different from any other I had ever known. He was a chick magnet, and I was quite pulled in.

At first, we were just friends. I had a boyfriend when I met him. But because my then–boyfriend was still in high school and I in college, most of my free time was with my newly-found college friends (some of whom I'm still friends with today). So, we started hanging out, and the more time we'd spent together, the more I realized I enjoyed hanging out with him. Something about him was very appealing to me. Where I was wrong is that I started allowing my heart to fall for someone while I was still in a relationship with someone else. Don't be this girl. If you're in a relationship with someone, you really don't have business hanging out with someone else you're interested in. If you sense that is what's happening or taking place, the best thing to do would be to cut off the relationship you're in, being honest with him that you are not ready to be in a committed relationship. While we wouldn't recommend jumping right into a relationship with the other potential love interest, if that should happen or be the case, it would behoove you to take it slow. But really what would be even better than that would be to take some time to work on whatever is going on in your heart, that allowed you to start two-timing in the first place.

So, back to my story … As most of you may already suspect, things with my then–current boyfriend ended quite badly, and without any hesitation, I jumped right into an official relationship with my college crush… the very next day! We thank the movies for teaching us how to do that. He was ready for it, and I was happy to do it. Red flag #1—this is a rocky way to start off a relationship. If you want a relationship to be laid on a good and solid foundation, there should always be time to reflect and do the work necessary so that your next outcome is better than the last. And hopefully, this relationship will stick and be something that grows into a lifelong commitment.

As you can imagine, any relationship that started off that quickly—regardless of the great chemistry that exists—is bound to go only so far. Of course, in the beginning, it was very exciting because it was new, we were hot and heavy, and very much into each other. Did I mention that he was a chick magnet? It was about four or five months into our relationship that his best friend proceeded to clue me in on the idea that though we were a couple, he was indeed cheating on me. Note: "Hot and heavy" does not equal fidelity, faithfulness and certainly not happiness. Sometimes when that's all it is, you're left with nothing once the excitement of it all goes away. For those of you thinking, "Yeah, well, not me," if this is all your relationship is built on, think again, sister. So wrapped up in his identity, and not seeing myself for the amazing person I didn't know I was, I ignored it, brushed it under the rug and continued in my quest for "happily-ever-after," which would end, and not very happily. Once I learned of his cheating, I became very distrusting of him, watching his every move, and seeing that though he professed to love me, he definitely had a wandering eye. He'd lightly flirt with other girls we went to school with, and the worst thing of it all is that he was not very kind to me, to those who I loved, including my closest friends, and my mom. Any respect we had for each other started to be thrown out the window. He'd accuse me of things, and in retaliation, I'd resort to physical abuse—hitting, punching, and even slapping him in those moments of intense anger towards him. Our relationship was so volatile and toxic. There would be times we'd be fighting, and I would be so upset, I would just start throwing up.

His best friend did offer to love me and take care of me in a way that my then-boyfriend apparently wasn't doing, but I would not have it. I stayed in the relationship, saw my friends get verbally abused, saw my mom be disrespected (what respecting boyfriend would turn on the Playboy channel, even when my mom asked him to turn it off?). It got worse, but my things with my mom came to a halt when he and his buddy found it necessary to climb up on top of our house and stomp on the rooftop. Red flags 2, 3, 4, 5, 6, and 7! There were actually several more red flags than that, but I was so naive and young at the time, I just wanted to believe the best in him, and the best in US. Never mind that I was losing myself to a man who didn't think very highly of me. You would think that once I ran into him with another girl in his arms, that I would have ended it there, but I didn't. I continued in this exhausting relationship, and like Iris, in those three years, experienced the worst birthdays, Christmases, and holidays of my life. Of course, there's more and the story doesn't end there, but for this point of where Iris is at, it's clear that three years of misery like this, is three years too many. I wish I had known then what I know now. I stopped settling for the crumbs and I am now all the better for it. This book is a result of the many mistakes I have made as a vibrant single woman, with the hope that *you* can avoid wasting precious years in misery with someone you're not meant to be with.

Head over heels for him, but you ain't nothin' more than a play thang, boo!

Please don't be this girl. "Why not?" you ask. What Iris describes as what her life looked like for three years in love with Jasper is not what any woman should ever go through for any boy or man. Period. Ladies, when we lift our heads over and above these dark scenarios, we can actually see the possibilities of real goals and dreams coming to pass. We see light that shines on us, promising love that does exist, but not from a man whose behavior is anything close to how Jasper treats Iris. This woman who is, "... head over heels...," is so very deserving of so much more. She is deserving of a love that is returned and even more than that, one who cherishes her, seeing and honoring her for who she is.

Now here's the thing—we realize no one is perfect, and that though not everyone is an Iris, many of us have done or walked out our fair share of Iris in our lives. Whether it's one-sided love, daydreaming, settling for someone who doesn't value our worth, if you're still single, you may have walked this out, as well. Even in all those miserable years, he only told her he loved her "...almost four times." That was one of the most embarrassing things she says in the entire movie. It's clear to see that even though Iris' words were saying it's over, she was anything but. He cheated on her. They remained as friends who'd email, sometimes talk on the phone for hours, grab lunch occasionally and apparently, who she was still buying gifts for. Iris had her friend, Anna, to confide in. We all should have at least one Anna in our lives. Annas are a must for accountability and to help keep your heart shielded from the daggers of cavalier men like Jasper. Or sometimes, we need Annas to help keep us from being the ones who cheat.

Ivette: There were two times—okay, maybe three times—in my love life that I did things that I'm really not proud of. I was doing it to get a person's attention (okay, not a good enough reason). The first time that I cheated on someone was totally a selfish move. He didn't deserve it and honestly that secret has never been told until this very moment. I guess I felt okay about it because our relationship was coming to an end, but we were still living together, so it was wrong. I was young and didn't really think about a lifelong commitment with someone. "It was just dating," I told myself.

The other time I began dating someone before ending the one I was still in. I was in a very bad place in my life, both romantically and emotionally. And I just wanted to get his attention. My boyfriend was living his life and coming home to me when he was done for the day. I felt alone and sad, and so the minute someone else showed me a bit of attention, I grabbed it with open arms. The problem here was not only that I was cheating on my boyfriend who, by the way, was living a destructive life I no longer wanted to be a part of, but the guy I was cheating with was married. *Oy vey!* Two cheaters will never be a good combination, for nothing worthwhile or meaningful will ever come out of it. So yes, I was very unhappy with myself, and my relationship and I just ran to the next thing, as if that was going to make things better. It didn't, it made things worse. But it did make me think that I needed to run away from both of these relationships and that is exactly what I did. I left my job, the city I lived in, my "home" and started over. It was time to grow up and make something of my life. This was the best thing I could have done for myself. And for some of you, it may be time for you to make some bold decisions for the life you know you really want to live.

Cyndi: The times I cheated I think it was because I knew I would never end up with the guy I was going out with in the first place. That's so wrong. Somehow, in knowing it was a short-term relationship heading nowhere, I cheated on two different relationships in my life. The hypocritical thing about it was growing up, I couldn't stand cheaters because of what infidelity did to our family. At the time my mom was going through this pain, I could barely stomach the woman my dad was unfaithful *with*. Why? Because she broke up our home. But then, here I was, at the age either 18 or 19, and though it wasn't anything more than kissing, I was still being unfaithful. It's a matter of the heart—if it's once, twice, or 20 times, cheating is cheating. I was being deceptive to my not-so-sweet boyfriend when I was in college (while he was still in high school). I managed to convince myself that it was okay, but in case you didn't know it, and we're telling you now: cheating is never okay. It doesn't matter how hurt you are emotionally or how mistreated you are by someone you are with. Unfaithfulness is not justifiable. It's better to break off the relationship with that person than sow seeds of unfaithfulness. You reap what you sow. It's a biblical principle that will forever stand. And, in my case, I reaped it painfully in one of the greatest loves of my life just a year or two later. "Do not be deceived … whatever a man sows, that he will also reap." (Gal. 6:7, NKJV)

Cheating never ends well. The question is asked, "Is it cheating if you're only dating?" Anna asks Iris. To us the answer is still, "yes." And yes, they were "shagging," as Anna puts it, but Iris loved him. He thought they were only dating. Not only is it an unfortunate pattern in so many relationships we see today, but we too, have both walked out this warped way of thinking. While she does understand that she is "pathetic," as Anna calls her, it's seeing him, hearing his voice, that all sense of sanity goes out the door. He knows what he does to her. And like many men out there who are not looking for commitment, to him, it was a game. He may not have considered it cheating, but he was definitely two-timing them both. He knew that all he had to do was come her way, and she'd once again be all his. Unabashedly gawking and gushing over him. He's selfish and he is cruel.

You're not the one

The gushing. Oh, how we wish we wouldn't … (ahem) we mean, *she* wouldn't. Jasper enters her office. At first, she's working and diligently trying to meet her deadline, then before you know it, she's gushing at him, quoting his article with all-eyes-adoring and somewhat-reluctantly-yet-flirtatiously smiling at him as he lures her in—hook, line and sinker. He's eating it up. He loves the attention and that clearly, she's still very much into him. This is what is so hard to watch—painful, actually. We see that she has a good head on her shoulders career-wise, but for us, we cringe at the idea that many women allow themselves to be treated this way. How do we know? We've done it. Whether because of his boyish good looks, charm, wit, talent, or all the above, many very smart, intelligent women get it right in every area, but this one. We are smart, but we allow some of what we see to be blinded so that we only see the good. This is a sweet trait to have, as 1 Corinthians says, that "...love believes all things…" (1 Cor. 13 NKJV), but not in the sense of being a doormat. And in Iris' case, this is not only what she is to him--a place to wipe his dirty feet on, but she's a blind doormat as well. For just when you think it won't get any worse at this moment, it does. He lies to her by telling her he got something for her for Christmas, to which she then does what any doting girl would do–she opens her drawer, pulling out a Christmas gift for *him*! Why? Why? Why? Well, the beauty of this story is that it is just that very thing, a story. So, for the story to continue, she must behave in this manner. Well, Jasper definitely hadn't planned on Iris having a gift for him. He'd only meant to flatter her as to keep stringing her along. But now that she foiled his manipulation through his lips dripping with deceit, he begins to backpedal by telling her the gift isn't there, but that he knows he bought her something saying, "Hope I didn't lose it … could be in my car." What a jerk. Have you ever fallen for a man like this? You see the disappointment in her face, immediately recognizing that look that wants to believe what he's saying, but at the same time, forgiving him as she is well aware he most certainly didn't get her a single thing for Christmas. Does this make you as angry as it's making us?! She gets him the most thoughtful gift and he has nothing in return. But he can say a few words to her, "Why are you so great?" and she finds herself back in the moment with this man she adores.

Oh man, have we been *there* before?!? More times than we can count on one hand. This is the part in the movie where we're literally coming unglued. What is he doing talking to her in her office and why is she still talking to him after we just found out that he has cheated on her and is a man with zero character? A kind-hearted girl, you can see she really wants to believe the words he is telling her, as she's soaking it all in, loving every bit of this waste-of-a-time exchange between the two. We are well-aware that most reading this book are kind girls, who unfortunately would believe a guy just like Jasper—and maybe right now, you are Iris. Well hang on, sister … you're the reason why this chapter is in this book.

Ever read the Proverb, "Like a dog that returns to its vomit, so is a fool who repeats his foolishness…."? (26:11, NASB) If there ever was a movie that was painful to watch because of foolish behavior—again and again, sting after sting—this was it. Still caring deeply for him, Iris' gift to him was not only generous, but it was also thoughtful—confirming that even though she'd explained to her friend, Anna, that she and Jasper were "very over," this couldn't have been any further from the truth. Had it been, she wouldn't have thought about getting him anything at all, but maybe instead, she would have given herself the gift of letting go and stop investing in someone who hadn't put her first in any area of his life. "Simpky," as he calls her, was not a priority for him and this is evident to everyone, including Iris, but still, she wouldn't let go. You see her melting at the sound of him calling her by her nickname. Gag. Things only get worse for Iris as their boss, who claims he has news to share, presents to the staff a newly engaged Jasper Bloom to his now-fiancée, Sarah Smith-Alcott. This is one of the most heartbreaking moments to watch as Iris courageously braves a smile at him as their eyes meet. Here he is—just having finished flirting with and teasing her in her office and yet, he is engaged. What a dirty rat. If a man has ever done that to you, he is exactly that. How dare he lead her on like that. Now, did she let him do that, knowing he was seeing another girl? Yes, but whether he was in love with Sarah isn't the issue--and we can clearly see, based on his flirtatious behavior with Iris, a faithful heart he does *not* have.

So, here is where we're going to put this movie on pause. If you're into someone who isn't into you, or if you're into someone who used to be into you, or if you're into someone who doesn't even know you, the gift-buying needs to come to an end. Ladies, while there are good honest men out there, the ones that aren't, will tell you anything just to get what they want. Stop letting this happen! Just stop. Save your money for a rainy day, a trip to somewhere fun or even to buy something extra special just for YOU!

Not that we're trying to break down every shot and scene (and we won't), what was all-telling of who this fool really was, the deal is sealed as we see what Iris finds after quickly heading back to her office—her thoughtful gift to Jasper, had been left behind in her office. He had not only stomped on her heart, but he also had no regard for a gift that to her was of great value. He treated both poorly—and for three years. Have you ever just sat in one of these types of relationships for one year too many? Or in Iris' case, three years?

Ivette: Me, me! As I frown with disbelief at myself. I have been in not one, but multiple long-term relationships similar to Iris' for way too long. It was not my greatest hits era for sure. I fell for that perfect guy—my friends were even excited for me. They all knew him to be a great guy, but apparently, we were all fooled. I always wondered why his parents treated me rudely but would soon find out that he was still living with his girlfriend. He swore to me that it was over, saying he was just waiting for a new apartment. Being so vulnerable and gullible, I believed him and went on to have a four-year relationship that was filled with lies and many other women. I can remember a time that I went to one of his shows (although he told me to not worry about going if I was tired). I was there to support him with some of my friends, but when we got there, I found that he was on a date with someone else. I was devastated but kept my head high and pretended that it didn't bother me. There were so many horrible situations in those few years. I honestly don't know how I got through it. All the broken promises, affairs and mental abuse finally came to an end (for a moment). I broke up with him, but it only took one night back in his arms to change my future forever. I became pregnant. I tried to stay in the relationship and make it right, but when my life and unborn child were being threatened by the other women, I realized this would never end. Unlike Jasper, this guy ran the other direction, so as not to have any responsibility as a father. This is one time I was thankful for his decision to run away, though it made my life harder in one aspect, I was able to raise my son without interference. The moral of this story is that I should have walked away the moment I found out about his live-in girlfriend, but I'm thankful that I didn't since I now have a beautiful son and daughter-in-law that have blessed me with my sweet granddaughter.

Heartbreak, healing and time

"When you catch your guy with another woman, you're not supposed to stay friends with him…," is what her co-worker tells her at the party just before finding out he's engaged. So, our rendition of this is, "When you find out your guy has another woman and/or is engaged, you're not supposed to stay in his life. It's time to cut the cord and go." It's time to stop settling for the crumbs, girlfriend! The daydreaming dilemma of whatever Iris had hoped for in her and Jasper needs to come to an end. For Iris, the party is over (in more ways than one) and now she's going home to feel the pain of rejection and (somewhat) public humiliation. He had his chance to tell her in private, and guess what? He didn't. That's all that needs to be said. But instead, what has happened is that Iris has had the "shagging" rug pulled out from beneath her, and we're glad it did. If this has ever happened to you, don't continue to be the other woman. You're better than that. It could have been done a whole lot kinder and more considerately—but this is Jasper we're talking about. He is neither of those things.

Now devastated, Iris has to face the music at home and process the reality of what will now become of her life. The love, excitement, heartache and pain this man once brought her has now come to an end. Faced with the hard facts about Jasper's romantic elevation, Iris in her misery, considers ending her life. Note to everyone reading. Note to you. NO man is worth you turning on the gas and attempting to breathe in the fumes. We're going to repeat that a little bit louder now: NO MAN is worth you turning on the gas, in an attempt to take your life. NO MAN is worth it. NO man. The good news is, if you have come to feeling like you are at the end of your will to go on, here is where it ends. Not your life, not your time, not your heart, not your energy, not your finances, but rather, your relationship with him—this is where it ends, and this is where for you, a new life can begin. This is where you arise. Up, we said, and let go of this one-sided relationship, so that you can start living a beautiful life with peace and strength. It's there for you, but you won't find it remaining STUCK in that relationship. Turning your back on unrequited love puts you in a position to walk forward.

How did Iris know it was time for her to move on from this one–way love relationship? When it was announced that he was engaged and getting married. Hopefully for you, you'll know much sooner than hearing about it from his engagement-announcement. Jasper found someone with whom he wanted to attempt to spend the rest of his life with (poor girl), and it wasn't Iris, who quickly bounces back after the fleeting "low-point" thought of breathing in the gas fumes, and good thing, too. Good things await her, and her life is about to drastically change…for the better. You know, that's one of the things in life, is that just when you start to wonder about why it's dealt you the hand that it has, something beautiful or amazing knocks at your door. Be expectant of those wonderful things, no matter if you lean in the pessimistic camp or constantly reside in the home of the optimist. Life has many beautiful things for you–if you'd just be open to it, and actually *wait* for it, some pretty amazing things are being prepared just for you. A favorite verse of ours encourages, "*I would have lost heart,* unless I had believed that I would see the goodness of the Lord in the land of the living." Psalm 27:13 (NKJV) There are good things He has for you. Believe it, and don't lose heart.

What we see happen next with Iris is extraordinary. In the midst of her most downcast moment, she gets an online message inquiring about possibly switching homes for a couple of weeks. Amanda, the other leading lady in this holiday film (who we should cover as well, but won't), has reached out and they've agreed to switch homes, which Iris is ecstatic to find out is in Los Angeles … and not a moment too soon! Ironically, Amanda is also getting the heck out of dodge as she just broke up with her live-in boyfriend who has told her that he slept with his secretary. Is it crazy that these two women are trying to get so far away from their realities? Is this what *we* have to do in order to get away from a bad situation that we've put ourselves into? Sometimes it is necessary, and in their case, it was. They're doing the switch the next day. This is an example of one of the beautiful things life can bring you when you least expect it. Iris' demeanor has changed. In one moment, she is hopeful for a brighter tomorrow.

Looking towards a brand-new day and ready for that fresh California air (which really only exists in the winter season), Iris is on a flight headed to L.A., and just as we'd expect from Jasper, he throws his hook and line to Iris through text, asking, "How can I reach you?" Seriously?! Selfish weasel. The nerve he has in reaching out to her knowing full well that: 1) She needs a clean break from him; and 2) He is engaged to somebody else and has no business texting her to begin with. He needs to leave her alone and get on with his new life. It almost seems that what has taken place in her overnight is a new sense of empowerment, for what Iris does next is as lovely as it is brave. She is honest with him. Thinking about what to rightly say before saying it, she texts,

> "Jasper, we both know I need to fall out of love with you.
> Would be great if you would let me try."

Way to go, Iris! Good for you! The reason she can be honest with him is because she has been honest with herself. Have you been honest with *yourself?* Have you been honest with him? If not, now is a great time to start. ☺ Some of the most empowering tools include honesty, reflection, work, forgiveness, and time. Especially if you're in need of healing, what is surely most needed is time. But not just time doing nothing, but time doing *some*thing. We keep talking about doing the work, but that's because it's so needed. So many of us grow up having lived through some traumatic experiences, affecting, and impacting the way we live out our lives as adults. The saying goes that, "Time heals all wounds," but in most cases, it requires more than just time to truly work on the issues that need to be healed in the first place. It looks like Iris was taking the first step in the right direction but leave it to Jasper to try to ruin that, by keeping his claws in her heart.

Cyndi: This reminds me of a time where I was in a relationship in my early 20s and we were very back and forth—it just was a very unhealthy relationship to be in. I remember finding out from so many others that he was into quite a few of us girls at the same time, so I made the decision I needed to be done with it. What helped is that I had attended a party where he was also at, flirting with a younger girl dressed in a much shorter skirt. There was nothing wrong with the skirt or the girl, but for me, it was the final straw, giving me the backbone, courage, and the unwavering decisiveness that I was never going there again, and would not be looking back. I left the party, I got in my car, and wouldn't you know it, the moment I jumped on the freeway heading to Pasadena, the song, "You Keep Me Hanging On," by The Supremes came on. Talk about perfect timing. I cranked that song up so loud and all the way down the 210 freeway I sang that song so loud with every fiber of my being in between praying in tongues—yes, that's exactly what I did, while tears of finality went streaming down my face. It was my declaration, and guess what? It was over and it was done. Ooh, that was such a powerful moment and I don't know what happened in the spirit realm that night, but what I can tell you is that when I woke up in the morning, I could literally hear birds chirping, the sun was smiling down on me, and my heart felt as though it had never cared for this guy a day in my life. It was a miracle, and I was thankful to God for it.

Walking away from the one causing the pain and time away from the source of pain gives you an opportunity to experience new things and different patterns. Though Cyndi's came overnight quicker than an Amazon delivery, healing will indeed take time, and for everyone and every situation, it will be different. Just like every surgery requires different tools—depending on the type of procedure and the desired outcome—there will be different tools needed for your healing. So that we can continue in this flow, the tools and resources for healing will be towards the end of this chapter. What we do want to address is that if you're in this type of relationship, please allow this chapter to open your eyes and give you this strength to be honest enough with yourself about it, and to muster up the strength needed to walk away from it. As women, many of us have the innate ability to nurture and to help, and so for many, receiving a selfish text like this could throw some of us into a tailspin right back into his arms, however, please note that if this is you, it is not the time for this inherent trait to kick in. You really do need your time away, time to hear and think without his influence, a time to quiet yourself so you can really hear what your heart already knows to do. This man is selfish and doesn't care for you. The only person he cares about is himself. You deserve to be treated well from a man who truly "sees" you—not one who drags your heart through the mud for three years, then throwing both, it and you off to the side so that he could marry someone else who he has also been unfaithful to. You're not the problem. He is, but some of the way you've allowed yourself to be treated and seen by men does need to change. It's time for a change and even if you don't feel like it, you are worth so much more than that. This is a great time to get to know who you really are. Do you remember who you are? Do you remember who you were before you jumped into that relationship? Sometimes we get so lost in that person, we forget who we are and what it is that we enjoy doing. Grab a hold of time, pick up a journal and reach out to trusting friends around you. Don't rush through it. Take as much time as needed.

You're a leading lady

Now the whole point of getting away was to get clarity away from Jaspar and his constant ability of stringing Iris along in person, and what better place for that to happen for Iris than in Hollywood! Leaving to LaLa Land was not only a great idea, but the fact that it was somewhere as exciting as LA—somewhere she had never been—was about to open a whole new world of lights, cameras, and action.

One of the things we loved seeing in the movie was the beautiful home of Amanda, where Iris would be staying while in California. Because of the neighborhood that Amanda lives in, Iris finds herself befriending colorful characters in the entertainment industry, one of which is a retired Oscar-winning screenwriter, bringing her—in just one night what she hadn't received in her three-years of therapy regarding the "schmuck" on the other side of the pond. It's over dinner that her sweet new friend tells her that instead of playing the best friend in a movie, her true role was that of a leading lady, which she is but she just hadn't realized it yet. This insight brings her to tears, and we are glad that it does. For one, someone on the outside is being honest with her, and taking the time to gently massage the truth she so desperately needed to hear; and secondly, crying is good. And finally … she gets it. Exhale. This was an empowering moment for her.

Hooray for Hollywood

In the midst of all the lights, glitz and glam of Hollywood, Iris finds what she truly needs—consolation and new friends. In addition to Arthur, she also meets Miles, a film composer in the industry. He's with Maggie, an actress who is non-committal. Iris is still getting over Jasper—well, trying to. But because of the circumstances of their meet-cute, a friendship has sparked, and really, that is how all relationships need to begin... as friends. What so many fail to realize is that at the base of every romantic relationship, should be the foundation of friendship. This is one of the reasons so many failed relationships don't work out, because it was mostly based only on physical attraction and chemistry.

It's always so interesting to see how a selfish guy responds and reacts to a girl he no longer has direct control over. And in this case, Jasper's fears of forever losing Iris comes through loud and clear—even all the way from England. Set on keeping himself in the forefront of her mind, he continues to contact and reach out to her, proving himself to be every bit the selfish slimeball we already know him to be. "I need some Iris," he tells her, referring to needing help with his book. "I don't want to mess you up ...have some fun..." and yet he very much does ... and is. By now we're yelling at the screen, "LEAVE HER ALONE!" He knows full well that he has crossed the boundary she has asked him not to cross. Only concerned about himself, he has the nerve to say he doesn't want to mess her up. Really?!?! Did he not know she's on vacation? Didn't he know it was to get away from her? And didn't she tell him that she needed some time away to get over him? What is he doing? Caring only about himself, this is what he is doing. It's what he's always done and is all he knows to do. Do you know men like this? It's cruel, and if we can be so honest to say this—he cares nothing about Iris. Meeting his needs *are his only priority*. We do find a very frustrated Iris, and while we're watching it unfold, we can't help but being equally frustrated with her in not putting her foot down, verbally telling him to "buzz off!" Did you know that you can actually do that? If you haven't yet and need to, we give you permission. Put your foot down. If you can relate at all to Iris, please stop putting his needs before your own. If there is no ring on your finger, and he is not showing you even a fraction of the attention and affection, you're trying to show him, that relationship needs to be cut from the root cut the cord and pulling out every remaining root that remains.

We have been given a voice, and as women, it's important that we use it. Iris needed to tell him that it was not OK for him to be calling her, even if the excuse was regarding a book. Why couldn't he consult an editor? Or better yet, his new fiancée? It was all part of a need for him to keep her tethered to his miserable life. Ladies, if you find yourself in this position, don't continue letting him treat you this way. The good news is, she's in California, in new unfamiliar territory, and has allowed herself to be receptive to the very sound advice of her newfound friends. This is great progress, Iris, keep making better choices to help you get over him for good.

Time away helped give Iris the strength that was needed to see herself as the leading lady she always was. It was that newfound community of friends, and her budding relationship with Miles, that helped to not only give her the courage that was needed, but it opened her eyes to the possibilities of things that could be. She was in a new, healthy place and space. That didn't prevent Jasper from calling, flirting, and bringing up past moments that made her think she meant more to him than she really did. What did that do? It stirred up her emotions for him. And if you can believe it, he went so far as actually flying to LA to see her—dirty rotten scoundrel! Even with his poorly executed endeavors at keeping his just-in-case-rebound girl available at his beck and call, Iris was triumphant. She had the better sense and came to the truth—that she was no longer deserving of sloppy seconds. Whether in a relationship or not— YOU are *not* a sloppy-seconds girl. Don't be this girl—no matter what you think your future might hold, if you've been dating for that long and he's still rejecting you and giving you no indication that there's any future for the two of you, he's not the one. Period.

The beautiful thing that we're seeing with Iris is not only the healing, but the restoration that comes from it. She's taking time to learn about herself, meeting new friends, and in the process, is truly developing a genuine friendship with Miles, who eventually realizes that his then–girlfriend was emotionally unavailable to him and was also stringing *him* along. Ouch. Come 'on people, it's time to stop glossing over what you already know—DEEP DOWN—is happening. Sometimes we leave the blinders on because we don't want to know, but yes, you do. And you should! The one thing we are sure to know about this Jasper, is "...once a Jasper, always a Jasper." Guys like Jasper will remain the same *unless* he has a catastrophic epiphany or a supernatural heart-transforming experience, like coming to know Jesus! No more of this, but "love is blind," excuse. We're done with that. It's time to live and breathe again. It's time for a new adventure. It's time for a few beautiful new friends to be a part of your tribe. It's also time for you to experience a love so beautiful and kind. It's a new season and can be one for you if you—like Iris—let it.

Of course, the story ends happy because she's kicked Jasper out of her life, and when she was ready, slowly allowed Miles in. This man was different than Jasper. Miles wasn't cruel or selfish. No. Unlike Jasper, he was kind, caring, patient, honest, talented (so talented), and equally as important, he lit up when he saw her. Isn't that the response we'd like to see in whoever we're dating? For some, we are so used ugly relationships, we don't know anything else outside of that, and we end up unhappy and miserable, thinking that nothing else outside of that exists. But we are here to tell you different. There *are* good men who are kind, respectful, fun, and who will treat you with respect —a "...one-woman-at-a-time kind of guy...," as Miles put it. This is a man deserving of a leading lady like Iris. If there is one thing we'd love for you to know and remember, is that you, too, are a leading lady.

Here are some questions below to honestly reflect on and work through. Take your time, and regardless of your answers, please don't be hard on yourself. You've gone through enough already.

1. Have you ever had a heartache you weren't fully healed from?

    _____

    _____

2. How did it cause you to act or behave?

    _____

    _____

3. Has the wound feeling healed?

    _____

    _____

4. If not, what do you need for the healing to fully take place?

    _____

    _____

5. Have you ever had a physical wound you needed healing from? How long did it take to heal?

    _____

    _____

6. What did the healing process look like? How did you tend to it?

_____

_____

7. What does that say about the healing process from the wound you still need healing from?

_____

_____

8. What will you do so that your heart completely heals?

_____

_____

Words to remind you of who you really are

These beautiful words of affirmation below will bring your spirit, soul, and body the health needed to get you back on track to taking care of you. "The words of the reckless pierce like swords, but the tongue of the wise brings healing." (Proverbs 12:18, NIV)

- ➢ I am a woman of value and of great worth. I, along with others in my life, see me as the wonderful person I am. I not only treat others kindly, but I am also treated kindly by others. I will be the first one to honor myself.
- ➢ I am awesomely and wonderfully made. (Psalm 139:14, NASB)
- ➢ I will not be afraid, for I have been chosen and called by name (Isaiah 43:1, NKJV)
- ➢ God has not given me a spirit of fear. He gives me power, love, and self-discipline. (2 Timothy 1:7 ESV).
- ➢ I am an incredible being who learns from my mistakes. Though I'm not perfect, I am smart, resilient, and a woman of value and worth.
- ➢ I am confident of this very thing, that He who has begun a good work in me will complete it until the day of Jesus Christ (Philippians 1:6).

> ➤ I will not allow myself to be mistreated and devalued by others. It doesn't matter what my past looks like or what has been done to me by others, today is a new day. Old things are behind me, and I am looking forward to the beautiful things life has in store. There is beauty all around me, and that includes me. I *am* beautiful.

No matter what your present or past looks like, if you find that you're unhappy, desperate, and that you have very much identified with Iris in how she was treated, things don't need to remain the same. There is hope and things can change. You are of value and worth. If you wrestle with low self-esteem and worth, return to this section of scripture and affirmation (also located in other chapters), reminding yourself who you—even when you don't feel like it. It is who you are, and we'll say it over and over again.

In the meantime, here are some of our faves to get the point across with some iconic notes that have stood the test of time.

The Holiday Playlist:

- ♫ *Quit Playing Games with My Heart* by Backstreet Boys
- ♫ *Just a Gigolo* by Louis Armstrong
- ♫ *You Keep Me Hanging On* by The Supremes
- ♫ *I Will Survive* by Gloria Gaynor
- ♫ *You Send Me* by Aretha Franklin

"Hi. You like me just the way I am."

Bridget Jones,
Bridget Jones's Diary

Bridget Jones, A Self-Devalued Girl Who Doesn't Know Her Worth

Bridget Jones's Diary

A light-hearted woman you want to see win from the get-go, we find Bridget Jones single and trying to navigate every area of life amidst the opinions of her family and closest friends. Still floundering through life in her thirties, we find a comical and silly girl with a lot of heart, stuck in unstable circumstances and relationships that seem to be on repeat. Feeling pressured by those around her, she is down on herself because she is single, overweight, and putting both food and her foot in her mouth at every opportunity. Can anyone relate? Even though we like Bridget, from the start you find a single thirty-something female who is a hot mess, who lives on her own, and attempting to be "set up" by her mom (who, by the way, is also still picking out clothes for her to wear). Let's just pause here for a moment. While this may not be a classic example of true "infantilization," we can already identify a parent-adult child relationship a little more coddling or catering than most, which helps us to better see why Bridget sometimes behaves the way she does.

So, early on in the movie, Bridget is already under pressure to find "Mr. Right," from her mom and others. Ever been this girl? Finding Mr. Right is on the forefront of her mind. If you're currently single, you might be able to relate. For Bridget it was magnified as she was in her thirties and not yet married. In so many of our cases as single women, we encounter external pressure from those in our circles, no matter how far out that circle may be. If you're single, someone is bound to ask you about your singlehood, wanting to fix it for you, as if it's something needing to be fixed. Newsflash: It's not. While some may be single and actively looking, others are single by choice—a topic we will be discussing further on in our accounts of colorful on-screen characters.

For the most part, people do mean well, but there are some who look at singlehood as though you have been plagued by a disease. In Bridget's life, this is evident in the painful scene where she was the only single attending a dinner party of "smug married couples," and the apparent point of focus through comments made at the dinner table such as, "...old girl...time's-a-running-out," or even the question, "Why is it there are so many unmarried women in their thirties these days, Bridget?" Talk about insensitive (and even demeaning) comments, making us super uncomfortable for her. She managed to hold her own, but it typified how many view single women over 30–unhappy, un-whole and, sadly, often ashamed. Whether or not people mean to intentionally hurt the feelings of unmarried women, this moment on-screen revealed what many single women do experience—embarrassment and shame. Bridget did handle the dinner party as best as she could, but even the strongest of women can only take so much.

Even though what people say shouldn't pressure you into doing something just to avert the opinions of others—especially when it comes to relationships—people will say things. Others may try and set you up, as we see Bridget's mom doing from the start of the film. What do you do if others do this to you? How do we respond? What we can't do is rush into something we're not ready for, just to avoid the pressure. Reasons to no longer be single shouldn't be determined by a holiday, your biological clock—no matter how old you are—by others, or so that you can "fit in" and no longer be lonely. Jumping into a relationship for any of those reasons will most likely do more harm than good. Anything else outside the perfect time for you, and anything outside of you truly believing this person is the one, isn't reason enough. Pressure or fear shouldn't dominate your decision to date.

Being single is the time to grow and be comfortable in your skin, and even though Bridget was in her thirties, as we will see, she hadn't yet done this. She hadn't yet learned how to be good to herself, because she hadn't spent the time learning and knowing who she was and understanding her worth. She was unhappy with who she was. Have you ever been this girl? Let's take a closer look at Bridget Jones, a single, unmarried "spinster," who drinks too much, talks too much, doesn't think very highly of herself, and believes she's running out of time on meeting "Mr. Right."

UNDER PRESSURE

Bridget was definitely under pressure to find true love. From her mom to the comments of others, we can see the heat was on. Have you ever been there? Feeling the pressure to no longer be "the unmarried," equating it with being unwanted (which you're not)? When you're in that space and you don't see any relief in sight, it can make you want to take matters into your own hands, doing whatever it takes to get into a relationship or even worse—settle for something less than what your heart truly desires, which is love. But it should be a love that is pure—a love that is patient, kind, and true. It's a love that doesn't seek its own. "To everything there is a season," but for the love we truly long for (and were made for), we need to be fully developed and ready before doing so. Being single allows the time to develop spiritually, emotionally, and in every other area growth is needed. It not only gives you time to learn about yourself but also to know who you are and to love yourself. We shouldn't underestimate the power of singlehood and what great things you can accomplish as a single. Even when others pressure you into no longer being a party of one, this is the time you can come to know and understand your worth. How do you see yourself? What kind of things do you say to yourself when no one is around? Being single is the time to treat yourself kindly. It's especially important to be comfortable in your own skin, learning how to enjoy yourself and working on whatever issues or shortcomings you may have carried into adulthood.

Timing really is everything, and not just in love, but to many things we walk through in life as well. Timing is also vital to being ready to be in a romantic relationship with someone, but Bridget isn't ready. Like many still-single girls in their thirties, she was not only open to love, but she was hungry for it. But had she done the work to be able to give someone what is needed in a relationship? We think not. She doesn't have what is needed to give to someone else, as she is barely hanging on by a thread to living life as a responsible adult herself. Is it just us, or have there been moments in our lives where we wanted something but weren't quite ready to handle or adequately care for it? Take a child, for instance, who wants to own or drive a car or even a bicycle that they've not yet learned to ride even *with* training wheels. It would be ludicrous to think that a child could handle something as massive as driving a car or even a bike with no training wheels. We wouldn't think of allowing a child to do that. Why? They aren't ready to handle the responsibility and the weight of what it is they're wanting. So, do we give it to them anyway? Heck no! There is a process. They need to build and learn what is needed in each season, which will lay a foundation for what's to follow.

The ugly side of alcohol

Of all our beloved characters in this book, Bridget is the one who "drinks like a fish," and because she mostly turns to alcohol to soothe her brokenness, she's often drunk, not having yet dealt with the issues causing her to drink in the first place. Drinking—or turning to substances—will never be the answer to whatever is causing your pain. To that, every former addict or recovered alcoholic would say, "Yes, and amen!" Time to do the hanky wave!

Though there is a jolliness to Bridget's character, she is clearly unhappy with who she is. With several scenes showing a drunken Bridget, you realize there is pain stemming from somewhere. From confessing to an eventual love-interest, Darcy—with whom her mom was trying to set her up—we embarrassingly find her revealing to Darcy—as she is both smoking and drinking—that she is, "...hung-over," and wishing her head was, "...in a toilet like all normal people." Normal? Okay, how have we come to a place where having our head in a toilet is normal? Is it just us? Well, it's unfortunate and while this alone is a reason to *not* be this girl, we've both walked out times in our lives where we have been this girl.

Cyndi: First of all, if you're trying to make a good impression, this most definitely *isn't* the way to go about doing it. Though it has thankfully been several years since the days of cooling my head on the rim of a toilet (I'm gagging even now just thinking of it!), I can relate to "Bridge" (as her friends called her) in some of these painful moments where she is working out the process of finding out who she is.

How long does it take for us to find out who we really are and what do we sometimes do in the process in search of ourselves? For me it was drinking. Initially the drinking stemmed from the loss of a child, but later in life it also had to do with feeling forgotten and overlooked. At the age of nineteen, single and pregnant, I miscarried at four months into the pregnancy. To this day I still can't explain the pain that was there–it was a hole that was so painful, and it remained there 24 hours a day, every day of the week. There was nothing I could do to make the pain go away and to make matters worse, the one I thought I loved at the time left me once I lost the baby that wasn't his (that's a whole other story). So, what's a girl to do? I did what I thought would remove the pain. I'd drink until I could no longer feel it, but in reality, I was really just making matters worse. I'd go from party to party, thinking that at some point, I'd start to feel the peace I once knew before all the turmoil began. Then I turned 20, doing pretty much the same, and guess what? The pain was still there. It was a huge ache in my heart that would not leave. Interestingly enough, I had never wanted to be a mom, or carry a baby, but once I found myself pregnant, I made a brave decision at that young age to do what, sadly, many are not willing to do today. I decided to keep the baby. Losing her was one of the hardest things I've ever had to bounce back from in life. I was 19 at the time. Twenty turned into twenty-one, and you know things didn't improve at *that* age, because now, drinking—for me—was legal. Before you knew it, I was 22. The ache was still there, and the choices I had continued to make were only making matters worse and making my life more complicated.

I came to realize that alcohol could never fix or remove the pain in my heart. And for me, getting drunk never ended well. Ever. I'd either end the night with my head in a bush, a toilet, or some random public place too drunk to care about what people thought regardless of what I was doing or saying—until the alcohol wore off and then I actually *did* care. It was a vicious cycle that went on for over two years. And not only had the hole in the middle of my heart remain, but it had become bigger. It wasn't until I turned twenty-three that I had this epiphany smack dab while dancing in the middle of a house party—unless I was drinking, I couldn't have fun. That made no sense to me. I, like Bridget, had been a pretty jovial girl my whole life. But here I was at my bestie's twenty-first birthday party, all of a sudden feeling very much like one of the donkeys in *Pinocchio's* Pleasure Island. All I wanted to do was get out of there so I could think (and hear) straight. So, while everyone else's hands were raised in the air to whatever the DJ was spinning (it had to have been good because it was the early 90's), I put the cheap beer down, walked out of the garage, to the back of the house, sat at the jacuzzi and started to think about making decisions that would positively impact the rest of life. I needed to make decisions that would change the trajectory of where I was headed, placing my feet in the direction of where I needed to go. I'd need to change the friends I hung out with, the type of guys I dated, and how I spent my time. By the way, Bridget could have used some friendship changes as well. Though loving and supportive as they may be, we saw some of their true colors when they had no problem kicking her out of the car, leaving her to fall drunk on her face, then driving off.

The journey home wasn't easy, but I did the work. I had to forgive myself and everyone else involved in losing my unborn baby. There was unreal vulnerability and intense moments of grieving that took place in my bedroom. And as I bitterly wept at the loss of the baby I never even really wanted, God met me, completely healing the pain and bringing me a true joy that I'd only experienced a few times in my life up to the point. If I could say it was miraculous, I would say it. And so, I will … It was a miracle. There was nothing else that could heal the pain, and in one night, it had completely vanished. I was healed and alive again. I was back to the joyful person I missed for a couple of years. Not only that—my face would never again be in a toilet, cooling off on the rim of the commode.

Ivette: Although I feel this should not be "normal," I do remember a time where I would drink for the competitiveness of it. How silly and immature is that? I would most definitely end up with my head in the toilet at the end of the night. But I was actually proud, because the friend I was competing with was a 260-pound, 6 '3 male that had gotten sick before me. Therefore, I was crowned the "winner" for the night. As I am writing this, I am disgusted by my behavior considering how old I was (17–18), and how does that make you a winner, anyway? What are you winning? Worst liver of the century? My drinking actually began when I was 14, but I always justified it, and so did my parents, with the infamous phrase, "If you're going to drink, I want you drinking at home." (I sense another book coming on, maybe one for parents). Not sure how that made things better, I just felt like it was okay and that I was a responsible and seasoned drinker by the time I was 17. Now being a mother and grandmother, I cringe at the memories of kneeling before the porcelain god, as some lovingly call it. I have made an effort to not make putting my head in the toilet the norm. I still scratch my head when full-grown adults are happily sharing their drunk stories with me.

Some things are better left unsaid

As we see Bridget's character unfolding, one of the characteristics so uncomfortable and awkward to watch was how frequently she says the wrong thing at the most inappropriate times—both in public, as well as in private. From the very beginning, we are squirming in our seats as we watch her initial conversation with the dashing Darcy derail faster than a runaway train going downhill on a 90-degree angle! She means well, but then she tells on herself and to someone she hasn't seen or really talked to since childhood. From confessing that she is unable to keep her New Year's Resolutions, to not following a simple speech format that would have kept her from on-stage embarrassment while introducing the featured author at his own book launch, she continues to word-vomit, time and time again, rarely learning from her previous mistakes. It was almost as if something was externally pulling it out of her and she couldn't resist, even knowing she had already said WAY TOO MUCH.

There is a proverb that says, "A wise man holds his tongue. Only a fool blurts out everything he knows; that only leads to sorrow and trouble." (Proverbs 10:14, TLB) There is a time and a place for talking about those dealbreakers, and telling this handsome barrister at their first re-meeting since they were children was not it. Had he asked her to divulge all that information? No, he didn't'. Maybe it stemmed from childhood, as her mother was known to make rude comments about others, and her uncle (who wasn't *really* a relative) blurting out inappropriate comments to Bridget. Regardless of why Bridget is this way, she's old enough now to where she ought to be holding her tongue and not saying everything she's thinking. Poor Bridge! Good thing for her, Darcy is a good guy. But how to tame the tongue? Is it possible to practice listening more and saying less? We think so. Very much so.

Cyndi: As painful as it was to watch, I felt Bridget's pain, for I, too, have had those types of these painful moments–more than I can even count or recall. Having won the "Most Talkative," Popularity Award all four years in high school, I relate to talking more than the average person.

My first memory of saying too much took place as a little girl. I couldn't have been more than 12 years old when my aunt called our house and I answered the phone, blurting out that my younger sister, "... Vonnie, might have the chicken pox!" My eyes were met with an immediate glare from Mom that said, "You've said too much." My punishment would be brushing my teeth with the worst-tasting Avon bar soap that existed at that time. I liked Avon, but this particular soap smelled so awful that I didn't even like washing my hands with it. I can still smell it now.

Talking too much as a child can be cute, but it's not the best characteristic to have as an adult, unless harnessed. While this trait had its perks of leading our student body, in addition to winning some other fun awards, as a young adult, I learned to get a hold of it through mentorship, working at it and from meditating on the Book of Proverbs. But how about working with that nervous energy that Bridget sometimes exudes when talking to possible love-interests? Being a people-person who enjoys talking to and meeting new people from all walks of life, meeting a new guy never really made me nervous; however, there is sometimes a stigma that unfortunately accompanies a single woman talking to a single guy in my line of work, which for a friendly person such as myself, has made me a little more self-conscious for sure. I recently experienced this while on a flight from LA to Nashville when bumping into a short-lived old flame 30,000 feet up in the air. Though I was truly happy to see him, I, suddenly didn't want him to think anything beyond our quick chat, and so what did I do? Cut it off prematurely, of course. I felt like an idiot for the remainder of the flight. How much fun would it have been to catch up with him? I mean, what were the odds of us being on the same red-eye flight? It would do us well to free ourselves from any thoughts of what others might think or say, so that we—as single women—can just enjoy a nice conversation with a nice single man without feeling awkward or judged by others. In case you're wondering, there were no butterflies, but it was great to see him. He's one of the good ones.

Ivette: What Bridget does in her conversation with Darcy, giving too much information that may not have been requested, is something that I painfully admit to doing myself. When I was younger, I was shy and didn't feel like I had much to offer in conversation. But somewhere down the line, I found that what I did like to do was get to know people and make connections. This is something called, "WOO," *Winning Others Over*, which is one of my top strengths from the *Strengths Finder* book (great book). So, I became that girl. However, after years of being the talker, I've learned that in order to really win someone over, you need to be a great *listener*. Even so, my husband will tell you that I was talking way more than listening the day we met. I knew that at 42 years old, I was running out of time to get married, and I was no longer willing to settle for someone else's version of life. I knew what I wanted, and I wasn't afraid to share it! It was funny—I literally asked him 21 questions, then I shared with him all of my "make-it and break-its," and he didn't run away—yet another sign that he was the one.

From Bridget, we can learn the importance of thinking before we speak. Even if you're prone to doing it the other way around, we can take some time to work on it. It's not too late. Are you the one who monopolizes the entire time of a "two-way" conversation? Do you often find yourself putting your foot in your mouth? Or perhaps in meetings or community settings you find that you're generally the one who does all the talking. Just because you've behaved this way possibly for most of your life, doesn't mean you have to stay that way. It is possible to work on this and change. But we're not just talking about giving it a try for 21 days and see-what-happens kind of change. Really, anything you put your heart into can help in this——and other——areas of your life. Can you see it now? Being in a group setting and enjoying listening to others share and not feeling the need to barge in. Can you envision talking with someone over a meal or on the phone, and really taking the time to hear what they are saying? Between excellent leadership tools such as, "7 Habits of Highly Effective People," great podcasts, webinars, wisdom-books like Proverbs, we believe that you can and will be the girl who doesn't say too much, but that instead, you think things through, listen to what others are saying, and share with thought behind it. It may take some taming, but through hard work and time, you can genuinely win others over and be *this* girl!

Inappropriate flirting and a case for sexual harassment

One of things dear Bridget does is fantasize about her boss, Daniel Cleaver, who, in this movie, is as slimy as they come. Initiating the first move via a direct message, he tells her she forgot her skirt, then commenting that her skirt was "out sick" that day. Enjoying the attention, she flirts back although she knows better enough than to go there. She flirtingly calls him out on "sexual harassment," and off they go. Losing all sense of self-respect at the attention she's apparently dreamt of for quite some time, she continues to ride out her curiosity with Cleaver, rather than doing the sensible thing she wrote of in her diary.

How do moments like these derail us from what we really want? She's writing one thing in her diary yet doing another. Not only that, but she is also being very intentional about it. Why, as women, do we allow ourselves to go there, even when we know darn well that isn't something that is right for us? We get that little bit of attention, and then it's as if all common sense goes out the door. We'd be better off responding to a fly that lands on you—at least its lifespan is short lived, so no chances of heartbreak *there*. Are we that desperate, that any attention we receive—whether inappropriate or not—is accepted and embraced? She wanted love and romance, but instead, what this led to was her becoming a sex-object for Cleaver, a man who had no character whatsoever. Sadly enough, she fell right into his trap. Willing to cross big-time boundaries with his employee, putting both of their jobs on the line ... we can see this was not the relationship Bridget really wanted, and yet, here she is, now purposefully wearing clothes (though still wrinkled and frumpy) now sheerer and shorter. For Bridget, taking a bite from this fruit was the beginning to a destructive and hurtful relationship.

Have you ever done that? Maybe you wanted so desperately to be married or be in a relationship, that you took second best—or in this case, last place. There are so many red flags about this guy, and yet now she's so high on cloud nine, she has become blind and oblivious to what she had at one point, seen so clearly. Everything from talking dirty to her via chat, to grabbing her behind in the elevator, he spells sleaze, and yet, she still allows her emotion to be won over by the attention from a great smile. Do you think that he hasn't done this before or that he wouldn't do it with someone else? But in that moment, we sometimes think, "I'm the lucky one," when in reality, you're nothing more than a one-night stand, which is what Bridget became to Cleaver. This couldn't have been more heart-breaking than when she (painfully) asks him, "What happens at the office?" For him, the answer was nothing. Nothing would happen there, because as far as he was concerned, they weren't anything more than what happened after-hours. Did she think that a one night-fling would bring her the man of her dreams? And why would she think that he would want to reveal it to anyone? Many men would willingly attest to this, and they'd have no shame in saying it. Many have and would say it again.

We see this happening in social media today when a relationship is not validated until announced on social media. Had social media been then what it is today, we know full well that he would not have been running to his phone to post about his time together with her. Why? Because in his eyes, this was nothing more than a fling. Maybe you've experienced this, maybe there have been times when your Mr. Man did not want to take a picture with you or perhaps, he didn't want to be out in public with you, because he didn't want to be seen with you out in public. Ouch. Instead of taking you somewhere beautiful and romantic, he brings you to one of the dingiest and off-the-grid places you have ever been. He wants you to be a secret. You want to make it known. It's time to come out of the dark. You are so much better than that. You are meant to shine and be seen, not hidden. In most cases, there is a reason he's not bringing you into the light. He sees her as nothing more than a sex-object. Now, while some of you might be thinking, "I'm good with that." Are you? Really?! How does that get you closer to what your heart truly desires? Stop rationalizing what he does and start realizing that how he is treating you isn't how you want to be treated. Oh sure, this song says one thing and your tribe tells you another, but none of that is who you are, nor is it what you want. How do we know? We've been there. Furthermore, in the case of Jones and Cleaver, that's a lawsuit in the making.

No longer tragic spinster, but yet still oh-so tragic!

They say talk is cheap, but something that's even worse than cheap talk, is cheap sex. "What is cheap sex," you ask? This is sex that is hollow, empty, and without attachment. It is what has taken place between Bridget and Cleaver. "No longer tragic spinster…," Bridget exclaims at a point in the movie when they're on a drunken weekend getaway, and she thinks they've passed the shagging phase and that they are now in an official relationship (they're not), later asking him, "Daniel, do you love me?" Well, the very fact that she's asking him this question, without first waiting for him to tell her (ladies, please don't fish for his declaration of affection!). If you have to probe for it, it's not authentic, and it's forced. What about forcing a relationship with a man is it that you're after? That only spells out another B R O K E N H E A R T. Stop this! Let him take the lead. It's what men are "men-t" to do. They are hunters, knowing full well how to get what it is they really want. If you have to search for it without him first telling you, you've already started going down that slippery slope.

What we see next isn't surprising, and Daniel's doing exactly what we thought he would. He is getting dressed in the morning, announcing to her that he is going back into town. His casual behavior isn't anything new. He's been casual all along. So let us answer that question for you. No, he doesn't love you—you're just the woman he is currently having casual sex with. But now, feeling used and a little anxious, she starts begging him to stay. Girl, wake up and please stop. Please. He is heading back into town because 1) He got what he wanted from you; and 2) There is someone else in the picture. Although it's only an on-screen character, we see not only the disappointment in her eyes, but it made us remember similar moments. Now, we wouldn't have dreamed of begging a guy to stay, but we can both recall personally doing the walk of shame in the morning. Although you may have acted as though it didn't bother you, it did. Didn't it? Wasn't there a hope that maybe you were more than just a one-night stand? The thing of it is, we weren't meant to give ourselves away in this manner to just any guy. The purpose of sex—which is meant to be a beautiful gift—is to consummate a marriage, as a sign of a covenant—a contract or agreement—with one another. If you want to look a little more into covenant, there's a great book called, "Marriage Covenant," beautifully depicting what a covenant is.

For Bridget, the romantic nightmare continues. Dismissive, he leaves her there and heads back into town to "work." She tracks him down, heading to his place without even so much as a phone call, which in itself is embarrassing because she still isn't his girlfriend, but even if she was, there is still protocol, ladies! They are not in an agreed-upon, committed, monogamous relationship, so *why* is she doing this? She suspects someone is in his flat, accusingly walking into his bedroom thinking she'd find someone in there. Well, as luck would have it, she doesn't. Why? Because the girl, Laura (a co-worker later referred to as an "American stick insect"), is in his bathroom, which is where Bridget finds her when she sees a women's sweater hanging in his entryway. Our heart breaks for Bridget, who thought she was out of the "tragic spinster," category, yet still being very much tragic. She feels defeated, depleted, and rejected. Who wouldn't? And at the end of a few additional conversations, including one which Cleaver tells her about being on a search to find someone special who makes you willing to go that extra mile. After this speech, he announces to her that he and Laura are engaged. You not only feel badly for Bridget, who until then was clueless that she was the "other woman," but also for Laura, his finance. Daniel was cheating on one and lying to the other.

Bridget is not only back to being "alone," but she's been used, lied to, has given herself to a man who cared nothing about her, and now she is heartbroken. How many of you think she would have been better off had she not gone the "Cleaver way?" Is this the way a healthy, promising relationship should have started? No! Additionally, she didn't even really know him. He was her boss. He crossed the line. And she responded to a man with no character. He was willing to cross lines at the office as her boss. He crossed the lines with her as his employee, and he crossed the lines with her as a woman who believed he was not attached to anyone else. And she did what many women mistakenly do–by giving him her body in turn, she had also given him her heart. Devastated, Bridget goes back to what she knows best—drinking. "I will not be defeated by a bad man and an American stick insect, instead I choose vodka and Chaka Khan." Still not the right choices, but at least she's seen the light.

This is where she begins to change the narrative, flipping the script on what her life has been. She chooses to do away with all the unhealthy habits in her life—the bad men, the heavy drinking, the cigarettes, her poor health, and a lousy job situation, tackling it head-on by working out, tossing out the toxic abuses in her life, and replacing her former books with better ones. Way to go, Bridget! And the best decision of all? Quitting her job, working for Daniel, and walking out to the Queen of Soul's "RESPECT." Anything Bridget can do, you can do. We've already noted that it will take work, and although it won't happen overnight, it is possible to have victory in every area of your life. You can overcome addiction; you can get on top of each of the vices that Bridget overcame. How? Keep reading, sister…'cuz you're on a roll. While all these changes were needed for Bridget (and to any who may be living it out in real-time), we were ecstatic that she was no longer working for a sleazy cheat of a boss. And let's be clear, though he was dishonest with Bridget, she wasn't the one he was cheating on. They weren't actually in a relationship to begin with. The cheating that had happened was on his fiancée, Laura. The fact that she too, was willing to stay with him after rolling around with Bridget on an English hillside, says a lot about the low self-esteem that Laura had, as well—a topic for another chapter.

Emotional pain from the one you love

While we are well-aware we've been sharing some hard-to-swallow issues, even though we don't *fully* see it here in Bridget, we do catch glimpses of it from her mom, and so want to address emotional pain we sometimes carry as adults, that so frequently can come from our parents—often the ones we love most.

It is not an unusual thing for adults to carry pain from things spoken to us as children by people we love, or from experiences in our lives. We see a slight example of this through Bridget's mom. Early on in Bridge's newly found pretend relationship with Cleaver, her mom not only breaks the news to her that she and her dad are divorcing, but in that same conversation also shares some pretty deep things, causing us to see that this could be why our dear Bridget is the way she is. It is likely she behaved in this manner for all of Bridget's life. Her mom, selfish and very much all about herself, painfully announces things to Bridget, without even giving it a thought of how Bridget would feel. In one of those conversations, she shares that if she had a chance to do it again, she might not have children. How and why would a mother say such a thing to her child? Well, she did, and many have heard far worse. Again, some things are better left unsaid, and in this case, it looks as though the apple doesn't fall too far from the tree. Ladies and gentlemen, we are seeing a generational curse recurring right before our very eyes. As an adult, this would still be painful to hear, causing emotional damage. Among many issues that could spring out of hearing something like that—rejection, abandonment, mother-child resentment—to name a few, hearing this type of hurtful comment can hold us back from fully being who we're meant to be. Maybe something like this has happened to you. If so, did it affect you and if so, how did it affect the way you live your life?

Ivette: This is a tough one to nail down. I feel—as women—we endure a lot of emotional pain from others from a very young age. We have so many requirements of how we should be as a young lady, what we are made for, as the capable body that gives birth to generations. How we should find Mr. Perfect and create the perfect family, all while obtaining a college degree, landing your dream job, and raising respectful little humans. And sometimes this is a job many of us end up doing on our own due to a failed marriage, relationship, or even some of the issues we will cover in the chapters to come. The emotional damage that can come from everything from negative words to external pressures put on us from our family, can be devastating and can be a reason we feel these are the only options we have.

Just as you are

Even if you're no longer single, now is *always* a good time to learn how to be good to yourself. Come to know and understand your worth. How do you see yourself? What kind of things do you say to yourself when no one is around? Being single gives you the time to learn to be comfortable in your own skin, learning how to enjoy yourself and working on whatever issues or shortcomings you may have grown into as an adult, and treating yourself kindly. In Bridget's case, cutting Daniel Cleaver off was one of the best moves she could have made. What she didn't do was go right into another relationship. She worked on her job for a bit, though she could have worked a little harder at it. She dusted herself off, picked herself up, got back up again.

To be able to get into a deep meaningful relationship, you have more to bring to the table when you have taken the time to focus on yourself and do the work. When do you jump back in the dating game? Should it even be a game at all? What about those who mean well—like Bridget's mom—who want to "set you up?" Do we make room for that? It's safe to say that should be a case-by-case situation. Like anything else in life, everyone's story is different. Some might meet others organically, while others may need a little extra help, like finding love online.

Back to being set-up. Bridget's mom had the idea of setting up Bridget with Darcy, and she wasn't wrong about the who, she was off about the "when." Whether someone is trying to set you up, or you're meeting a potential someone for the first time—what are you sensing? Do you feel at peace about it? Or is there something on the inside of you that senses it's best to wait and keep working on you? Now granted, no matter how long or hard we work on ourselves, we will never have fully arrived, because we will always be a work in progress. However, there should be some parameters you have already set in place about this new relationship possibly entering your world. You don't want devastation. You don't want the heartbreak, so, ask the questions. It's okay—this is you we're talking about. You have the permission to ask the questions about his character. Is he a serial dater? Do you have similar religious beliefs? What is his relationship like with his parents? Chances are that if he is kind and honors his parents, treating them with dignity and respect, he will treat you the same. Has he been married before? Does he have kids? And let's not forget something that should be equally as important—do you find him attractive? That's not to say he has to have the charming boyish looks of Luke Wilson, or the handsome jawbone structure of say...Viggo Mortenson, but this potential person should be someone you'd be attracted to.

Cyndi: There have been countless times where I have been asked if I could be match-made with someone, and while I'm definitely not against it, I have to say, I just don't feel like that's how it's gonna go down for *me*. But then again, life does tend to surprise me—as it does for many of us. In fact, I have not one, but two dear couple friends of mine who are happily married and all because of their willingness to be set-up on a date. Maybe I'm a little too controlling. Who knows? There was one instance about twenty years ago where a friend of mine and her hubby set me up with someone I had a very small crush on. When I got to their house, not only was I surprised to find him there, but I was also so upset as the last thing I wanted was for him to think I had anything to do with it. I didn't. I'll say this to those of you who like to play matchmaker. To this day I'm pretty sure he still would think I had something to do with it. Oh well. People, please let the individuals know your intentions of setting someone up, so that the two being set up aren't blindsided and uncomfortable. I wasn't pleased at all. What it *did* do for me, was it ended the crush. That same night.

Ivette: Sometimes we give into the pressure from people around us, to appease them, not necessarily because it's something we even want to do. Let me encourage you to stop caving into pressure and wait for the right moment, that's how my husband and I met. We both had been in horrible relationships, not knowing exactly where to go from there. I had literally just put my hands up and said, "I just want to be single forever and never deal with another bad relationship again." That is when the right moment presented itself. My now-husband and I had been hanging out in the same place and even hanging out with some of the same people for years, yet we had never even laid eyes on each other until the day we met. We had a quick encounter, which truth be told was slightly annoying. But I'm so thankful that I looked past that first impression which had nothing to do with him per se but was more about me being annoyed with his phone notifications going off every five seconds (which, let's be real, is not necessarily a character flaw). In fact, I was actually interested in how quick-witted he was when I asked him to silence his phone, as I was trying to have a conversation. Any man that was that quick on their feet, while being funny at the same time, was someone I was interested in getting to know. We ended up talking all evening and realized that we knew the same friends. What was pretty amazing, was that a dear friend of mine was actually his neighbor, whom I had recently invited to speak into my life, where dating wrong guys was concerned. He came over to me and whispered in my ear, "Oh, he is perfect for you," so I continued to get to know him and later we both knew that had we met even two months before, it would not have been the right time for us.

Let patience have its perfect work

Ladies, timing really is everything, and not just in regards to love, but to many things we walk through in life. Timing is also vital to being ready to be in a romantic relationship with someone, but Bridget isn't ready. Like many still-single girls in their thirties, she is not only open to love, but she's hungry for it. But has she done the work to be able to give someone what is needed in a relationship? We think not. She doesn't have what is needed to give to someone else, as she is barely hanging on to living life as a responsible adult herself. Is it just us, or have there been moments in our lives where we wanted something but weren't quite ready to handle or adequately care for it? Take a child for instance, who wants to own or drive a car or what about a bicycle that they've not yet learned to ride even *with* training wheels. It would be ludicrous to think that a child could handle something as massive as driving a car or even a bike with no training wheels. We wouldn't think of allowing a child to do that. Why not? Because they aren't ready to handle the responsibility and the weight of what it is they're wanting. So, do we give it to them anyway? Heck no! There is a process. They need to build and learn what is needed in each season, which will lay a foundation for what's to follow. It shouldn't be any different for us. Many of what we learn as kids are principles, we should be building our lives upon, but at a greater level.

As we've already stated, we love Bridget's resilience, because even though she has made more than her fair share of poor choices (Daniel Cleaver among them), she got back up on her two feet and moved on. One of the beautiful facets about life is when things are working on our behalf that we don't necessarily see until it's staring right at us.

So, we haven't talked much about Darcy, who Bridget believes is a man of no character, based on lies fed to her by Cleaver. Did we already say he was sleazy? Yeah, we did. Okay, so back to Darcy. Darcy and Cleaver had been close friends, until Cleaver was caught cheating with Darcy's wife. Getting to Bridget before Darcy ever had the chance, Cleaver deceives her, pitting the two childhood friends against each other. Even though he didn't really want her, he made sure that Darcy wouldn't have a chance with Bridget. It wasn't until a fateful night at a dinner party, that Darcy and Bridget were able to connect for a moment, having a short-but-honest conversation, in which Bridget confesses she feels like, "... an idiot most of the time...". This was in part, because everyone at the party was a couple, except Bridget and because of that, she and her singleness were the focal point of conversation. Being singled out is a thing, folks—especially by those who have forgotten what it's like to be single. How do we know? We both have experienced it—at gatherings, events, church—it's all the same. Different venue, but same questions. "When are you going to start dating someone?" "Maybe it's' because you're too picky," or a personal fave of Cyndi's—" What about *him*? *He's* single...". Yeah, it's a thing. For Bridget it was slightly worse, so she managed to call it a night. Here's the thing, if you don't like the scenario, you *can* leave. We give you permission. Darcy tells her he doesn't think she's an idiot, and wraps it up by saying these words you have wanted Bridget to hear from a man as kind as this: "I like you very much ... I like you very much... just as you are." Touched by his words, Bridget is speechless (for once!), but the moment is spoiled as Darcy's date interrupts this moment by snapping at him, not once, but three times. That's a whole other book, but until then, let your man lead, ladies, and don't be *that* girl.

Darcy's confession of liking Bridge the way she is, is the starting point of what ends up becoming the relationship she has longed for. We cheer and applaud this beautiful new turn of the tide as Darcy's gestures to Bridget are caring and honorable. Bridget seems to have a better handle on the kind of guy she not only truly desired, but who was also worth waiting for. We think things are going smoothly for her and Darcy until Cleaver shows up uninvited and unannounced in their lives one more time. Though this scene is hard to swallow, we all knew it was coming, as that lie told by Cleaver needed to be addressed. Ending in a pretty intense fight between the two, Bridget comes to Cleaver's aid, turning on Darcy who punched Cleaver one last time. Little did she know it was his wife that Cleaver had cheated with. Darcy was the victim. Hurt with Bridget's siding, he leaves, leaving her alone with Cleaver, who then proceeds to tell her, "If I can't make it with you, I can't make it with anyone." Jerk.

This is where we see a mature Bridget defending her worth. She boldly tells Cleaver, "I am not willing to gamble my whole life with someone who wasn't quite sure. It's like you said, I'm still looking for something more extraordinary that that." Which is basically what he told her in defending himself after being found with another woman the day after their weekend getaway. Bridget is now back to being single, and we are thrilled. Though the minutes of the movie are winding down, we feel this is the best place to be for a woman caught in a love triangle between the admiration of two men, to make the best decision for herself. Move on, girl...move on!

Bridget and Darcy do end up together at the end of the movie, which like most Romcoms, is what the plot climaxes to. We are thankful for the character of Bridget Jones, because while we believe she'd make a great friend, we don't want to be this girl when it comes to how we see ourselves, allowing ourselves to be treated by those who don't know our value.

If you find that you, like "Bridge," have veered off into destructive patterns in life and love, there's hope. Is there work to be done? Yes. But there is hope! Take some time to identify some of the issues you see Bridget dealing with. In a journal or even your laptop, write them down.

1. What are some ways you already know you can easily stop or change?

    _____

    _____

2. Who are the true friends in your life who will act as guardrails?

    _____

    _____

3. Write their names down, following through by asking them to speak into the areas of your life where you need help.

    _____

    _____

4. Do you have some personal goals or things you've been wanting to work on but haven't because you've been too busy being in a relationship to not be alone?

    _____

    _____

Now's the time to be honest with yourself. What are those goals? Write them down, using this time to work in your favor. Finally, build yourself up with declarations of who you really are—a beautiful, amazing, capable, responsible, smart, woman of value. Proverbs 18:21 says, "Death and life are in the power of the tongue and those who love it will eat its fruit." In other words, your words are powerful. Watch what you say. If you have a habit of tearing yourself down with your words, here are some things you can say about yourself–and not just once, but over and over until they come alive to you at the core of who you are.

Not sure what to say or what that sounds like? Here are some examples of declarations you can repeat several times a day, every day. Although there are thousands of declarations that exist, we've included seven below—one for every day of the week, which is a great place to start! Some can be said by looking at yourself in the mirror or writing them on Post-it notes, but at the very least, open your mouth and let these words come out of your mouth about yourself! Speak these words of life, saying them over and over (and over) again, throughout the day—especially if you feel yourself slipping back into those old destructive patterns.

These beautiful words of affirmation will bring your spirit, soul, and body the health needed to get you back on track to taking care of you. "The words of the reckless pierce like swords, but the tongue of the wise brings healing." (Proverbs 12:18, NIV)

> I am a woman of value and of great worth. I, along with others in my life, see me as the wonderful person I am. I not only treat others kindly, but I am also treated kindly by others. I will be the first one to honor myself.

> I am awesomely and wonderfully made. (Psalm 139:14, NASB)

> I will not be afraid, for I have been chosen and called by name (Isaiah 43:1, NKJV)

> God has not given me a spirit of fear. He gives me power, love, and self-discipline. (2 Timothy 1:7 ESV).

> I am a girl who learns from my mistakes. Though I'm not perfect, I am smart, resilient, and a woman of value and worth.

> I am confident of this very thing, that He who has begun a good work in me will complete it until the day of Jesus Christ (Philippians 1:6).

> Because I've been made in the image of God, I will not allow myself to be mistreated and devalued by others. It doesn't matter what my past looks like or what has been done to me by others, today is a new day. Old things are behind me, and I am looking forward to the beautiful things life has in store. There is beauty all around me, and that includes me. I *am* beautiful.

No matter what your present or past looks like, if you find that you're unhappy, desperate, and that you have very much identified with Bridget, as if someone were writing an excerpt about you, there is hope and things can change. You are of value and worth, and from this point on, the strides you take will be in that direction. If that's something you've struggled with, open up to this chapter, remind yourself who you really are by declaring those affirmations over you and about you, for those affirmations are who you really are—even if you're the only person who believes it. There is another who does, as well. And what He says about you is all that matters. "Fear not, for I have redeemed you; I have called you by Your name; You are Mine." (Isaiah 43:1, NKJV)

Finally, for all you melomaniacs (music lovers), this movie has an OUTSTANDING soundtrack, by the way!

Playlist:

- ♪ *I'm Every Woman* by Chaka Khan
- ♪ *RESPECT* by Aretha Franklin
- ♪ *Ain't No Mountain High Enough* by Diana Ross & The Supremes
- ♪ *Someone Like You* by Van Morrison
- ♪ *Stop, Look, Listen (To Your Heart)* by Diana Ross & Marvin Gaye

"I've loved him all my life."

Sabrina Fairchild,
Sabrina (1995)

Sabrina Fairchild, A Smitten Dreamer Void of Reality

Sabrina (1992)

Dear, darling Sabrina. Oh, how we love our naive Sabrina. If there ever was a deer in headlights character through-and-through, Sabrina is it, in both the old version, played by the dashing Audrey Hepburn, and the newer, played by Julia Ormond. Because the newer version's Sabrina had us in severe protest of her weakness at even the sight of her beloved David, *this* was the girl we *knew* we did *not* want to be.

From the very beginning of the movie, we meet Sabrina, a young lady who is playfully and curiously climbing up into a tree as she hears music at what she knows is a Larrabee party. Her eyes are dreamingly glued to the scene, taking in the beauty of it all. Lights are twinkling, with a moonlit ocean serving as the backdrop to an elegant party of elites sipping champagne and swaying to the orchestra as people float across dance the floor in tuxedos and formal gowns. The daughter of the chauffeur to the Larrabees—known to be one of the wealthiest families on the shore of Long Island—she has lived there for a good portion of her childhood. However, now as a young adult, we find she is infatuated with the youngest of the Larrabee men, David, with whom she had her first dance with as a little girl. David Larrabee, a deadbeat rich kid, is the playboy of the family who lives off the fortune of his family; Though he is indeed magnetic, his *creative* charm is lacking when it comes to wooing women, scoring him a solid "0." Now watching him dance with a woman from afar at one of the many Larrabee parties, David, a player who is a creature of habit, goes to the bar, grabbing

45

a bottle of champagne and two champagne flutes—as he often does at their family night parties—is now on his way to the solarium to meet with his new lady-friend. Hearing a noise behind him, he turns around. It's Sabrina, who has jumped down from the tree hoping to get his attention, to which he responds, "Oh, it's just you Sabrina. I thought I heard somebody." Looking at him like a scared little doe, she replies, "No, it's nobody." This whole scene is painful and hard to watch for so many reasons, but we'll just focus on two. First-off, she totally lacks the ability to hold a conversation with him. There was no opening line to hold his attention as he was walking by, so why did she feel the need to jump down from the tree? This would have been the perfect time for her to intrigue him with something interesting to say, causing David to see her as the beautiful and talented girl that she was becoming. But as we can clearly see, she is not up to par yet, as she was still so young in thought and behavior. We also see this when she asks her dad (when she was still in the tree) "Am I witty ... Do you think I'm funny?" This is when her dad, being annoyed, told her to get down, stating, "... full-time observation of David Larrabee is not a recognized profession." We hate that she thought so little of herself, that she felt she needed to tell him she was nobody.

Ladies, we've said it before when looking at Bridget Jones' character, but we'll say it again. You *are* somebody. You *are* of value, and you *are* of worth. For some of us, we base our value on what we do for a living, how much we weigh, what we drive, or where we live. These factors—though external—have nothing to do with our value. The simple fact that you are a woman created in the image of God (Genesis 1:27), you are of worth. Proverbs 31:10 breaks it down this way, "An excellent woman [one who is spiritual, capable, intelligent, and virtuous], who is he who can find her? Her value is more precious than jewels *and* her worth is far above rubies *or* pearls" (Amplified version).

So, here's the thing—our worth is not based on feelings or how others view or treat us. In Sabrina's case, she was so wrapped in this fantasy world created in her mind that she felt that her worth was based on the Larrabee's value. If you have ever found yourself in this situation, or maybe you're there now, the negative imaginations we have of ourselves need to be eradicated from our thoughts and minds. One of the biggest mistakes that we make in our youth and sometimes into our adulthood, is to think negatively about ourselves, which in turn, affects how we talk to and about ourselves.

It is important to note that, "A soothing tongue [speaking words that build up and encourage] is a tree of life, but a perverse tongue [speaking words that overwhelm and depress] crushes the spirit. (Proverbs 15:4, Amp Version). Most people don't automatically function this way. There are various reasons for this—brokenness, rejection, or maybe others have spoken this into your life. No matter the reason, you need to know you are of value and worth. We realize that changing a faulty mindset that has been plaguing you for most of your life doesn't come quickly or easily. It will take work. Even for those who may not struggle with it as much, there is still a tendency to talk down to ourselves when others aren't around. The good news? There is hope. We believe in you and will be addressing ways to walk through this towards the end of this chapter. We're not here to just say don't be this girl, but having been this girl to some degree, we understand the struggle of low self-worth, knowing that there is victory no matter where you are on the spectrum.

Sidenote: Before we go any further, we must point out the comedy we see in Sabrina trying to get David's attention as *he's* walking to the solarium in a tuxedo, while Sabrina—on the other hand--is wearing a denim jumper and Converse. That's fine if you're running errands or painting a piece of art, but given the circumstances, David's attention is clearly on a lady who is dressed to impress as she has primped and prepped for the party.

Sabrina's character lacks confidence, and though she is sweet, she initially comes across as pitiful and perhaps even slightly delusional. Raised in nice quarters by her single dad, on Larrabee property, she has grown up living above the garage and is the Fairchild's (the English chauffeur's daughter). She has spent way too much time watching the lifestyles of the rich and famous from a tree on her side of the world. We know and understand ... this movie is a classic. "How can you say such things?" We get it, for we too, have enjoyed watching the likes of Sabrina for years, but with romantic-grooming like this, it's time for a wake-up call. So, it is with strong hearts and sound minds that we mutually agreed on this movie. This, friends, is our next chapter: Sabrina. Don't be this girl.

He doesn't even know you exist

Have you ever had your head so very high up in the clouds that you couldn't quite see straight? Maybe like Sabrina, it's been someone you've been crushing on for quite some time. While we too, are smitten with the person of Sabrina, we kinda just want to shake her and say, "Hey, girl. Get your head outta the clouds and take a lesson from *En Vogue*, and come 'Back to life... back to reality.' It's her dad that truthfully says, "You've spent more of your life on that tree than you have on solid ground." Solid ground. That's exactly what Sabrina needs, and we're SO thankful that her plans include moving to Paris so she can hopefully start living the life she was meant to live—one not chained up to the "idea of a man," who barely knows she exists. Even up to the night before leaving for Paris, she asks her dad, "What if he forgets all about me?" Really?!? Her dad honestly and quickly delivers a response, asking her, "How can he forget someone he doesn't know exists?" Ouch. He's being brutally honest, but she doesn't hear a single word he's said. His words have fallen on deaf ears. Even in the midst of a wonderful opportunity to work overseas for a fashion magazine in Paris, she's still thinking about David. Ooof. She's got it bad.

So, though we haven't really wanted to break our chapters down scene by scene, we just couldn't leave this out because of how ridiculous this precious girl is. And, who knows, maybe you're this person, or maybe you know someone like this. But even with all that her dad has said, even though when David sees her, he doesn't really "see" her, as she is packing, she feels the need to say goodbye to David. Say goodbye? What for? Your dad already told you he doesn't know you exist, and yet you still feel the need to say goodbye. This is obsession, folks. And it is delusional. So, she barges into their home, walks up the stairs and with shaky determination goes into his room. His room, as in his *bedroom*?! Yep, his room. We feel that's a little intrusive, encroaching on his personal space, but it is what she musters up the courage to do and so does it. What she doesn't know is that it's actually his brother, Linus (played by Harrison Ford), who is in the closet. She proceeds to tell him she's leaving for Paris saying, "I don't expect you to think about me while I'm gone. You haven't thought about me while I was here … I think I know you better than anybody else … whatever they think or say, I know the truth … you're kind and generous (by this time Linus is rolling his eyes) and we are laughing so hard. Oh, Sabrina. Why are you doing this? She continues, "For what it's worth, know that someone very far away is thinking of you … and if there's ever anything I can do…," she is cut off by Linus who comes out asking her to bring him an Eiffel Tower paper weight. She can't believe she just poured her heart and soul out to Linus and so runs out of David's room, which—let's just be clear—she had no business being in there in the first place. Furthermore, why would she ever think there'd be anything she could do for David Larrabee? He barely knows you exist. Stop doing this.

Cyndi: I remember talking to a gal who let me know there was a special someone in her life. But when I started to ask questions, I came to realize the person she was talking about, didn't actually know she existed. It was a shared moment they had in a specific space they both happened to be in, but he didn't know her, he didn't know her name, and so, of course, didn't pursue her. Why? Because it wasn't a real relationship to start with. As women, we can probably all agree that there have been times we've maybe daydreamed. I've had my fair share of being obsessed with a few actors in my life. Once season my crush was actor, Viggo Mortensen, after *Lord of the Rings* came out. And with all my resources, I managed to land in the same spaces as Viggo from time to time. However, one thing was clear. I knew he didn't know me from Adam, and to think otherwise would have been *delusional*. Have *you* ever found yourself daydreaming of someone, only to realize that they may not have a clue as to who you are? If we're going to make headway in healthy relationships, we must be very clear about the difference between what's real and what's fantasy. Unfortunately, with Sabrina, even with all the talks and David not giving her a second thought, she doesn't get a clue. Even if someone knows you exist, but they don't think of you or look at you romantically, read their language correctly and don't read into something more than what it is. He either likes you or he doesn't. He either knows you exist, or he doesn't. Like Sabrina, don't daydream about something that might never be, or even worse—something that doesn't exist.

An American in Paris

Even in Paris we see that Sabrina has a hard time letting go of the idea of David, which is proof enough that a geographical change doesn't necessarily affect matters of the heart. We must address the heart. This is a man she has had affection for, for many, many years. He doesn't even know she exists, so how do we continue to live with thoughts of what could be if there never was even a hint of interest from the other party. Ever heard of strongholds? "What is a stronghold" you ask? *Wordhippo* defines it as, "A place built to withstand attack."[1]

In this case, Sabrina's strongholds in her mind wouldn't necessarily protect it against attack, but what it has built is a fortified a place in her thoughts and mind, so that even though she is now on an entirely different continent, the stronghold of her obsession and fantasy of David remains.

The unfortunate truth of the matter is that we see a smart, beautiful girl who has spent years dreaming about someone who she really means nothing to and who may very well end up belonging to someone else. What a shame. Can you relate? Have you been living in a fantasy world, spending countless hours thinking of someone you don't even know or who doesn't know you exist? If so, it's time to start focusing on what's real: the people around you and being present in the space where you are.

Can you imagine having the opportunity to live and work in Paris and yet, that time isn't fully enjoyed because you can't seem to get *him* off your mind. Girl, wake up and please smell those Parisienne Roses. You're. In. Paris. Let Long Island be a thing of the past so you can move forward and progress. Learn to speak the language, enjoy those croissants, that good coffee and delicious French food. Learn all you can from the best of the best in Paris, shop those beautiful couture stores, enjoy the Champs-Élysées, take it all in and fully immerse yourself in that whole new world that has been waiting for you. Jump in—all in—and forget about that little boy you left behind. It's time to grow into the sophisticated woman you are, with a bit of French flair. You're in Paris now!

· · · · · · · · ·

1   "What is a stronghold?", *wordhippo.com/what-is/the-meaning-of-the-word/stronghold*

She is introduced to Louis, but her heart still belongs to the all-American boy. A transformation starts to take place, but it's more of an inward one, that you start to see affecting the outward. We never want to stay where we are. We should always grow and develop into the person we are meant to be. There is reflection and introspection. She begins to see life through a different pair of glasses—rose-colored glasses. In fact, the ones she wore when living in the States even come off. Her style changes. A more confident, not as clumsy, Sabrina emerges. Seeing the change in Sabrina is refreshing. "America is my country … and Paris is my hometown," saying she'd always feel that way about Paris.

Not a little girl anymore

You've heard the saying, "All good things come to an end," and Sabrina's time in Paris was no exception, except that her time there seemed to be best spent towards the end of her time living there. It appears that she did learn a little about herself, but she didn't quite let go of the idea of David, even hearing the news that he was finally engaged and soon to be married. There is something very wrong with this. You know he's engaged. You haven't seen him in years. He was never your boyfriend to begin with, and you can't seem to let him go? Get over him already. *Be* present in Paris, soak it all in, let go of what never was, and be fabulous with someone who actually sees you. We just can't with this one.

The next time we see Sabrina back in the States, having just arrived from Paris, she comes into town, arriving on a shuttle, taking it all in, she sees it. Yep, it's David's red Ferrari. Just almost as quickly as she spots his car, he sees a sophisticated woman looking as though she stepped out of a Chanel ad, wearing a chic, new coiffure (hairdo), accented by an all–black tailored pants suit, glamorous black sunglasses, and a beautiful black hat. Paris has transformed her, indeed. But other than aging, he didn't change much. The man with wandering eyes (even though he's newly engaged, which is proof that a ring doesn't always change a man from the inside out), almost gets hit by a car, as he is distracted by this beautiful woman. Now looking more French than American, he doesn't even recognize her. "Hi. How are you?" she asks. He replies, "I'm great (pausing), how are you?" The exchange between the two is slightly awkward for David—who offers to give her a ride home, still has no clue as to who she is, and she is gushing from cheek-to-cheek with a hue almost as red as what is most likely a perfect Chanel lipstick color. Accepting the ride, she playfully flirts with him, as she hides behind her Parisienne sunnies, and although she has removed both hat and sunglasses by the time they're turning on the street she tells him she lives on, he still has no clue who she is. Arriving at his house, he invites her to his mom's birthday party—something she has dreamt of since the first day she fell for him. Enters Linus, saying, "Hello Sabrina … have a good time in Paris?

You look all grown-up …," breaking the flirting between the two, as she answers Linus, now embarrassed her identity has been revealed and as David is not only in disbelief that it's Sabrina, he is actually shocked. Knowing his brother all-too well, Linus looks at him after Sabrina leaves saying "David, no … No." It's a little too late for "no." Yes, he's engaged, but he's now infatuated with the new-and-improved-sophisticated Sabrina. Guess she needed to get out of those sneakers and overalls after all.

The issue? David is engaged to someone else. And so now we have Sabrina oblivious to that fact, because he has now indicated interest in her, and all she can think about is what she's in for—having grown up watching him do it to other women for years—the dance, the romance, the champagne, and the solarium. There wasn't much to his method, but why should she care? David had invited her to a Larrabee party.

Be where you have always wanted to be, but with a man of your own

There is no reason whatsoever that Sabrina should have been excited at David's invitation to his mother's birthday party. He was engaged to be married, and yet she was acting as if he wasn't in a relationship with anyone at the moment. Not only that, she already knew the drill of what he'd do, what song he'd do it to and where he'd take her to do it. She was looking forward to a night that she'd seen so many others experience with him. What's with these women thinking it's okay to be "second best" or to get someone's "sloppy seconds"?

The night of the party, she walked over from the "help" side of the property, looking stunning from head to toe. In the most beautiful of gowns, she was elegant, beautiful, sparkling, and dazzling, outshining all the beautiful ladies at the party that night. The moment David saw her, he couldn't take his eyes off her. It made the entire scene so uncomfortable to watch. "Where was his fiancée?" you ask. A doctor, she was out of town attending an event in California. Sabrina was a lovely sight to behold, and everyone there watched their chemistry–Linus, their mom, David's in-laws, the help … all eyes were on Sabrina and David. Her behavior was not only foolish, but it was also unfair. Why do we have to do that? Why not realize who we are—women of value and worth—and accept the fact that if you have to try and win someone over who is already with someone else, you need to let it go. It's not yours to begin with. Do the work, spend time reflecting, but move on. We're not talking about a man who's a free agent, we're talking about a man who is engaged to be married. He's already taken, miss. Leave the man (and his fiancé) alone. Even if he has a problem with a wandering eye that failed to keep his eyes only on his fiancé, why are you okay with contributing to his unfaithful heart? Does it go back to the low self-esteem we see at the beginning of the movie? Maybe, but it's still not acceptable and doesn't make it right. No woman—no matter how low your esteem is—should be the reason a man cheats in his heart, while acting it out in person. What we really want to say is, "Didn't your mom teach you any better?" But Sabrina's mom had long since passed, and in some cases, to answer the question more broadly, many moms don't.

Ivette: We see this so often, when someone meets a nice guy or gal and their close friends decide they want to see if they might be a better fit with this person, not even thinking about their friend's feelings. For years I had a friendship that, as an experienced woman, my mom would tell me that this friendship wasn't what I thought it was. She'd point out that this friend was jealous of me and that our friendship would end badly. She was right. Thanks for your wisdom, Mom. Too bad I didn't listen to it until it was too late. This friend would always want to meet my newest boyfriend. And when she did, she'd take him aside and even flirt with him or try to get him to be with her. Y'all, this was my best friend! She said that she was trying to see if he was worthy of being in a relationship with me. And although maybe her head was in the right place, her actions were not—not to mention she was married and had no business putting herself out there as bait!

In David's case, Linus is the one who determined he'd be the one to run interference, stepping in to change the trajectory of where his younger brother was possibly headed with Sabrina. Though it'd be nice to think he was doing it merely for his little brother's love life, there was something in it for Linus. Though he, too, saw Sabrina as a breath of fresh air, he was now using her as a business scheme pawn so as not to interfere with the marriage of his brother, with whom he had entered a powerful and pricy business merger. Nothing was clearer about his intentions than when he said, "I'm not about to kiss off a million dollars. I don't care what she did to her hair."

His plan worked, only all too well. David ends up injured, eventually sitting on the champagne flutes meant for him and Sabrina. Linus steps in at an awful attempt to get her mind off David, as now it seems to be her desire to regularly check in on him after the glass broke off on his behind (that had to hurt–you could feel the pain when hearing them break the moment he sat on them). Why he put them in his back pocket, we don't know, but it's one of the more humorous moments in the story. As for Sabrina, she continues to embarrass us as we watch her feeling the need to visit and check in on him. As she does, we find ourselves yelling at her inappropriate behavior on-screen, "You're not his fiancée. He already has one, who happens to be a doctor. Leave him alone!" What we can't seem to realize is why she thinks it's okay for her to do this. Perhaps had she not been in "Lala land," daydreaming and pining for David for all those many years, she would have had her head on more straight saying, "I appreciate the invite. Thanks, but no thanks. You're engaged to be married." End of story. But now she's here being played like a fiddle because she crossed boundaries never meant for her to cross.

What we see unraveling next is a series of manipulated events set up by Linus to keep Sabrina pre-occupied, which again, had she known her "place" in David's life, that would never have happened in the first place. Have you ever found yourself in a similar situation? Maybe your answer is, "No way. Never have and I never will." Do you know others who maybe don't quite know their place? Friends who are okay with being the other woman?

Cyndi: Being raised in a single-mom home due to my dad's unfaithfulness, I've had a difficult time understanding the reasoning or thought process of the other woman. And for a while, it was very hard to forgive what my family endured for at least ten years, if not more. As I watched Sabrina being okay with receiving his affection and attention, knowing full well he was engaged, I lost all sense of respect for her, making it difficult for me to feel for her as the lost character that she was. And that's probably what many women who find themselves in this position are–lost. Ladies, I'm sorry, but if this is you, this is not okay. It is not okay to be a homewrecker. I realize it does take two, but if and when you find out he's married, that's when you cut it off. Period. None of this, "Oh, but I love him," or "But, you don't know how he makes me feel." Well, what you're doing isn't love, it's lust. And secondly, that is a selfish statement to make, because you know what? You don't know how that makes his family feel. You don't know how that makes his wife feel. You don't know what that does to his kids. It's not okay to be this woman. I've always said, if every woman joined forces together to support each other, "the other woman," wouldn't exist, for she would care more about the wife than she does for herself. If you are the other woman, or have been her, you can still do the right thing, and say goodbye to the man who isn't yours to begin with. Ask God to give you the strength to do it. You don't want to do this to his family. Would you want it done to you?

> *"Therefore, whatever you want men to do to you, do also to them…".*
>
> ***(Matthew 7:12, NKJV)***

Although she's never apologized to my sisters or me, I have since forgiven the other woman, but sometimes I have to return to that place of surrender, forgiving her again. It's okay to do that. Do whatever it takes to allow forgiveness to flow freely in your hearts. I forgave my dad long before, because I loved him, but forgiving someone who I barely knew and didn't love was difficult. It may be difficult, but it is possible. "With man it is impossible, but not with God. For all things are possible with God." (Mark 10:27, ESV)

Sabrina became the other woman when she came back, knowing full-well what David's intentions were and that he was engaged. She was so focused on having her moment with him--a moment she had wanted for years, that she was willing to not only disrespect herself, but also his fiancée. But let's talk a little about David. He is a spoiled young man—a womanizer with too much money. And no purpose since we're being honest. Why does she even want to be with this guy? Is this guy attractive to you? We hope this is someone you'd want to run away from—far away. This type of situation brings heartache and drama. Even though he comes from a wealthy family, he has absolutely nothing to offer. This is not the kind of guy we should be looking for. We already know that money is not the key to happiness. In fact, it's been said, "the love of money is the root of all evil."

All in the family

Doing business is what he does best, and so Linus orchestrates as many romantic outings and business-type events created just for Sabrina, using her new-found talent of photography as the reason behind their trips. So now, both Linus and Sabrina begin spending a lot of time together–on the beach, eating out, flying to beautiful beach towns, and the list goes on and on. In the process of capturing beautiful candid shots which she thinks is for the Larrabee Company, she captures him, seeing him in a newer and softer light. As Linus' strategies with Sabrina are working, what we also see in the process of the two of them now spending time together is that she begins to have a change of heart. A transference of affection has taken place, and Sabrina starts developing feelings for Linus, David's brother. Girl! What are you doing? Can you just *not* for a little bit? Losing feelings for David is great, and so now would be a great time to focus on you, and quiet any feelings you may have towards anybody. Just take a break. But not Sabrina. She goes from one brother right to the next. Interestingly enough, Julia Ormand plays the same type of character, creating havoc between not just two, but three brothers in *Legends of the Fall*. Don't be this girl. While most of us may never experience doing the George-of-the-Jungle swing from one sibling to the next, many of us can unfortunately relate to going straight from one relationship to another without any second thought of healing or reflection, no time to stop and process. Nope. Just full-on transference–from one brother, to another. Has this happened to you?

Ivette: I have to say that I know this all too well. As maddening as it was to watch Sabrina do this, I watched this scene wanting to shake our sweet little Sabrina back into reality. But as I watched on, I realized I had done this myself. I had fallen for one brother who was a childhood friend and years later had a moment with the other. The worst part of this scenario was that I was old enough to know better. But I thought, "Hey! I'm single, so it's okay." It wasn't okay. This isn't acceptable.

How did Sabrina handle going from one brother to the next? The switch was a little rocky, but once she was locked in on Linus, she was all in because she was still hungry for love. Linus' wooing of Sabrina was heartbreaking. What she perceived as romantic gestures from Linus, were in actuality, calculated occurrences to deter her from his younger brother. And it worked; little by little, her desire for David began to wane. Had it been the other way around, you kind of got the feeling that neither she nor David would have known what to do with their emotions had that first night at the Solarium taken place. But now, we'll never know. She's full-blown fallen in love with Linus. It must have been an emotional roller-coaster for her. Imagine experiencing the initial excitement with her fantasy about David seeming to come true, only to immediately be followed by disappointment as Linus shows up, instead of David, at the Solarium. Isn't it crazy that while we can easily identify it while watching it on screen, it's not so obvious when we're the ones going through it. Have you ever found yourself on an emotional roller-coaster between two guys? Has it been as quickly as Sabrina's three weeks-ish record? We saw something very similar in another movie great, *The Family Stone*. The great news about seeing it unfold before our very eyes in Sabrina is that we can allow ourselves to be mentored in how *not* to be and what *not* to do, taking notes, journaling even, on this very character. If you haven't, you should. The heartbreaking thing of it all really, is that even though she perceives these special moments with Linus as romantic interludes, he's still playing Sabrina to keep both her and his brother separated.

I hardly know you

Now, one thing is for certain. Sabrina isn't into Linus for the money. Though she is wishy-washy between the Larrabee men, you see her really trying to make sense of it all. And just when she's trying to sort out her emotions, Linus does the unthinkable, inviting her to Paris with him. But just when you see her starting to make sensible conclusions, can someone please explain to us why she feels she must talk to David after Linus has invited her to Paris? Sabrina, you are not his girlfriend. He is engaged to someone else. Why do you need to talk to him? Leave. Him. Alone. Ladies, this may be a tough one to swallow, but if you—like Sabrina—are into a man who belongs to another woman, for the last time … LEAVE. HIM. ALONE. Find a man of your own who isn't committed to another woman. One look at the tickets to Paris for Sabrina and Linus, and she's all affection for him. Almost in a blink of an eye, her emotions have entirely done a 180 for the older Larrabee now taking her to Paris declaring after kissing his face, "I don't understand what happened … I hardly know you … I wasn't even interested … I wrote in my stupid journal … and cut my stupid hair…," she is giggling with all the glee of a silly schoolgirl. It's hysterical that she exclaims, "I hardly know you," as she barely knew David either. She only knew him from the tree. Does she feel she doesn't know Linus because she hasn't obsessively longed for him all these years? Either way, she's beaming, "I'm so happy. You've made me so happy!" (Eye-roll) Is it just us, or has sister-girl gotten a little carried away? And a little too soon? She's gone between both brothers in a matter of maybe three weeks max, and now she's reveling in *his* invitation to love? Linus has become uncomfortable, pulling her away from him. Why? He has something to tell her (uh oh)! He is about to drop a bomb on her, and she is going to get wrecked yet again. What had she not seen coming? Ladies, beware of relationships that feel like they're going a little too fast. Take your time. Get to know him. Even though Sabrina didn't get it 100% right, what she said to Linus was correct—she barely knows him. This shouldn't be our story and it shouldn't be yours, either. Don't let it be. If we find ourselves in this position, we've missed something.

It's here where Linus finally comes clean, telling her, "I can't do this…". Confused, she's not quite getting it. It's even more painful than how we're describing it. He proceeds to say, "It was all a lie … I was sent to deal with you. There was a marriage. There was a merger. You got in the way." If you think that's bad, there's more. No girl should ever hear this. He continues to break her heart even more, "The plan was to take you to Paris, then leave … to get you out of the way." Wow. A man should be so ashamed of himself, and what's even sadder is that there are men who are really like this and have no problem playing our hearts like a pawn in their game of chess. She's been played like a fool. There was a mousetrap with the best tasting Brie dangling right over it … and what did she do? She ran right into it. I wonder how many times we as women have done that very thing without even realizing it. Now granted, he had an apartment ready for her and a bank account with $500,000 for her, so in that regard, a trip back to Paris to get out of this mess of a situation ain't all that bad. But had she known who she was, and not felt the desperate need to follow David's lead, she wouldn't be in this situation in the first place. Oh Sabrina. So foolish and now oh-so brokenhearted for Linus, a businessman to the core … even in matters of the heart.

To Paris or not to Paris? Sabrina, hurt and confused, decides to go, but first, she visits David, however, this time, it's not for the reason we think. She's not declaring her love for him; she's not declaring her love for Linus. Having smartened up a bit (FINALLY!), she is going to say a proper goodbye before packing up to leave for Paris. Sabrina should have walked away from David once she made the decision to leave for Paris the *first* time. This time it's different. And although she didn't ask him to, David honors her in confronting Linus about it all, and here is where things get good, and what has been hidden in hearts is revealed. Willing to blow a billion dollars on canceling the merger, David, although originally really upset at his brother, sees that Linus actually does love Sabrina, which is great news, except for that by now, Sabrina is taking off on Air France. And while Linus thinks he's calling off the merger,

David has—by now—come to his senses, inviting Elizabeth (his fiancée) into helping all the love triangles end up where they need to be. She's a strong woman, and apparently must really love David, to not only come to his aid, but also to still be willing to marry him (another book for another day!).

With both the Larrabees and Tysons present, we find that David has taken care of everything, prodding Linus to go after Sabrina, which he does. On the way to the airport to pursue Sabrina, her dad—still the family chauffeur—tells Linus that he doesn't deserve her, to which he replies, "I need her … and I don't need anything." The music swells, he's now running through the streets of New York to get to Paris via the Concorde before Sabrina does. She arrives and he is there waiting for her. Never mind that she has had to sit with his hurtful words and actions replaying in her mind all day. Never mind that he rejected her in one of her most vulnerable moments of affection to him. Never mind that he played her like a pawn. Still admitting that it was a lie, she questions his authenticity, having been lied to by him this entire time. We applaud her reluctance. We're like, "Girl, don't believe him just because he's saying it. Ask him the questions and find out what you need to!" And that, she does. He's being truthful and with his guard finally down he asks her to save him. And with that, hers comes down, too. He's with her in Paris--her home—her heart has melted, her heart appears to have been mended and with that, she will be a Larrabee, after all. That will most certainly lead to interesting family gatherings—especially if David and Sabrina ever find themselves dancing together at another Larrabee Party.

What Sabrina teaches us

➢ Spending time obsessing over a man is not an emotionally safe place or space to be.

➢ Don't ever take the liberty to find your way into his room or personal space. Can you say *stalker*?

➢ Don't waste your time on emotionally unavailable men.

➢ If he belongs to another woman, he's not yours for the taking. There are plenty of *other* men in this world to choose from.

➢ Don't believe everything a man tells you.

➢ Don't get caught in love between two men, especially two men who are brothers. There are plenty of men in this world to choose from.

➢ Take the time to get to really know someone. It can't all be based on looks. If it's true love and meant to be, it'll happen for you at the right time.

Something to write about

> What are some of the personal takeaways that stood out to you in watching this beautiful doe-eyed character, Sabrina, on screen?

> Why did they stand out to you?

> Were there any qualities in her that resonated with you?

> If so, what were they?

> Are those areas you need to work on?

> If so, how will you work on them and when will you put them into action?

P.S. As far as movies go, let it be stated that of all the characters we're breaking down in our book, if you felt you needed to see ONE movie, this is the one to watch. And really, make it a double-hitter–watch both the Audrey Hepburn and Humphrey Bogart version, as well as the Julia Ormand and Harrison Ford one. The 1992 character will annoy you as all get out because she is so inappropriate and stuck to David as if they had ever been a thing. That is irritating, for sure, but when the time is right, you'll do well to watch them both from the comfort of your home, with a bucket of delicious popcorn and a freshly brewed cup of coffee. These two movies won't disappoint. And now from brothers...to sisters.

"You cannot start a relationship based on lies."

Jane Nichols,
27 Dresses

Tess Nichols,
A Manipulative Phony

27 Dresses

In this movie about two sisters falling in love with the same guy, we find not one, but TWO very flawed female characters we felt were important *not* to emulate; Jane is a single girl who apparently doesn't know how to say, "No," to all the brides whose weddings she's been in and who has many bad habits we'd love to see her freed from:

- ➤ Attempts to make everyone else happy.
- ➤ Overextends her time, not paying attention to her own needs.
- ➤ Seeks the adoration of the brides and others.
- ➤ Always the bridesmaid, never the bride.

Shall we go on? No, we'll stop there since this chapter's focus isn't on Jane, but on her younger sister, Tess, who is a hot mess of a young adult woman. Now while this sounds like many of us who have been—or still are—a hot mess, Tess takes the meaning to a whole new level.

To give a little back story for those who have never seen the movie, Jane, a perpetual bridesmaid to 27 brides in her lifetime, is secretly in love with her boss, George, who though he relies heavily on Jane for everything from administrative assistance to the dry cleaners, is unaware of her existence romantically. Jane's little sister, Tess, comes in for an extended visit to NYC, staying with Jane, and thus Tess and George meet at a company party, right before Jane's very eyes. Jane, faithful administrative assistant to George, is at the work party with her friend, and George. In walks confident, beautiful, sexy Tess. George spots her, she spots George, and the two instantly connect, eyes locked on one another, as they make their way to each other. The way George looks at Tess is the way we should want a man to look at us when he takes notice—interested, yet not lustful. He does not hesitate.

Why? Because men don't need help in letting someone know when they are interested. They don't need *our* help in coaxing them into it, either. Ladies, we need to learn to let the men be men. And if they've not manned up to it, either: 1) They're not ready or 2) They are ready but aren't into *you*. Ever heard of the book, "He's Just Not That into You"? Hello … It's a very real thing and it comes right out of the horse's mouth, as it's co-written by a man, Greg Behrendt. The book, though brutal, with colorful language and a very in-your-face style, is not just about the way a lot of men think but reaffirms the obvious signs and ways to tell if a man isn't into you.

Okay, so back to Tess, who is back in town, sans a boyfriend, admitting there were problems in their relationship. She is staying with Jane, and within her first few moments on-screen, you already detect who she is. She is beautiful, charming, a model who is very fashionable, and a little selfish. As the movie progresses, we learn a little more about Jane's celebrated sister who, up to this point, enjoys being the center of attention. Entering the party, she brings it to a halt for George, making her entrance wearing a beautiful, short, sequined dress, in the striking color of canary yellow (think Kate Hudson's look in *How to Lose a Guy in Ten Days*). Spotting her across the room with her beautifully layered blond locks of hair complimenting her dress, their eyes have locked, which is unfortunate, as Jane was just about to tell George how she felt about him. Ladies, leave your bosses alone! Even if he *is* single, this is not what we do. It will only lead to turmoil, an aching heart, and possibly even job termination. But once she and George have locked eyes, and they meet each other in the center of the dance floor, it's apparent that there is great chemistry. It becomes a whirlwind romance, but it's about to be built on sinking sand for two reasons, yay, maybe even three, but we'll just focus on two. The first of which is, she isn't settled in life yet. She just flew back in town and has no idea where she's living or what she's doing for work period is she already in a career? No matter how badly we want to be in a relationship, there should be some aspects of settled-downness in our lives. We're not saying that you have to have everything altogether as we will always be evolving season to season, building foundation upon foundation until the day we breathe our last. But for Tess things were still so up in the air in just about *every* area of her life, entering a serious relationship is the last thing she should be doing.

Cyndi: I remember being in my early 20s and meeting a guy that I thought I could really like. There were so many things we have in common, plus he was fun, smart, musical and we really got along! I remember really thinking about if this would be something I should be embracing in my life as at that season I hadn't finished college yet, so I was still working on my degree, and I was in between jobs, as well. It's amazing how wisdom is quick to come when you call and ask for it. One morning this proverb jumped off the page while I was reading: "Prepare your outside work, make it fit for yourself in the field; And afterward build your house." (Proverbs 24:27, NKJV) there was no doubt about it, I knew exactly what wisdom was saying. I was being instructed to get all my things in line first period who knows how long that would have taken, for me, I did not end up getting my bachelor's degree until about five years later, so good thing I didn't get into a serious relationship. Some people can do it, but with how easily distracted I was at the time, I really needed to stay focused on the things at hand. I also had no clue what I wanted to do in terms of my career and calling, and it was in that season of singleness that I came to understand the first layer of my calling.

Tess needed to have some of these basic life essentials in order, as well. The second reason she wasn't ready to be in a relationship is that as fashionable and beautiful as she was, she had no idea who she was, and was willing to conform to what she *thought* someone else wanted her to be. These two factors alone tell us, Tess isn't ready for real love.

A fake, a phony, and a fraud

George, though obviously smitten with Tess, is a vegetarian, outdoorsy guy who owns a dog, a philanthropic company, and loves helping people. What he doesn't know about Tess—because she's not honest with him—is that she has found out his likes and dislikes from her sister. Although she is a total carnivore, she tells him she is a vegetarian, then pretends to like hiking and animals. We find through her conversation with Jane when George isn't with them, that she in fact was disgusted by even the drool of her own family dog, Tobi (who she mistakenly called, "Tori,") growing up as a child. And from that moment on, she latches on to every lie that will bring her closer to George. It's true, he *is* a catch, which is why Jane was so drawn to him to begin with, but to have to lie to someone to get them to like you or to make you think you are soul mates who have many things in common, is a bad place to be. Lying will never get you where you are trying to go.

"The getting of treasures by a lying tongue

is a fleeting vapor and a snare of death…

The way of the guilty is crooked,

but the conduct of the pure is upright." Proverbs 21:6, 8 (ESV)

When Jane calls her out on lying to her boss and actually hating their dog, Tobi, Tess defends herself saying, "… I could like soy milk and hiking if I tried it … maybe!"

Unfortunately, deception and lying has existed since the beginning of time. But it most certainly isn't how one starts a healthy relationship of any kind. What we unfortunately see in Tess is that more important than having integrity and being honest, she wants the guy. What we do know about lying is that if someone is intentionally lying repeatedly to one person, they are most likely doing it to the others in their lives. So here is Tess, not only deceiving George—who quickly becomes her boyfriend-turned-fiancé—but she also lies to both her sister and dad.

To discover where, when, and how we as women began to lie, we can go back to the Book of Genesis, where we see the first woman to lie—Eve. For this reason, we, as women, should work to not behave this way. Don't be this girl. Liars never prosper. Whether behavior that our family taught us from childhood, or something we picked up later in our teens or adult life, this trait should never be the norm in our lives. Some might say, "Well, what about a little white lie? Would that be okay?" The answer is no. It all starts so innocently, or does it really? We don't think there is anything innocent about lying. You've deliberately made the choice to be dishonest and now you are putting all sense of trust on the line. Have you ever found yourself caught in a lie that got so out of control that you didn't know how to stop it from snowballing into a giant avalanche? That's what happens when we find ourselves lying. The only way out is honesty. You may be afraid of what that honest confession might look like, but just go there, and allow those lies to be shattered.

Cyndi: I think I mentioned I was 19 years old when I found myself pregnant, caught in a love triangle and for about a month I didn't know which of the two was the actual father of my unborn child—the one who had been my first love, we'll call him Baby Daddy #1, or the one I was actually in love with—Baby Daddy #2, who though we were on a break, was my *true* love. The even worse news came after taking an ultrasound. I learned that I was actually one month further along than I had hoped, meaning it belonged to the man I was no longer in love with. Devastated with my newfound news, what did I do? Did I tell one I really loved that it wasn't his? No, I stayed quiet, saying nothing to him, even though I knew he was not the father. Talk about living out a Jerry Springer moment. I still was unsure as to what I was going to do about the pregnancy. I was already confused, overwhelmed, scared and now this?! I was going through a lot with both guys, with my mom, as well as a handful of friends who felt it best for me to abort my baby. I came from the school of thought that since I was old enough to get pregnant, I was going to put on my big girl pants and go through with it.

If there's one thing I know about lying, is that when you're doing it, you don't feel good about yourself. Whether you are making a false statement or are intentionally omitting information to lie, that is deception. There's no inner peace—whether it's a "little white lie," or a big, fat red one, a lie is a lie, no matter the size. Once you've lied, trust has now been undermined, making you a pawn in the hand of the master deceiver—the father of lies. This is why you struggle internally, producing inner turmoil—because in all reality, we are meant to be honest and truthful beings. Once the truth was out about who the father of my unborn was, I could finally exhale. Was the man I loved (who wasn't the dad after all) upset with me? Absolutely furious. He was more upset with the fact that he wasn't the baby's dad (we were on a "break" when I became pregnant). And now that he knew the truth, I felt so much better. Why? Because there was no longer anything to hide.

Ivette: I can remember the biggest lie of my life. It altered so many relationships and broke my heart at 12 years old. The sad thing was, that it was a lie that came from my own mother. I could have thought, maybe this was one of those moments that "could have been left unsaid" but really it needed to be addressed. But the collateral damage that came from something that my mom told herself, shared with her family and friends and kept from me caused a break in trust. My mom, God rest her soul, was a great woman, but the one fault that she had, was making up stories to look better to others—lies. We've all done it, in one way or another, or at least most of us can admit to it. However, her story that she created would change my relationship with her for years.

She, like many of us, fell into a relationship with someone that did not serve her wants and needs. From what I know he was an alcoholic and although they had two boys together, it didn't last. The story I was told at 12 years old was that I was a product of rape, by my brother's dad, and the man that I knew as my dad my whole life up until then, was not my dad. Being a daddy's girl, that was a blow to my heart, and I was crushed. I want to stress that a lie or any kind of deception not only hurts the person you tell it to, but in most cases, it will cause you to be the one that loses respect and trust from the ones you love.

My mom and I had a hard relationship after that. I acted out even more and did not want much to do with her. As for things between my dad and I, we became even closer as we were able to talk more freely about the truth. I did end up forgiving my mom and restoring the relationship, but it wasn't until I was in my 30s that I started to enjoy time with her again. All those years lost—because of a lie.

They say that love is blind, and so in the case of George, this is especially true. You can see that he is a smart guy having accomplished all he did before the age of 30, but he has now been blinded and has fallen in love with Tess, a girl he barely knows. We said things were moving quickly, and so not too long after he began courting her—something men are capable of doing when they are interested or in love with someone—he asks her to marry him, and we know the answer she gives him. Having gone through all the trouble to lie to him about who she really is, she accepts, never once thinking about how George will feel if he finds out the truth. Have you ever been this girl? Are you this girl now? She is so into herself, for the most part—even though she is also into him—that's why she's lying. We see she wants to have someone swoon over her and spoil her. George is this guy. He is great at it. So many scenes in this film were hard to watch—especially when it came to Tess being a fraud to win George's heart. It worked, but it was all built on a lie.

Ladies, if there is something we can exhort you on in this chapter, it's to please just be you. If you are a carnivore and he's a vegan or vegetarian, man up, and be authentically you in your likes and dislikes. No relationship is worth faking just so you can be with someone you're "into." And why would you want to start a relationship on false pretenses? Even if you're, say, self-centered, don't take it so far as being a fraud. Don't be Tess. While watching her gawking over her sister's boss is extremely painful to watch. In this movie, *this* is the girl not to be. There were horrific things she did that were extremely insensitive to Jane. Everything from cutting their mom's beloved dress that Jane—a hopeless romantic—always hoped to wear, to not even noticing that Jane also liked George, which by the way, would never ever have worked out because he wasn't into her, Tess is clueless and doesn't seem to care about Jane.

If you've ever been in that scenario or you are in a relationship built on lies, there's good news—we're here to gently lead you off the ledge. Because that's where you're at, and it's time to S-L-O-W-L-Y get off. But we'll help ya down, so that you don't hurt yourself ... or others.

Lies, lies, lies, yeah (they're gonna get you)

It is the official wedding dinner and things get ugly. By this point, Jane and Tess have had it out over many issues—the biggest one being that Tess cut up their mom's wedding dress, to sew it into a more modern one. So, with the dinner about to begin and Jane giving the speech that Tess wrote, Tess is a tad bit worried that Jane might do or say something that might reveal the truth. Building upon another lie, now she is trying to control everything to keep the truth from really being exposed. Unfortunately, Jane has had it with her selfish, lying sister who she believes has only stolen George's heart because been lying about who she *really* is. Compiling a video that shows George—and everyone else—who the real Tess is, she stuck to the script, but through photos showed that Tess was none of the things George believed her to be. That whole scene was uncomfortable to watch, but in the end, the truth came out and bit her. George–now with eyes wide opened—called off the wedding. Some may have thought it to be Jane's fault, and those closest to her were not at all pleased with what she did, but in the end, had Tess not lied about who she was to begin with, there would have been no truth to unveil. Don't be this girl. Let the man of your dreams fall in love with the real you. Don't lock someone into a relationship based on lies, as it will come out in the end.

Nowadays you must be a little crazy or have a ton of faith that something like this could work after only a few weeks (there should be a book for men, too). George had only met Tess a few weeks before proposing to her. *Don't* be this guy. What was George doing? And what was he thinking? He was taking her for what he saw only with his eyes. And really when you think about it, in a sense, he was objectifying her. It makes us think of another Rom-Com, *Brown Sugar*, when Dre (played by Taye Digs), was so smitten with his woman, Reese, he was bragging to his best friend about her, but not once did he mention a thing about loving her. It was all about her features—what she looked like, and what she could give him in the bedroom. "You know, we all looking for wifey material. A woman that's fine, smart, classy, but not a snob. You know, hella... hella sexy, but not a ho. That's brown sugar. That's my Reesey. I mean, don't get confused by her business suit. She is a freak in the bedroom...". Don't get it twisted, girls. Giving it up too soon—even before marriage—presents many problems for many married couples even once they've said, "I do." You are *not* the exception to the rule. Statistics will affirm this (Google it), couples will even attest. And now here is George—heading down this road both, blindly and dangerously. Blinded by her beauty and taken for a fool, he moved down the path towards marriage much too quickly, not knowing a thing about the true Tess. Before you knew it, there were photos of them on his desk, she was winning her way—based on lies—into his heart, but you can't deny the chemistry they had, and so the movie left us hopeful that now that the truth came out, maybe Tess has learned from her mistakes. Initially, she didn't. Girl, look in the mirror before hollering at your sister. You're the liar, not Jane.

It's sad to say that while the truth came out, Tess was still not willing to fully come clean, still blaming her sister telling her, "The wedding's off. I hope you're happy." Well, of course, being the big sister who did play a part in wreaking the wedding havoc, she wasn't pleased with herself, either. What is the one good thing we see from this scene? Jane stomping on her people-pleasing ways.

As most romcoms do, this ends on a good note for Tess, who after quite some time, see George at her sister, Jane's wedding. She re-introduces herself to him, telling him the real and truthful things about her and what she's currently up to. No longer trying to be a phony, she is real with him telling him that she eats a hamburger a day and that her idea of a pet is a rock. Don't we feel better when we can just authentically be who we are without any pretense? There is something so freeing about being honest and coming clean. *This* is the girl we want to be—the girl who isn't afraid or ashamed to share and tell the truth—even if there is fear involved. It is freeing.

Are there things you've built on a lie? In your heart of hearts, do you already know what you need to do to fix that situation or circumstance? Is there a lack of peace in your heart because you're still living the lie? You are deserving of a love that is honest, beautiful, and real. Don't keep lying to yourself about why you need to stay in a relationship founded on lies and deception. Jeremiah 17:9 says, "The heart is deceitful above all things, and desperately sick…". It's the same if you find that you've struggled with it your entire life.

You already know what you need to do. It's time to say goodbye to that dishonesty and let it go–like, out loud. Say it out loud. Say to deceit, that it shall no longer have a hold on you. Go ahead, say it. And once you do, forgive yourself for behaving dishonestly and start making those decisions you know in your heart you should be making. We agree with you and know you can do it. Isn't it time to stop making agreements with the father of lies, who John 8:44 (ESV) says, "… does not stand in the truth, because there is no truth in him. When he lies, he speaks out of his own character, for he is a liar and the father of lies."

We know that breaking down some of these characters may resonate with some of who you are or how you maybe too, like us, have been this girl, but we are proud of you for your willingness to do the work. Here is a little something for you if you look a little (or a lot) like Tess.

Get a journal or your laptop and honestly answer these questions.

1. What are some of the more recent lies I've told?

   ----

2. Who were those lies geared towards?

   ----

3. Why did I feel I needed to tell those lies?

    ----

4. What do I know I need to do to come clean?

    ----

5. What resources or help will I need to walk this out?

    ----

6. What freedom do I believe I will experience once I've done this?

    ----

7. Who can I be honest and maybe even accountable to, to help me with this area of my life?

    ----

8. What scripture or truth can I keep in front of me to help me overcome the tendency to lie?

A favorite verse that we both love comes from John 8:32, which says, "And you shall know the truth, and the truth shall make you free." (NKJV) Today is a new day for you! The heaviness of lying and deceit will lift right off as you start to walk in truth *and* in knowing the truth. Be glad in the new you because that old you, isn't you anymore!

"Jules, do you really love him, or is this just about winning?"

George Downes,
My Best Friend's Wedding

Jules Potter, A Deceptive Manipulator

My Best Friend's Wedding

Don't call yourself a best friend when you're everything *but. My Best Friend's Wedding* is a story based on the friendship of Julianne and Michael—best friends since college. Julianne (aka Jules, played by Julia Roberts) is determined to "... break up a wedding, steal the bride's fellow," once she receives the news from Michael (played by Dermot Mulroney) that he's about to get married in just a few days. Okay, so maybe she isn't *really* his best friend, after all (or else why would she be behaving in this manner to begin with?), but we see it all unravel as she painstakingly calculates one (failed) move after the other.

It's a classic, but this one was hard for us to critique for two reasons—first-off, this is one of Ivette's favorite movies, and while she adores it for so many reasons, this movie was difficult for Cyndi to get through almost immediately. From the moment Julianne began plotting ways to stop and ruin the wedding, Cyndi was already over it. Needless to say, this is the girl we don't want to be. And so, if you're a scheming conspirator, or one who intentionally tries to ruin other people's happiness thinking things are going to work in your favor, think again.

As the movie begins Jules, a food critic, receives a voicemail from Michael, who, in our opinion—has one of the dreamiest male voices in Hollywood. This is where it all begins. Hearing this while having dinner with her friend, George, indicates he's desperate to talk with her. At first, she thinks nothing of it, but as she shares this update with George about her other male bestie, she reminisces about a silly little bet they had about marrying each other if neither of them was married by 28. About to turn 28, they get to wondering if this could be what Michael wants to talk about, and you can just see the wheels turning in her mind as this isn't just a best friend since college, but she also reveals that the two had one "hot month," in college, before realizing they were better off as best friends. So, from the get-go, we already know that as a couple, they were a wrong fit from the start. It was when she got on the phone with Michael (who *told* her why he was really calling—to let her know he was getting married in just four days), that the break-up games begin. Now, as women we understand the shock of it all, since it had been months since they'd talked, and now he's getting married–and in four days, no less! So, what would a best friend do if they were to hear this news? What would *you* do if you were in Jules' shoes?

Would you be bummed that you didn't have enough notice—because what best friend would tell you four days before the wedding that they were getting married? Maybe you'd be on the first (affordable) flight out there to help in every way you can. This is what a bestie would do or how they'd respond, right? In Jules' case, she did neither. What she proceeded to do was not only cunning and devious, but it was also despicable.

Caught off guard

So, you're caught off guard about someone you once deeply cared about. While some might say they'd rather respond than react, let's be real—if there are unresolved issues, it might be more of the latter than the first. While we would all hope that none of us would ever be caught off guard with someone you were very close to, it's life and it happens. This is what happened to Jules. She was so caught off guard about Michael marrying someone he'd just recently met, that she fell off the bed. She begins drilling him with questions about his wedding, and you initially do feel for her for two reasons:

1. Apparently, she didn't matter enough to be invited to, or informed about the wedding until just four days prior to the day Michael and Kimberly (aka, Kimmy, played by Cameron Diaz) were to say, "I do." I think any of us would agree that this would be somewhat devastating to any best friend—even if they had never met the person (knowing that they were *engaged* would have been a nice start!).

2. Michael hadn't *just* been Jules' friend. He was someone she had slept with.

72

How do you feel about someone you have had sex with? What about someone you've slept with more than once? Was that person ever easy to just "get over"? While some of you might be saying, "Oh yeah. It was no big thing," for those of us who are willing to be honest about how we felt about anyone we've given ourselves to sexually, it was never just an easy thing to move on from. And because of that, even if you moved on, there was a part of you left with him, having experienced one of the most intimate connections—if not *the most* intimate form of physically connection with someone. Reasons for this are many—one we know to be scientifically true is that a hormone—oxytocin—also referred to as the "love drug" or "love hormone," is released into our bloodstream, "... when people snuggle up, have sex…"[2] So, while we're not scientists here, we are definitely confirming that there is more to what happens to people when we engage sexually with someone. And for this reason, Michael was not just Jules' bestie, but someone with whom she had bonded with significantly. Needless to say, her attachment to Michael was more than merely platonic friendship.

While we slightly feel bad for her, our emotions begin to shift the moment we realize she's not hurt or crushed by the wedding news, but rather she's afraid of losing him—the man who has seen her through thick and thin, through pain, loss, and life. And if we're going to push a little further, she's mostly upset about losing him to another woman—someone he's known for only a short amount of time. Rather than it surfacing like the graceful emotion it should have in a best-friend-only status, it's now rearing its ugly head as she's now outwardly manifesting what has been in her heart for him this entire time—nine years to be exact—knowing full-well that he adored her, as she did her own thing, living her own life for all that time, all while keeping him in sight, until he met Kimmy. It's a classic case of REO Speedwagon's[3]. however she's months late on this one. Why? Because he's getting married. It's time to take a backseat, sister. Kimmy's in the picture now and, in four days, they're about to tie the knot. But as far as Jules is concerned, she's going to do everything in her power to not let this happen. He hasn't been a priority for her emotionally for all these years, but now that another girl is in the picture, he has her undivided attention to a fault, for now not only is she upset, but she's upset and if her manipulative gifts were dormant, they are now awake and dusting themselves off for a fight she intends on winning.

Have you ever found yourself in a similar situation? Hit with this news you never dreamed of hearing, a blow to your heart has been delivered. Had she always had a thing for Michael? Most likely. But even though she was still most likely attracted to him, had he been the one, she would not have left him dangling as a best friend for nine years. What she thought would always be there, will no longer be, and now she's panicking. She suddenly feels this need to

· · · · · · · · ·

2   Wu, Katherine, "Love, Actually: The science behind lust, attraction, and companionship," *sitn.hms.harvard.edu*

3   "Can't Fight this Feeling," by REO Speedwagon. Album: Wheels Are Turnin', 1984.

get him back, though they haven't talked in months. All of a sudden, she's smitten with the memories of many years ago?

Why do we hang onto memories of "what was"? If you need to, write down why you hold on to thoughts from the past. If you don't do it now, we're fairly certain we will ask this question again later on in the book. It was years ago; he's moved on and so have you. Let it go. George nailed it by telling her, "It's amazing the clarity that comes with psychotic jealousy." Here's the thing, relationships are not a game. And jealousy is not love. If you love someone, you love them, which means you want the very best for them. If you love someone, you don't start to play games and manipulate situations to work in your favor. That is not love. That is selfish behavior which is the opposite of love.

Has someone knocked the wind out of you, catching you off-guard? If so, one of the worst things you can do is to start grasping at the wind for what once was. While this has got to be a tough spot to be, the best thing to do would be to hold both hands wide open, allowing it to take flight. It was author and writer, Richard Bach who said, "If you love something, set it free; if it comes back, it's yours, if it doesn't, it never was." Our advice? Even if you don't love it, if it doesn't reciprocate your feelings, hold your hands wide open to let it go.

Sadly, Jules isn't taking our advice. She is jetting off to Chicago for this four-day wedding extravaganza. However, she isn't going there to support her friend, but rather to steal him away from his bride-to-be—Kimmy—who not only is so adorable in this character, but you see all the reasons why she is so very *right* for Michael. Get a clue, Jules. You aren't it.

Already taken (so stop flirting)

We've heard the saying, "Men will be men," but knowing several pretty amazing ones, we're not sure why it is that *some* guys think it's okay to flirt when they're already committed to someone. Whether it's because of being dissatisfied, feeling unappreciated or, in this case, just wanting to swim in familiar territory, it shouldn't be happening for any of the above-mentioned reasons. And shouldn't be happening at all. We simply aren't impressed with Michael's behavior with Jules when she arrives to Chi-Town. Why? Seems like brotha-man-Michael needed to have some personal things in his *own* heart sorted out before asking Kimmy to marry him. True, it seemed as though she was the one he wanted to settle down with, and we see, as time goes by, he really does love her, but he was sending some pretty heavy, "I'm still-attracted-to-Jules" vibes when she came into town, and this ought not have been so. For example, why was his face pressed up against hers when they greeted at the airport in Chicago? Um, no. This is not okay. It's not okay for you to be all up in her grill when your fiancé is just few yards behind. It wasn't okay for you to walk into Jules' dressing room and not turn around when seeing that she's in her bra and undies, and it certainly wasn't okay for you to tell her, "I've seen you a lot more naked than that," while still not looking away. Ladies, should you *ever* find yourself in a position where you see this happening (either *to* you or in front of you), call him out—and don't waste another minute of your time watching him do that. It's disrespectful, and guess what? Time is too short. We've wasted enough of our years watching people do things they ought not have been doing and so it's time to say, "Enough is enough." You shouldn't be the one he's flirting with, and you shouldn't be the one with him, while he's flirting (with another). We goin' repeat that so you get it (yes, it's spelled correctly, and there's a little side-to-side neck attitude going along with it). You shouldn't be the one he's flirting *with*, and you *shouldn't* be the one with him while he's flirting.

It's so interesting how we can see something so clearly looking at it from the outside, but when you're in it, why do things get a little foggy? May this scenario help to paint a clear picture of what it looks like to have your man flirting with another woman, toying with both of your hearts. Michael looks straight at Jules, and he had the nerve to tell her, "You look really good ... without your clothes on." Really? What is he doing?! Why is he playing on her mind and emotions? Would he have said that to her in front of Kimmy? And would he have been standing there staring at her in underwear had Kimmy been right next to him? Why is he even getting married right now? Is he ready to make a life-ling commitment right now? He's literally holding Jules' maid-of-honor gown in his hand, while telling her she looks good. That should give you your answer.

Cyndi: The scene had me so aggravated, it triggered me into recalling a horrific memory, but one I must share. I was 19 and just starting college, and though I loved where I worked, I remember constantly arguing with one of my co-workers. What I didn't know at the time, was that there was physical attraction-tension between the two of us, and so that is why he would instigate fights with me. I knew he was in a relationship, and I did remember meeting her, though I didn't know her well. I was pretty naïve at the time and also had a boyfriend. The arguing continued, but they intensified until we were fighting almost face-to-face one day. And that was when he grabbed my face and kissed me. Well, I wasn't quite sure what to do with that, but rather than pulling away, my reflex was to kiss him back. This was not a wise move as 1) We were both in relationships; and 2) We worked together. I must admit, the initial newness and excitement of it all was invigorating, however, it would only be a few more times of intensely making out that I could no longer carry on in this manner with this guy. It was so secretive, and I just knew it wasn't right. Have you ever been there or ever done anything like that? I was thankful that what little moral compass I had at the time was screaming, "NO! This must stop." I knew it must be done, but what I needed was the strength to stop it. Even though I knew it was wrong, I did care about him, and so I also didn't want to hurt his feelings. After all, we were co-workers and meant something to each other as friends. So, out came the strength and scissors, cutting off what should never have started to begin with. Not only did that sow awful seed into my then-relationship, but it was also what started our relationship on a downward spiral. I don't know what became of my ex-co-worker, but it wasn't too long before I didn't see him any longer. Flirting with someone you have no business flirting with never ends well. I'm glad it didn't go too far or last that long, but I'm sad to admit that it even started at all. If either you or he is in a committed relationship, neither of you should be flirting with or looking at anyone else but your better half.

Ivette: It's true that we all want to be loved, but we should want to be loved by the person that is the *right* person for us. Remember the guy I told you about—the one I met after my reunion? I wanted him to be with me, as much as I wanted to be with him. Honestly, I don't even know why, he had nothing to offer me—zero. He was a liar, a cheater. But still, I made a point to go to him, call him, and still try to have a friendship with him, even after I found out about his family. So why *this* guy? Was it because he didn't show me the attention that I thought I needed or thought I deserved? Yes— that is exactly it. I knew he wasn't that into me after the truth came out. And I still put myself out there. Girls, there is so much we can learn here from just this one character. It's more than just not going for the one that's not into you, it's about not going for someone not worthy of you. You are amazing. If I'd known then what I know now, I would not have wasted my heart, energy, or time. It pains me to even think and talk about it now. I'd like to think that it would eventually be the same for Jules. As we go deeper into this movie, we will see how self-centered Jules really was. Cyndi was right—I love this movie and have so many one–liners that I love sharing with my son. But what we find Jules doing in this movie is just wrong. No one should be taking pointers from this character. Please, don't be this girl!

For a mere moment we were proud of Jules for letting Michael know that things were different, which didn't faze him at all, but we felt that for a quick moment, Jules had some sense knocked into her and so exhaled at the hopeful thought that she might not be such a bad person after all. But the moment she heard Michael's words, "You look really good ... without your clothes on …," Jules' playing nice came to an end, picking up the phone, telling George, "...she's toast." Not exactly what the best friend of the groom-to-be should be saying about the woman he's about to marry. "Hello, Kimmy! It's me, Ms. Jules Nasty, and I'm coming after your man!"

Keep your enemies close

Ever heard of that saying, "Keep your friends close and your enemies closer?" As the day of Michael and Kimmy's wedding quickly approaches, this is Kimmy's plan-of-action and, with what she has up her somewhat-sinister sleeves, rightly so. Although she had no idea of the wedding-sabotaging Jules was devising, Kimmy was no dummy and, if you find yourself in a similar situation, you shouldn't be either. All Kimmy had heard about from Michael was—in her words— "Julianne this," and "Julianne that." She had never even met Jules, but she had the sense (but maybe not the sensibility) to ask her to be her maid-of-honor? Whatever reasons she had, she was probably pretty much on the nose, as she didn't know Jules from Adam, but most likely wanted her to be right by her side so she could keep an eye on her every move. We don't really find this out until later, but Kimmy had an agenda of her own. Furthermore, she knew that Jules meant everything to Michael (and probably the other way around), and that was a lot for her to live up to. Here is the thing, ladies—if you have to try and live up to someone else's ex or reputation to please a boyfriend or someone you're dating, turn him loose. Let him go—not only is it not fair to you, but it will also save you a whole lot of insecurity and heartache. And that's what we're going for—to keep those heartbreaks minimal, as we learn from these characters in how not to be and what not to do to protect your heart, mind, body and emotions.

So, while this may have been an okay plan for Kimmy, it wasn't the most forthright plan. It would have been better for them to sit down and have a genuine heart-to-heart. This would also have avoided the fiasco at the bridal shop while Jules was getting fitted for a maid-of-honor gown to a bride she met just minutes before. Awkward! What a game. And in the real world, games like this usually blow up in someone's face. We think that honesty is the best policy. We didn't always make the best choices, and so this is why we're pulling out our past junk from the hat—to help keep you from making the same mistakes we made in our earlier years. So, both girls are playing each other, with an agenda of their own, and can we just say, we don't like it. Young, supportive Kimmy is telling Jules way too much about her relationship with Michael, both even going so far as to sharing about his bedroom habits—initiated by Jules. That was way past the line, but at the end of the day, Kimmy lets her in on her acceptance that even though they had a past (which Jules has no qualms about sharing—to a fault), that she felt jealous and competitive when it came to Jules, knowing and that she'd always be, "...in his mind, this perfect creature that he loved for all those years." She resigns to the fact that Jules wins, telling her, "He's got you on a pedestal, and me in his arms...," immediately afterwards being greeted by her cousins as the "...the woman she'll never live up to."

Let's keep it real, ladies. Young Kimmy may have resigned to this, but this won't work for Kimmy after three or so years of marriage. You're gonna marry someone? YOU had better be the woman on his pedestal *and* in his arms. None of this sharing your husband with another woman. Are you nuts?! That will never work. If you want your marriage to last, be a one-stop woman for your one-stop man. No need to bring another person to the mix, it's just you and him—husband and wife—for the rest of your lives. What does that mean? It means, "Adios, Jules! You don't get to be a third wheel in my marriage." End of story. And if Jules is a self-respecting woman—which she is not in this film—she'd concede, surrendering the pedestal spot. What we're not saying is that the friendship needs to end, but if you're going to be in their life, you are now a friend to them both.

Let the games begin

Since the moment she arrived in Chicago, the very smug Jules has been soaking in all the info, *not* because she cared for Kimmy, wanting to help her relationship with Michael, but because she wanted to demolish what they had, with hopes of canceling the wedding and winning. Anything Michael or Kimmy shared with her she craftily used as ammo for the two, pitting the two against each-other. UGH, it just made us literally yell out, "Stop being so deceptive... stop being this girl!" The thing of it is, Jules is not to be trusted with either of them. When she's alone with Michael, she's not talking great about Kimmy, and when she's alone with Kimmy, she does the same with Michael. We don't trust her, and neither should either of them. The fact they couldn't see her pitting them against each other baffles us, but then again, it is the movies. However, in real life, please don't be this girl. And if you're not, but you know her, steer clear (*very clear*) from her. Now, granted this is only on-screen, but this happens in real-life. Just think of all the energy and time exerted in all that plotting. What about the lack of inner-peace, and we'd even go as far as to say lack of trust in your partner.

Cyndi: I experienced the same type of emotions when watching "Bridal Wars," a movie about two besties who end up rivaling against each other and their weddings. I just kept thinking and saying to myself, "OMG. This is awful. May I never have friends like this." Almost the entire movie was a trainwreck of these two friends loaded with fighting, conniving, jealousy, self-seeking, competing, doing awful things to each other to the bitter end—and yet, it was so painful, I couldn't pull away from watching it until the very end. Thankfully, it was a chick-flick and so wasn't reality for the two; however, it made me wonder if there were friendships like this that existed. And while I'd like to think that if friends like this exist, they'd do whatever is needed to no longer act like that, the truth of the matter is, they'll continue to behave similarly to the two characters in that movie until they do the inner work needed to not be driven by selfishness and the need to win. It was a game of survival of the fittest, but in games like that between two people who claim to love each other, no one wins.

First introduced by sociologist Herbert Spencer, "survival of the fittest," is the idea that a group or individual is "more likely to survive if they fit into the [surrounding] environmental conditions." The idea of winning has always existed since the beginning of time, long before the likes of TV shows like, "Survivor," "American Gladiator," "Gossip Girl," or taking it way back—"Battle of the Network Stars," but it *isn't* how we are to approach people in relationships. Though we would think or hope to not approach people this way relationally, the games between Jules and Kimmy intensify, and in this case, Jules being older and more experienced pulls out the big guns of deceit and plotting against Kimmy. It's almost as if Kimmy doesn't stand a chance, for Jules is now on the prowl, determined to end this engagement, and her hidden fangs begin to surface after meeting Kimmy's family at the bridal brunch once she's whisked off to a ball game to hang out with Michael and "the boys."

You're an imposter

Seeing her opportunity to pounce with Kimmy nowhere around, Jules cranks up the heat, and we continue to cringe. She's no longer viewing those around her as people she is in relationship with, all she cares about is winning. Now a full-on game for her, not only is she being flirty with Michael, but she forces herself to be someone she's not with someone who has known her well for many years. Everything from sitting on Michael's dad's lap after kissing him on the lips (that is so gross), to pulling his much younger brother, Scotty, into her (eew), reminding him it's his duty to dance with her at the wedding, the capacity to which she flirts with all these men in one scene is super uncomfortable to watch. Girl, have some decency! There are some women who love being the center of attention in this way. They want to be seen by men and will stop at no cost. This is Julianne at certain points in this film. She's cranked up the charm—and it's embarrassing. This is not the kind of attention we want, ladies. We should be known for being genuine, loving, kind, and caring. We are smart, intelligent beings who are mindful of others. At this moment, Jules was none of these things. And what she was showing wasn't really who she was, either. It was written all over her face. Michael called it. "Imposter! What did you do with my best friend?" Have you ever played this game pretending to someone you *weren't* for the sake of winning or getting something or someone, you considered as the prize? And above all, how important is it to remember that people are *not* a game to be played.

Michael is someone who has meant a lot to Jules over the years. But let's be real—they were never meant to be in a long-term relationship together. The things he needed or desired from her, she was unwilling to give. We all have different love languages; his was clearly touch—and hers was not. Of Kimmy, he said, "When I hug her ... even in public, I don't have to let go right away." Jules pretending to now be this type of girl, functioning in this love language lies, "Well, I've changed. I'm not the girl I once was. This is not about longevity, Michael, this is about being comfortable with the yucky love stuff ... and I am." Girl, you are lying through your teeth!

What tangled webs we weave

now comes the part we frowned on for a majority of the time—Jules' plots against Kimmy are deployed—one right after the other. In trying to keep Jules close, Kimmy revealed way too many of her secrets, flaws, and fears, which is fine when you're sharing that with someone who actually cares about you. Jules didn't and so used those little-known issues about Kimmy against her. Doing everything from bringing up the honeymoon, school, career, her wealthy financial status, his not-so-prestigious job —poor Kimmy—she didn't know what was coming to her!

What a devious thing to know something about someone and use it against them in an attempt to bring them down. Jules was this person. Knowing full well that karaoke bars intimidated the heck out of Kimmy, she jumped at the chance to make Kimmy look bad in front of Michael, luring into a karaoke bar. And just how did Kimmy do when put to the final test of singing in front of everyone? Well, she sang terribly, but the fact that she stood up and did it, brought Michael so much joy he couldn't restrain himself from keeping his hands off his adorable and courageous fiancée. While we were celebrating with Kimmy in this scene, sadly, Jules was not.

Another ploy created by Jules was in direct attack at his career. Michael worked as a journalist, a "zero respect paying job," that he happened to love. Jules uses that to plant seed that maybe one day, his soon-to-be-very-wealthy-family might want him in a more prestigious job (his father-in-law-to-be owned the White Sox). Dressed to kill, she shows up to dinner, where she's planted this idea in Kimmy's mind, prodding her to bring it up to Michael. So now, Kimmy's up to bat—to bring up this discussion about Michael's job and career, and how she's giving up her life by not finishing school for Michael, which ignites an immediate argument between the two of them. Pretending to side with Kimmy, Jules is so pleased with herself thinking that this plot will help win her best friend back, you see the devilish gleam in her eyes as they argue. It's sick. But what she underestimated was the power of love and meeting your man where he is to make things work. Crying, Kimmy apologizes, clinging to Michael, and so what it does instead, is causes them to work it out right then and there in front of Jules, ending their fight with hugging and kissing—an extreme PDA—which Jules has never been comfortable with. Kimmy is vulnerable with Michael; Jules is not and has never been. Furthermore, you see the disdain in her face regarding their making up. Her plan has failed, again. We must admit, though, while watching her try and try again is unnerving and uncomfortable, we took pleasure and delight in seeing her schemes against Kimmy come to no effect. Round three? Before we go there, we want to pause here because while we don't want to be Jules for many reasons, the vulnerability we see in Kimmy is something to be admired. How are you in that area of your life? Do you find that you're more like Jules or Kimmy when it comes to vulnerability?

So, now at the end of her rope, Jules puts an APB out to George, exclaiming that Kimmy double-crossed her. Really?! Wow, she is so deep into it, she can't even see straight. That's exactly what she has been doing this entire time from the moment she arrived in Chicago. Double-crossing Michael and double-crossing the bride-to-be. Talk about denial. We're so over her, but unfortunately there's more. She's running on empty, running out of time and out of ideas, but as Michael's best friend, can we just take a moment to stop and see, that you are no longer his #1? Time to wave that white flag, Jules. And yet, she doesn't.

Cyndi: Everyone wants to be loved, but at what cost? Girls, if you love someone and they don't love you back, move on. Not only is it not the right time, but it's also not the right person. And that's okay. Rejection is okay. Will it sting? Umm, yeah, but better to experience that pain early on, than years later when it will really hurt. Getting stung is always better than an actual break.

Ivette: Jules should have just supported her friend. Even if I had thoughts about someone else's pick for a husband or wife, I would say my peace and move on. I mean, who has time for that much plotting and scheming? I would rather have been in a fine restaurant critiquing food with George.

I have to be ruthless

If you've ever been this girl, you have felt the exhaustion of it all. We don't even know how she sleeps at night—surely there is torment and anxiety as she does, and whenever she has the time to quiet her mind. We're exhausted just watching her. The games and deviousness continue, but now George has arrived to help his friend in need. And though we are hopeful that he will help turn the tide in Kimmy's favor, Jules is bulldozing over all parties present, George included. He thinks he's come to help give her the strength to do what's right, but she somehow manages to also pull him into her web. So yeah, basically, George has now become an insect in her world of spinning webs.

The fact she now has someone with whom she is honest with is good. But her perspective is all wrong, telling George, "He was in love with me every day for nine years … I can make him happier than she can ... I am breaking her heart in the short run ... but really, really doing her a gigantic favor....". Really, Jules? Why don't you leave that decision to the two that are really the ones in love with each other? He's watching her and listening to her, sympathetically, but you also see that because he is a friend who loves her, he's somewhat pitying his friend who seemed rational and had it altogether just a few days prior while they were at dinner.

Sharing her reasons why she felt it necessary to do the insane things she's doing all boiled down to an unspoken claim, "You [Michael] belong to me." We still don't feel sorry for her. Why? Because she's had nine years to have this discussion. And though George tries giving her honest advice, his input isn't the answer either. Telling Michael that she's loved him for nine years, but has done nothing about it, isn't what you should be telling a man who 1) Loves someone else, and 2) Is about to be married. It's selfish, insensitive, and cruel.

You see that he is a true friend in asking her the hard question, "Jules, do you really love him, or is this just about winning?" Nailed it. Thank you, George! It's what we've been saying all along. For her, it's about winning. She could have professed her love for him in the nine years he loved her. But it isn't until now that she's realizing it? Girl, come on. He's marrying someone else, and unless he approaches *you* and asks *you* if you still love *him*, you have no business telling him that you do. It doesn't matter that you're afraid of love, which you are. Now's not the time.

Have there been times where maybe you—like Jules—have stopped at nothing to win the emotions or heart of a man? How did that make you feel? What did you feel like after that victory passed, and you were all alone in the celebration? Was there a part of you that didn't enjoy doing it? Did you learn anything from that? Do you still have the prize you fought for?

Proverbs 14:12 says, "There is a way *that seems* right to a man, but its end *is* the way of death." In so many cases, there are things we do for self-serving reasons, but that shouldn't be the reason we do what we do. It may seem right, or it may feel good at the moment, but once we've taken a bite from that fruit, a type of death takes place. The peace and joy is gone. Maybe it's an ending of a relationship or good friendship, or now having the name of a bad reputation, when really all that was at the root of winning was selfishness, that isn't love at all.

What is love? "Love suffers long *and* is kind; love does not envy; love does not parade itself, is not puffed up; does not behave rudely, does not seek its own, is not provoked, thinks no evil; does not rejoice in iniquity, but rejoices in the truth; bears all things, believes all things, hopes all things, endures all things. Love never fails...". (1 Corinthians 13:4-8, NKJV) That's what real love is. Anything outside of what we just read above, isn't love.

What are you afraid of?

We don't hear or really know the backstory of why Jules is afraid to love and be vulnerable, but clearly, she is. We know many a girl who professes to being a "hopeless romantic," however, when it comes to them personally loving someone, they admit that it's difficult for them to be vulnerable, opening themselves to love, but we're all created to love and be loved, so if this is a problem for you, now is the time to do a little bit of digging so that you don't find yourself in the same shoes as Jules—loving someone all these years, but never giving their heart the time of day to let them know until it's too late. Has it ever been difficult for you to verbalize or communicate to someone how you feel about them? Was it always this way? Are you this girl? Her character leaves us with some questions that we need to honestly ask ourselves. We will ask (and answer) some of these questions at the end of this chapter, because if you are anything at all like Jules, we know you don't want to be this girl.

Cyndi: I get it. I get it. There were definitely times where I was more vulnerable on dating in high school, because I hadn't experienced a whole lot of hurt and heartbreak at that point in my life. Though I had witnessed my mom experiencing heartbreak, pain, and rejection, I wasn't the one personally walking it out, so didn't have too much understanding of what it actually felt like to be the one hurt and devastated by it. So much of the unfortunate relationship-pain happened between the ages of 19 through 21, so by the time 1992 rolled around, I had extremely well-built thick walls all around me. These walls pretty much stayed up for about six or seven years, and they were there because I determined that I would never be hurt again the way I had been broken by my college sweetheart.

You already know how I feel about working through all the issues—it's a must, but I do need to point out that although several of the guys I dated from '91 to '97 all said the same thing—I kept them at a distance, not letting them into my heart. I don't believe that was a bad thing. None of them were "my person," and so I'm thankful. It still wasn't fair to them. Finally choosing to somewhat let my guard down, there have been two guys *since* that I allowed into my heart, allowing myself to feel deeply for them. And what happened was what most of us don't want to happen—getting hurt. It's tricky because on one hand if you're going to be in a relationship, you should be all in, however, on the other hand, why would we need to be "all in" with every guy we date? Now older, I think the answer is clear—we really shouldn't date, just to date. We should date when we feel he could possibly be our person. Until then, spend time investing in yourself, your spirituality, goals, dreams, health, finances. Protect and keep your heart for one who is doing the same for himself. I had to fight hard at getting "myself" back as one of them was so devastating and we had only dated for a month, and never even kissed (yes, girls, it is possible to have some self-control). Being vulnerable can be costly and you might be the only person of the two paying the price. Besides those last two, I really do believe that's why I never was vulnerable for all those years—because none of them were the person I was meant to spend the rest of my life with. Shoulda kept those walls up after all.

Encouraged by George to tell the truth, she starts off on the right foot, then almost immediately forgets she was on a mission to do what was right somewhere in between starting to come clean to Michael and him giving her Kimmy's ring to hold for him. So rather than telling him how she felt, she led him to believe she and George were not only an item, but that *they* were engaged. Well, you can imagine the joy that Kimmy had finding out that Jules was engaged to the dashing George, who happens to be gay unbeknownst to her family and friends in Chicago. But with Kimmy finally comforted in the fact that Julianne has someone she is in love with and marrying—amiss the comments about Jules' broken relationships and how tough it must have hurt going through all those men and never finding the right one—George plays right into it, engaging in PDA, singing to and about Jules … the works! Until he jumps on a plane and heads back home, leaving her with the stark truth that it would never work out for her and Michael, that he'll choose Kimmy, but that she'll stand beside him at the wedding. What would you do if you were in Jules' shoes, and you're told that's how it's going to be? Do you take the high road? Or do you continue to give it one more try?

If she had planned on taking the high road, Michael's confession of being, "crazy jealous," of her and George put an end to that right there. They spend the afternoon hanging out, and though he does love Kimmy, we find that he's still fishing for answers from Jules. Michael explains how Kimmy says, " … that if you love someone, you say it … you say it right then … out loud … otherwise the moment just passes you by," as the scene shows the boat going under a bridge, neither of them say, 'I love you,' and at that moment the boat comes out from under the bridge into the sunlight and that moment passes. He finally put the word "love" out there to her, without saying that he loved her, almost as if to give her one final chance to say it, and to say it out loud. Their eyes are searching deep into one another's, but the moment passes. He is disappointed and she—with tears in her eyes—is devastated. We, however, are not, because it doesn't take rocket science to see that these two are all wrong for one another. They don't belong together. It's true that Jules has made it hard for him to stay focused on Kimmy, which really is a matter of his own heart, but nonetheless, she has set up every ploy to take his mind and eyes of his soon-to-be-bride, and though she hasn't been fully successful, it's caused him to think about his two girls—when he should only be focusing on one. Swaying to their song, "The Way You Look Tonight," they dance their last dance as best friends while riding a boat on a beautiful Chicago River, for what will be their last moment before he gives his life to another woman, his wife.

But wait! There's more...

As sad as it was, it was a touching moment, right? Well, it would be if it had ended there. But rather, she's gonna give another scheme one final chance to help steal him from Kimmy. And this time, it's really bad—doing it right underneath the nose of Kimmy's dad, using his computer at his company. She will stop at nothing. She's quite naughty and has absolutely no respect for Kimmy, Michael, or Kimmy's parents, who have welcomed her into their lives.

Ivette: I don't know how she can even sleep with all these plots going through her head. George's advice didn't sink in and now she's desperate. I think when we're in these moments of mental clutter and chaos, it would help us out if we could just stop and take a breath, asking ourselves all the questions we need to honestly answer, rather than just acting impulsively. If you find that you tend to have an impulsive behavior, prayer and journaling really are some of the best tools and ways you can do the inner work, experiencing the healing needed to not be this girl.

Cyndi: Amen to that! If you are anything like Jules, please take note. You *are* in need of inner healing, and for this there is help ... and hope! You'd think that Jules would realize that she has continued to fall into the little holes she herself has dug out for Kimmy to be ensnared by. So far, none of her plans have worked. There is a lesson to be learned here, ladies: devising plots and schemes against innocent people will always backfire. Always. And, so knowing that, maybe we ought to think twice before attempting to sabotage anything in someone else's life ever again.

> *"Whoever digs a pit will fall into it, and he who rolls a stone will have it roll back on him. A lying tongue hates those who are crushed by it, and a flattering mouth works ruin." (Proverbs 26:27–28 NKJV)*

Given the opportunity to pick up Kimmy's dad from work, Jules pulls out what we hope is her last card, as she goes into his office—with his permission—and drafts an email from his email address to Michael's boss, asking him to let him go so he can work with Kimmy's family. You literally can see an angel on one shoulder and the devil on the other. She struggles in whether to send it and decides to save it rather than deleting it, once she sees Kimmy's ring, then putting it on. Well as you know how movies go, Kimmy's dad, Walter, has his secretary send all his emails he drafted that day, and so out goes the email to Michael's boss. How it unfolds is pretty gnarly, and we keep wishing Jules would just come clean. But as liars are used to, she continues to build lie upon lie, deception on deception. Before she has a chance to retrieve the email (already gone out), Michael receives a telegram from his boss, about the email informing him of the type of family he's about to marry. Knowing full well that Walter didn't send it, but rather, that she did, Jules still couldn't tell him the truth. "I do bad things to honest people," is what she tells the bellhop as she is sulking in the hallway, not knowing what to do as Michael calls Kimmy to call off the wedding.

Jules is hating herself. She knows that she has hurt her best friend and an innocent girl. She's gotten what she really wanted, and the ring is now also stuck on her finger. He tells her it's over. Now's her chance, but still a deceiver even in her best friend's brokenness, she can't find the decency to tell him the truth. She's seemingly there to pick up the pieces. Win, right? Wrong. Ladies, would this be the way to get the man of your dreams? Is this the way we want someone's love? Is this a way to start off a romantic relationship? The sad thing about it is that she was perfectly okay with it. She thought she had won but imagine the blow to her ego when Jules opens her hotel room door to find a note from Michael letting her know he's going to the wedding breakfast after all. The fact she had the nerve to show up at the wedding breakfast to coach him back, "off the marriage ledge," is telling of just how selfish she really is. He's clueless and has no idea that all of this is happening because of his so-called, "best friend." Wake up, dude.

I can't make you love me

Bonnie Raitt's song[4], "I Can't Make You Love Me," has some strong truth-telling lyrics like most country songs do, and it is especially true of Michael's relationship with Jules. He loves her, but not like that. It's Kimmy that he loves and wants. He wants Kimmy. This is clear.

Why they still trust Jules to be the messenger between the two, we'll never know, but he sends her over to make sure Kimmy is okay. They still love each other, yet Jules is still trying to

. . . .

4   "I Can't Make You Love Me," Bonnie Raitt, Album: Luck of the Draw, 1991.

break them up. Never taking the blame for the email, she puts it on Kimmy. How many times have you played a telephone game like this and changed up some of the information to make yourself look or sound better? That is what Jules is doing. She can see that they still love each other, and she is desperate to get Michael to let go. This is because she's only focused on her love for him, and not his love for Kimmy. Hollering to Kimmy about needing to come clean to her parents and trying to convince her she's never going to be the "Jell-O" he needs because she is a crème brulé, it's clear that Jules is psychotic and has serious issues. Even though all the turmoil, confusion, and drama that has occurred is solely linked to Jules' presence there, she still trusts her, asking her to talk to Michael for her, saying, "You're the only person that I trust." We honestly want to strangle her at this point, praying that we never, ever, have a "friend" like this. After all is said and done, he commissions her, "Tell her I'll marry her at 6 o'clock, if she'll still have me." Yes! Wedding back on. It's time to celebrate. We are thrilled. After all the conniving, lies, and deceiving she has managed to squeeze into these few short days, there will be a wedding after all!

Do you think it ends there? NO, but we'll wrap it up here. At the end of the day, Michael still chooses Kimmy (we knew he would), even after Jules professes her love to him, asks her to pick her and marry her (we knew he wouldn't), and if that wasn't the kicker, selfishly, she kisses him, and Kimmy sees it. But while one might think this is a wedding dealbreaker (it actually should be a reason to postpone it, at the very least), what happens next is nothing short of glorious for we see a now-matured Michael chasing the one he really loves. He is chasing Kimmy. Granted, she is running away from him, yet he's still chasing her—even while Jules is chasing him. Ladies, don't be this girl. Why would you think it's okay to be chasing after a man on the day of his wedding? It's not, nor will it ever be.

So yes, we do not suggest being this girl. The crazy plots and lies are just too much for one person to deal with. Imagine how exhausted she was. Just be the girl that knows when it's time to step to the side and let love run its course. It found them, and it will find you, too. Romantic love didn't find Jules that day, but she finally came to her senses and told Michael the entire truth. It's about stinkin' time! She did what was right. She finds Kimmy, they work it out, they hug, she takes her to the church, and she stood beside them both as they said, "I do," ending the night by lending them her and Michael's song, "The Way You Look Tonight." It's sweet and touching and wouldn't make a good ending if her now new best friend, George, hadn't surprised her at the reception, bringing the clever comedy and final resolve for the win. Yes, she was still single, but she now realizes that Michael's happiness was more important than her obsession to win.

So why not be Jules? Here are some of key reasons why Jules is not the girl we want to be:

- ➤ She's manipulative.
- ➤ She's sneaky and untrustworthy.
- ➤ She's an imposter for personal gain.
- ➤ She doesn't know who she is.
- ➤ She is still afraid to love and be vulnerable, meaning there is inner work to be done.
- ➤ She lies to Kimmy.
- ➤ She has deceived Kimmy's family who trusted her.
- ➤ She uses her friends, playing them like pawns.
- ➤ She is inappropriate with a man who is engaged to someone else.
- ➤ When she's with Michael and Kimmy, she leaves Kimmy out, reminiscing about the old days.
- ➤ She crosses relationship boundaries.
- ➤ She is physical with a man who is engaged.
- ➤ She has no regard for their relationship, professing her love to someone getting married that day.
- ➤ She has tampered with someone else's identity, falsely sending out something on their behalf.
- ➤ She chases after the one she wants, rather than the other way around.
- ➤ She is selfish to the umpteenth degree.

These are just a few obvious reasons why we don't want to be Jules, and if we broke it down a bit more, there would be many more. You can count on that. So, as we wrap up this character, you say, "Well, that's just the thing, ladies—I'm a lot more like Jules than I'd like to be. In fact, I've been manipulating and calculating schemes, interfering with people's lives just so that I can get on top or get the prize." We're so glad you're here! It's time to come to terms with some things. It's time to forgive yourself, as well, maybe even asking others to forgive you, and here's where we'll start.

First, we talked about journaling. This is a good place to bring out that journal to honestly answer the questions below. And hear us when we say we would love for you to *honestly* answer these questions. If it's true that you have been scheming and conniving like Jules for years, then the only way to get that to stop is to start addressing some of the behavior and calling it out for what it is—lies and deceit.

A time to reflect & heal

We will be using some of the same exercises as in each of our cases, we had to do these same types of exercises repeatedly before it sunk in, bringing us true victory. Think of it as a workout. You never really see the results you are after, until doing the same exercise over and over again.

1. In what ways does your life or action mirror Jules' character?

    _____

    _____

2. What are specific traits or characteristics you see in yourself in relation to Jules? In what ways are you this girl?

    _____

    _____

3. Proverbs 6:18–19 (NKJV) calls out the person whose heart, "... devises wicked schemes," whose feet are "...quick to rush into evil...a person who stirs up conflict...". Are you ready for your heart to no longer plot schemes against others?

    _____

    _____

4. In the Lord's Prayer, Jesus prays, "Forgive us our trespasses, as we forgive those who trespass against us...", take a moment—taking as long as you need to do this, asking for forgiveness. Once forgiven, those actions are separated as far as the east is from the west. (Psalm 103:12; Isaiah 43:12)

    _____

    _____

5. What are some things you know you can implement to change that behavior to one you know is trustwior?

----

6. Has it ever been difficult for you to verbalize or communicate to someone how you feel about them?

----

7. Why is that? Did someone you love or care about break your trust?

----

8. How did you process that?

----

9. Did you know that no matter how you feel about yourself, or what your past holds, you are not defined by your past?

----

10. John 8:32 says, "You shall know the truth, and the truth shall make you free." Now is the time to ask for truth to be revealed to you, renouncing the lies that have led you through some of these years. Write down what that looks like for you. It might be to ask for forgiveness, it will most likely involve you also forgiving yourself.

Replacing lies with words of truth

Here are some examples of declarations you should repeat several times a day, every day! Although there are thousands of declarations that exist, we've included seven below, one for every day of the week, which is a great place to start! Some can be said by looking at yourself in the mirror or writing them on Post-it Notes, but at the very least, open your mouth and let these words come out of your mouth about yourself! Speak these words of life, saying them over and over (and over) again, throughout the day—especially if you feel yourself slipping back into those old destructive patterns.

These beautiful words of affirmation will bring your spirit, soul, and body the health needed to get you back on track to taking care of you. "The words of the reckless pierce like swords, but the tongue of the wise brings healing." (Proverbs 12:18, NIV)

> ➤ I am a woman of value and of great worth. I see me as the wonderful person I am. Because I am of worth, I am not only treated kindly by others, but I will be the first one to honor myself, as well.

> ➤ I am awesomely and wonderfully made. (Psalm 139:14, NASB)

> ➤ I am a seeker of truth and therefore will find it. Because I know the truth, the truth shall set me free. (John 8:32, NKJV)

> ➤ God has not given me a spirit of fear. He gives me power, love, and self-discipline. I can therefore be honest with others, without fear, because I am led by true love and there is no fear in love that is pure and true. (2 Timothy 1:7 ESV).

> ➤ I learn from my mistakes. I know I'm not perfect, but I am smart, resilient, and am a woman of value and worth.

> ➤ I am confident of this very thing, that God who has begun a good work in me will complete it until the day of Jesus Christ (Philippians 1:6).

> ➤ I will not allow myself to mistreat others, nor will I be mistreated and deceived by others. It doesn't matter what my past looks like. what has been done to me by others, or what I have done to others, today is a new day. I walk in forgiveness, forgiving any wrong done to me, and I also will ask others to forgive me for any wrongs I've done. The old ways are behind me, and I am looking forward to the beautiful things life has in store. There is beauty all around me, and that includes me and means that I now walk as a woman of integrity and of a good reputation.

"A good name is rather to be chosen than great riches, and loving favor rather than silver or gold." (Proverbs 22:1, NKJV) Let today be a new day for you, giving you a good name. We both love this scripture, "I do not count myself to have [a]apprehended; but one thing *I do,* forgetting those things which are behind and reaching forward to those things which are ahead." (Philippians 3:13, NKJV) May today be a beautiful new day for you. You don't have to stay stuck in that place. If you started to feel ashamed or embarrassed about Jules' behavior thinking of some of what you may have personally done to manipulate people or circumstances, you can start fresh today. Remember that you are not defined by your past. In the words of Digital Underground, "Stop what you're doin...", and turn from walking in that way. That's the old you. There's a new you ready to emerge. It's been in you all along, you just needed a little eye-opening to see that you don't need to deceive, plot or scheme for things to work out for you. There is a God who does love you, and who has already made a way for you to beautifully (not perfectly) walk out who you are. We need the real you to stand and as you do, we're applauding you and are so very proud.

But for the record, if we were in Kimmy's shoes, that wedding would have been postponed until Michael worked out all his business. Just sayin'. And since we're on a roll with Julia Roberts' characters, we're moving right on into another Julia fave of ours, "Runaway Bride."

Playlist:

- ♫ *The Way You Look Tonight* by Tony Bennett
- ♫ *Say a Little Prayer for You* by Dionne Warwick
- ♫ *What the World Needs Now* by Jackie DeShannon
- ♫ *You Don't Know Me* by Jann Arden
- ♫ *I Can't Make You Love Me* by Bonnie Raitt

"I guarantee there'll be tough times. I guarantee that at some point, one or both of us is gonna want to get out of this thing. But I also guarantee that if I don't ask you to be mine, I'll regret it for the rest of my life, because I know, in my heart, you're the only one for me."

Ike Graham,
Runaway Bride

Maggie Carpenter, A Brutal Serial Relationship Conformist Who Can't Commit to Marriage

Runaway Bride

The directors of this film already had a box office hit from the get-go. Pairing Julie Roberts with Richard Gere was a great pairing in Pretty Woman, and this movie was no different. In this movie, Roberts is Maggie Carpenter, a bride who runs away not so much from love (for it appears that she runs *to* romance), but it's once she's at the actual altar, that she decides to bail. Unable to commit to a man for a lifetime, she leaves her men on their wedding day almost as fast as the speed of lightning, for all who are present to see. While we may know a few women who have commitment issues, Maggie's character stood out as a little different than others. While the plot definitely makes for a good story, her character makes an excellent case for the girl we don't want to be. We're not fans of how she ditches her dudes at the altar, but as awful as that would be, if Maggie were a real-life character, there are plenty of other reasons why we don't want to be this girl.

To everything that lives and breathes, there is progression, and such is the same for relationships. In fact, from all the thousands of studies about relationships, there are four known stages to relationships. Before we take a good hard look at Maggie, let's take a quick look of the four stages not only outlined by several love experts, but also widely accepted by many.

Four stages of relationships[5]

Stage 1: The euphoric stage:
6 months to 24 months (2 years)

Stage 2: The early attachment stage:
12 months (1 year) to 60 months (5 years)

Stage 3: The crisis stage:
60 months (5 years) to 84 months (7 years)

Stage 4: The deep attachment stage:
84 months (7 years) and beyond

The first of four, the euphoric stage–is generally the time when most people tend to fall in love, as it's anywhere from six to 24 months. In this stage, many tend to be forgiving or overlook flaws and "red flags," and so can be somewhat blind in the beginning stages of their relationship. In the case of both Maggie, and her men, this may be the case as to why the men were oblivious to the fact that her pattern showed her leaving every previous groom at the altar and could also be why she quickly ran into the arms of the next man—because of that "lovin' feeling" you get when you're falling in love. While there are other stages in a relationship, Maggie didn't stick around long enough for her to experience Stages 2–4 with any of those poor souls she left standing at the altar, for all to see.

As this story beings, we find Ike (played by Richard Gere) —a reporter low on his writing mojo and time—who writes an article about Maggie, hearing about her from her most recent victim, devastated by the public humiliation of the altar-jilt as she escaped on horseback from having to vow, "... 'til death do us part." Framed by the soundtrack of Hall & Oates' "Maneater[6]," Maggie has been painted—in the words of Ike—as a woman who "... likes to dress her men up as grooms before she devours them," but in the midst of doing so, he loses his job and thus decides to get the *real* story on this girl and why she finds it so easy to walk away from her grooms just moments before saying, "I do." Well, if you've seen the movie, you already know how it ends, but no worries, if you haven't, 'cuz we're about to break it down on Maggie Carpenter.

· · · · · · · · · ·

5   Abrams, LCSW-R, Allison, "Navigating the 4 Stages of a Relationship," *erywellmind.com*

6   "Maneater," Darryl Hall & John Oates, Album: H2O, 1982.

Untethered heart

Can someone please explain why she continues to say, "Yes," victim after victim? No one likes admitting they've failed relationship to failed relationship. Whether you're the one in it, or you're watching from a distance, it's pretty pitiful. Even more so is when the pattern of having an untethered heart always points back to you. This is how we find Maggie in this movie. A small-town beauty with the biggest of smiles, she doesn't finish what she starts—a classic example of a Type B personality.[7] She's enthusiastic in the beginning and has an easy-going and friendly personality, but finishing what she starts is a recurring problem. Right before the commitment is ready to lock in, she calls it quits. Yes, she's a quitter, but not necessarily because she is weak in that sense, but mostly because it appears that Maggie still hasn't stepped into her own sense of being. This couldn't be more apparent than the last three men she called it quits on at the beginning of the ceremony. Here are the names of the grooms Maggie has so far left behind at the altar: Gill Chavez, Brian Norris, and George Swilling.

Now, we've got to give it to Maggie, because at least she stays committed as far as the whole girlfriend thing goes, but when it comes to lifelong commitment, that is where we see her failing. Aside from all the money spent on what it costs to throw a beautiful wedding, think of all the time and energy spent—not to mention the gifts purchased for her by friends and loved ones in her small, quaint town—one wedding after the other. What we're wondering is why ya gotta have all these weddings when you know darn well that what you'll end up doing is either hopping on an escape motorcycle, fleeing on foot or on a horse to get as far away as you can from marrying the man who had the courage—but not the smarts—to get down on one knee, proposing to you, the one who just can't seem to settle down?! The moment she marches down the aisle to her grooms-to-be, you immediately see the conflict on her face. Before you know it, she is heading for the door, with a man in love being thoroughly humiliated before the ones he loves most. Poor Gill—he turned around for just a split second, and before you know it, she was jumping on the back of someone else's motorcycle. Tragic.

If the idea of life-long love gives you anxiety, or if you get squeamish even thinking about living with this person for the rest of your life or become nauseated at the idea of growing old with your person, this is your chance to stop and consider if this is someone you should be loving in this capacity for the rest of your life. Or maybe it's not the idea of love but loving a specific person. In Maggie's case, this could very well be the case (we'll talk about that later). Follow your gut—no matter how big or small. Or maybe your dream is to marry this person, but you have commitment-phobia. Do the work, work on it, and work it out. Isn't it time for

. . . .

7   "Understanding the 4 Personality Types: A, B, C, and D," *hiresuccess.com*

you to get to the root of it? What is it that has prevented you from walking down the aisle to your best friend you love most? Or maybe that's it—maybe they ain't your best friend and perhaps you've only known them for less than a handful of months. Take your time. Take time to get to the root of it, understanding why you carry on the way you do. When you feel ready, the work has been done, and any small amount of fear is bombarded by the excitement and joy you feel when you think about being with them, it may very well be that you are ready to say, "yes" to the one you want to be hitched to for the rest of your life. No little boys being dragged on the floor of the church, hanging on for dear life to the end of your bridal train. Rugburns on the ring bearer is no way for a bride to behave. The good news is you don't need to be this girl.

Cyndi: They say when you're in love, you're an open book. If that's the case, there are only five guys I've ever been an open book with, and these relationships took place 1) Two were in high school; 2) Another when I was 19 and in college; 3) When I was 30 and in graduate school; 4) and in the year of 2004—I think I was 35. Five times. There were far more that I dated, and a few others I deeply cared for, but none that I would allow myself to bear my soul to. None that I felt I could or should say anything about how I felt. In fact, I'd be dating a guy for a few months, and then he'd ask me if I even really liked him because I never "said" that I did, or because I never called or verbalized my feelings for him. I've already shared that my walls were up big time. However, none of these factors should exist when wanting to settle down with someone. If you have issues or pain not yet resolved with walls taller (and stronger) than the Great Wall of China. None of these are factors that should exist when you're with someone, either. Just sayin'.

She'll chew you up!

While some women take pleasure and joy in dating a guy only to chew him up, spit him out, and leave him as is, we don't get the idea that Maggie is this girl. Are her relational tactics brutal? Yes. But as much as we didn't care for the way she treated any of her ex-fiancés in the movie, we find that she does care about them as individuals, but not enough to actually marry them. Now engaged to someone new—Bob—she seems to still be friends with most of her exes, which can be endearing, except that she sometimes uses their past to cross boundaries. You don't get to tell a priest that ten years ago he had his tongue down your throat. Know your boundaries and have some respect. He may not have been a priest ten years prior, but he is now. Between Father Brian and musician Gill, who realizes her tattoo (which they both got together) was a sticker, she never removes herself from their lives even though she completely humiliated them at the altar. The part that makes her a "maneater" is that she leaves her men wounded at the altar. But we might as well face it, though she doesn't quite yet know who she is and what she's all about, what Maggie also doesn't know or "get" about herself is that she's addicted to love.

Now ladies, if there is anything at all that resonates with you about chewing up men with no regard to what state of being you've left them in, it's time to stop, put down the book, and visit our website for resources of licensed marriage and family therapists who can assist with some healing that may need to take place. Don't worry, we'll hold the place here for you!

Cyndi: There was a season I was hurting so badly from the miscarriage I was on a mission to ruin the lives of any guy I dated, starting the with the father of my baby. I was out to hurt them the way I had been hurt. Realizing this was not only wrong, but it was unkind, I began to do the work to receive the healing needed. Once healed, the eyes of my understanding were opened to the horrible things I'd done, I eventually reached out and called him; we talked, and I asked him to forgive me for my actions towards him. They weren't very nice, and I was more than well-aware it had been my goal to not only hurt but to humiliate him, so he could feel the pain of what I felt in losing our baby. Don't be this girl.

If you *are* this girl, no shame here, but we do want to say it's important to take some time to counsel with someone who can help in the process. Cyndi had to go through this by intentionally meeting with someone who could help deal with the pain and trauma she experienced, going as far back as when she was six-years old. She said she felt like a new (and different) person. We're glad she reached out and got the help needed to do the healing work, as painful as it may have been. There should be no shame in admitting this, and when you are ready to do the same, know we are applauding you for being willing to face the funk. Some of us have had some painful pasts that lead us to make poor decisions in adulthood, and so we want you to know that it takes courage and strength. But we know you have both. Yes, you do, and we are cheering you on!

Addicted to love

Addiction is real, and so while we've seen this person in real-life—not just in some women, but also in the case of some men—and while we often think of drug, alcohol, sex, or food when you hear the word "addiction," there are many other forms as well. For Maggie, it's possible that falling or being in love was one of hers. In this movie as we see the number of men she was engaged to in such a short amount of time. Now we've already agreed—thanks to Ike—that she was a maneater, which was how she left her men—with hearts almost left for dead. But this is one of the why's to Maggie's behavior, and before we go forward we need you to know, ladies, it's a thing.

Cured Nation, an organization that helps individuals who struggle with addiction, states that love addiction is, "...characterized by excessive passion-driven behavior and unhealthy … obsessions with romance or an individual. Love addicts typically do anything to find and keep love, even at the price of … lost identity."[8] Before you think, "That's only in a song," that same citing shares statistics showing, "It's estimated that between 5% and 10% of adults in the US suffer from some form of love addiction." And it's estimated that, "Between 12 and 30 million people in the U.S have a type of sex and love addiction.[9] In Maggie's case, she didn't know what she liked, who she was, who she loved and why she loved him. She just loved love. She loved being in love. She loved the newness of each guy she was engaged to. And she also enjoyed flirting—with former beaus, as well as with future potential male victims. She was addicted to love, and such an addict that she still had no idea who she was, or what she even liked.

How do *you* like your eggs?

This was a question Ike kept inquiring about Maggie. At one point, he heard from her former fiancée it was, "Scrambled with salt, pepper and salt … same as me." From another ex, he heard it was fried eggs. The third jilted fiancé's response? "Poached, same as me." As you hear the differing replies from each of Maggie's exes, plus her conformity to her wedding themes looking very much like the grooms she left behind, you get the funny feeling Maggie hasn't a clue as to who she is, what she likes, or how she likes it. Confirmation? Seeing a fake tattoo on her back in ditching Gill Sanchez, by hopping on a motorcycle giving a "peace" sign on her way out of the wedding, validates this. Don't fake a tattoo for the one you are planning on marrying. That's just wrong. Not only is it deceptive, but why doesn't she have the courage to tell him the truth? Either 1) She's "scurred"; or 2) She just doesn't want one; or 3) Tell him she could just get a temporary one, but other than that, she won't be inking a permanent one. Maggie doesn't even know who she is, which is foundational to any strong relationship. "But I love him and he's such a good kisser," you say, "...and that's all I need to know." Sister, a good relationship is actually better when it isn't built on the physicality of it all. The first thing that is key and crucial, before anything and everything else: know who you are. If you don't know who you are, you're not ready for that type of commitment.

One of the beautiful things about adolescence and growing up, is it gives you time to find out who you are—what you like, what things don't you like, what things you enjoy doing, discovering your makeup, personality, what you enjoy studying, do you even *enjoy* studying,

- - - - - - - - - -

8   Cured Nation, "Love Addiction: Definition, Common Signs & Options for Help," *curednation.com*

9   Cured Nation, "Love Addiction: Definition, Common Signs & Options for Help," curednation.com

some of your favorite flavors and tastes, the list continues—along with the time needed, embracing all the things that make you, you. Knowing who you are is key to living out a life of authenticity and purpose, free of fraudulent behavior and characteristics. What is even *more i*mportant than that is already knowing **who you are** when in a relationship. In other words, if you don't know who you are, you should not be in one. We repeat—IF YOU DON'T KNOW WHO YOU ARE, YOU SHOULD NOT BE IN A RELATIONSHIP.

We crack up at the scene where Coach "Bob," her latest fiancée has her doing visualizations. "Focus on Maggie," … "Focus on Bob." He's treating her like an adolescent, and with her history, it's understandable on his end, but for marriage-sake, not even close. He's a good guy, but he's proposed to a gal who doesn't even know what kind of eggs she likes. Knowing who you are, what you like, and what you're all about is so important before getting serious with anyone.

Cyndi: As frustrating as this movie is to watch, I resonated with many of the flaws we discovered in Maggie. If there was one thing I didn't know at the age of 19, it was my identity. First-off, even at 19, we are way too young to even know what we like. Oh sure, we may have a "general" idea, but by the time I was 19, I had gone through so many phases and fads. Pressured by friends, society, and the need to feel accepted, I sometimes acted differently than the person I knew I really was, and this for me was detrimental, taking years to later undo—all because I wanted to belong. Have you ever done anything like that? I often see adolescents teeter on who they are. I'm thankful I had the ability to hear clearly for myself, about myself without all the noise surrounding the adolescents of today—it's quite heartbreaking. For me, the "coming to myself," stepping into who Cyndi Galley really was happened when I was 27 years old. The best way I can describe it is like a perfectly fit hand-in-glove, taking 27 years to figure it out. A little over a quarter of a century. Prior to that? I was "searching for who Cyndi Galley was," rather than just being who she was meant to be. And when you're still searching for your identity and meet a controlling person who'll tell you who you are, that's never going end well.

While I was still searching for the real Cyndi Galley, I found myself in an extremely toxic romantic relationship —the same relationship mentioned earlier on in Iris' story. I was so in love with this guy, that I let his likes and dislikes determine what *I* did and didn't like. He was so very different than I was, which isn't a bad thing, unless you allow it to infiltrate and control who you are. Being with someone shouldn't come at the expense of losing your identity to his, which is what I did. I began to take on his identity, likes, dislikes, ways, habits, embracing his identity as mine. And for the entire time we were together, this seeped into just about every area of my life. Being with him changed my music, what I wore, how I talked, what I did in my free time. It even changed the entire decor of my bedroom. Born in Michigan, he was very much a fan of almost every sports team that had anything to do with it. Not only that, he was also quite controlling, and so he started purchasing posters for me of the things he liked, strongly suggesting that I hang them up in my room, and so like a young obedient girlfriend, I did exactly what he said, losing myself in the middle of it all. Can you believe it? What was once all cute, girlie 80s-and-90s-themed wall-art and decorations on my wall in my room, soon became a Detroit sports & athletes' shrine. From Barry Sanders to the Detroit Tigers, to Pistons' Bad Boys, Rick Mahorn, and Isaiah Thomas—there wasn't a Pistons or Red Wings game in L.A. that I didn't go to, and if you didn't know me, you would have thought I was born in Detroit, though I had never set foot there a day in my life. How stupid was that?! The same pretty much happened to my wardrobe. A lover of clothes and fashion, my personal style of clothing found at Contempo Casuals, Robinson's-May and Broadway and other places, slowly became a closet of Levi's, Detroit-team tees, and jerseys. I could go on, but you get it. I lost myself in who he was. If he liked it, I liked it...if he listened to it, I did, too. And the things I used to like—if he disapproved—I made myself not like it anymore. It's quite sad writing this out, and it actually angers me to not only think I allowed a man to control me to that degree, but that I completely gave up my voice and who I was. Others in my life were so very aware that I had completely changed and become a female version of my then–boyfriend.

When we broke up, I literally did not know what to do with myself. I couldn't remember what I did, I didn't remember what I liked, it was as if I almost had to start from scratch, though thankfully, we'd only been together for a few years, so the things that I enjoyed doing slowly started returning to my life—I eventually started to find my voice again. If you're reading this, and you know that you are in this situation, wouldn't it be wonderful to get the *real you* back? Wouldn't it be amazing to be the *real* you without being concerned about others judging? Well, you can. And we're gonna help. People need the *real* you back. *You* need to get the real you back. Don't allow yourself to be quieted, silenced, or squashed. Don't let a man dictate who you are and what you like.

One of the reasons I believe some women are depressed is because they are not allowed to be who they really are. My hope, heart, and prayer for you today is that things are going to turn around. We will be declaring some things, and we encourage you to write everything down. Write down your questions, your thoughts, your regrets, and what you forgive yourself and others of, knowing that your best is around the corner and your best is yet to come. I have done some serious work, and even in the release of it all, there'll always be more to do. And when you do, there'll be peace, a joy and a freedom that comes from the inside out. May today be your day of freedom, peace, and joy!

Ivette: As I shared in Chapter Two about the lie that my mom told me, that seemed to throw me into a slight identity crisis of my own. I feel like knowing who I am was a question that I've had to ask myself since then. I can remember a time in school, when we were all dressing up for a school carnival. My mom and I had created the cutest clown outfit with full make-up. I looked great, the outfit was perfect, and the clown make-up would have competed with the best that Barnum and Bailey circus clowns had to offer. But when I got to school, I didn't see too many people dressed up, so I freaked out. I didn't want to be the only one dressed up. I was afraid my friends would make fun of me. So, I threw a fit and made my mom take me back home (what a brat, I know). Then the next school day came and the award for the best outfit went to another classmate dressed as a clown. This was so upsetting because I wasn't confident in myself. I just didn't know who I should be, let alone who I really was.

Recently, I read a book called, *Fasting with God.* In that book it describes God by His many names. The name *Elohim* describes Him as the Creator. He has created us in His image, therefore we have the ability to be creative. But when I was young, the fear of what people would think of me always made me question myself. This has gotten better since I was a child, but I can tell you that sometimes, I still struggle with it. What I don't struggle with is knowing who I am, being bold and unapologetic about it. Some may think that I am "too much," and that's okay. I get that my personality may irritate certain people out there, but I know who I am, and nothing can change that. Be confident, my friends, learn to know your worth and your creativity or other amazing characteristics that you have and embrace them. Don't be this girl—that just wanted to be the girl that someone *else* needed her to be.

Maybe you're reading this and are thinking, "But I don't yet know who I am—I'm still figuring that out, well, that's okay, too! And we're so glad that you're taking the time to do that because that is of extreme importance. Learning about and finding who you are will take some time. It took Cyndi 27 years and then some change, and Ivette found herself at 28. This isn't something that should be rushed. Take your time and be confident when that time comes, that you know exactly who you are, and that you are ready to genuinely be 100% you.

A flirt to a fault

The Oxford Dictionary describes a flirt as one who behaves, "... As though attracted to or trying to attract someone, but for amusement rather than with serious intentions."[10] While most of us adore Julia Roberts in her larger-than-life smile, her contagious laugh and her (sometimes) sweet girlish ways, it's the flirting that's not so cute. Maggie doesn't just flirt,

. . . .

10   "Flirt," *encyclopedia.com.*

but she *is* a flirt. Let's take it a step further, her continued flirting with men is inappropriate as she's engaged to be married. She has no boundaries with married men, which is another a recipe for disaster. Maybe you know someone like this, or maybe you are like this, get ready, 'cuz we're 'bout to step on some toes.

In the movie, you see an insecure woman who, in some way, has this strange hold on the former loves of her life. Now, there may be some asking, "What's wrong with that?" If you are still so connected to your exes, or should we say, "ex-fiancés," that you have easy access to face-to-face conversations with every one of them at any given time, that's a little unnerving, or maybe it's just us being old-fashioned. As the movie progresses, we see that she remains a little playful with some. It's like she doesn't know another way to be. Is it because she still wants to be the number one woman in each of their lives, even though she has clearly moved on? Is it to perhaps help her get out of an uncomfortable moment or situation? Or is she just flirting to flirt?

Now, we get that there are definitely some female personalities who are very comfortable talking to and engaging with men of the opposite sex, and that's not what we're addressing here. One of the most irritating moments of this movie for us was the scene at the baseball game where Maggie—who perhaps just views herself as "one of the guys" —was with her best friend at the field watching her bestie's husband play baseball. It turns out in a conversation between Peggy and Ike, that Peggy's husband, Cory, and Maggie, used to be a thing in high school. What made this extremely uncomfortable and awkward to watch was how Maggie went about cheering him on, proceeding to do a "little dance" they shared for so many years —it was this little thing they had between just the two of them, and it was all centered around the nickname ("Magpie") he'd given her while they were dating. Ummm, NO. This is not okay, ladies! Just stop. While it may be okay to have guy friends who are the husbands to your girlfriends, it isn't okay to go way beyond boundaries, even if he weren't married. Are you this girl? Have you ever said something like, "Well, we were friends before they got together or before she became his wife, so if she isn't confident in their relationship, that's not my problem!" If any of your answers to these questions are a "yes," then read on, sister!

Ivette: This one is hard for me as I have always been a bit of a tomboy and most of my friends to this day are men. However, I've also learned the hard way (before getting married), that even your best friend may have feelings that they may not share with you. In this scene where Maggie is being supportive and fun in her own way, she was not at all considerate about his wife, who was her best friend. It can't possibly feel good to watch your husband chest-bump his ex-girlfriend—your best friend. But that's what Maggie did to Peggy, and it wasn't the first time either. Apparently, they'd carried on this way for years—they'd high-five, jump up while chest-bumping ... the whole nine yards. That's just wrong, ladies. Please, don't be this girl. If that's you, stop and think for a moment, "What if this were me? What if I were in her shoes? How would I feel if my husband was all about his ex-girlfriend—my best friend?" Would you be 100% secure? Probably not. And don't let your, "I'm good with anything," attitude try to tell you otherwise. Again, the heart is above all things deceitful.

This reminds me of one story. There was a guy friend that I liked in high school but never went out with. Years later at a reunion, we were having a great time talking about life and old times. And unbeknownst to me, his wife was about to take me out for the count. Why? Because she had heard a lot of good things about me, and she was feeling threatened. Unaware of what had just happened and what was going on, I was shocked. Which brings me to another point and something else to watch out for—don't be the girl that tells her new beau about all your best guy friends and how much you love them. If they are indeed still wonderful guy friends in your life, allow everyone to get to know one another. It takes time to know whether your new beau—and your guy friends—can accept that (and each other). Be kind, girls!!!

Cyndi: Agreed. I remember dating someone in college, but I had a best guy friend. Because I've grown into an independent woman, I remember getting so annoyed whenever the guy I was dating would come around without asking. One time my bestie and I were going out, and the new guy came over without so much as giving me a call or a heads up. I was so annoyed. Not only did I ask him what he was doing there, I told him that I was on my way out with my best guy-friend and that he could either wait or we'd connect later. I wasn't about to invite him to hang out with us. I realized later that not only was that inconsiderate, but it was also rude. Should he have asked before coming over? Yes. But he was a person and that's what we should (always) remember. Men are people, too. ☺ I was a bit harsh during that season of my life. I had a lot of healing that needed to take place and even though I still don't believe I should have changed my plans for his spontaneity, I could have *definitely* been more gracious about it. Grace, ladies. If we want grace extended to us in these romantic settings and situations, we must also be gracious.

As for you when dating someone new, your new guy needs to know he is your number one and that even though you care for and may love your bud, if there is any chance you think this is the man you may want to spend the rest of your life with, the new man in your life needs to be given the priority over all others. The male-besties need to take a back seat, and if they love you like the sister you believe you are to them, they'll treat him right and honor your new love-interest. Use this time to get to know each other. And as for the guys in your life, think of it like when male dogs are getting acquainted. They rarely meet on one of their territorial places. It's best to meet somewhere neutral, where no one feels threatened. And just like you see the "sniffing" nature taking its course within the canine community, let the men take their time getting to know each-other before that official handshake. Once the information has processed and that genuine handshake has taken place, that's a good sign of a green light on both sides.

As we get older, it would do us well to become wiser in this area, as well. This was something Maggie hadn't done yet. We saw it in how she behaved with men—even as a woman who was engaged. That didn't stop her. I have to hand it to her, though. She impressed me when she approached Peggy to ask her if she thought she flirted with Cory. Peggy was honest and flatly responded, "Yes." Way to go. Ladies, if a friend asks you something, be honest in your reply. Don't tell them what you think they want to hear. Tell them what they *need* to hear. If you're telling them three or four years later, never having been honest enough to tell them the truth while it was going down, you're not the friend you think you are. Help them be a better friend, by being honest at the time they need it. Peggy's honesty warmed my heart. While this is only a movie, she is a good friend. *This is the girl you want to be.*

Okay, so now that we've identified the girl we *want* to be—an honest friend, like Peggy—here's a list of some of the ways we can help eliminate the Maggie-ness from our lives. By the way, this is a great exercise if you either feel you connect with Maggie on several of the points above, or if you feel yourself becoming a little defensive, this is a sure sign that some beautiful feathers have been ruffled. Take a moment to breathe. Inhale. Exhale. Inhale. Exhale. How do you feel? Ready to move on? If so, great! If you feel a little flustered because you see glimpses of yourself in some of what we're sharing about Maggie, feel free to take that little break. Go outside, get some fresh air and don't beat yourself up. When you're ready, we'll be here.

Something that has helped us both immensely in leveling up in the various areas of our lives has been journaling. You can write your thoughts. You can vent, pray, write letters to people, and express your feelings about certain situations. Journaling is a beautiful tool that assists you from just "keeping it all in." Now, while there are other exercises that assist with that as well, for this section, we'd love for you to grab (or go buy) a journal so you can write, process, and reflect. Again, this is about us doing some of the work we've just never taken the time to do, or we've been too afraid to do it, knowing we may not like what we feel or how it feels when we are addressing some of these things. But there is a verse that says, "Therefore, confess your sins to one another and pray for one another, that you may be healed." (James 5:16, ESV) There is healing that happens when we share things we're going through, with others. And ladies, you are worth this. There are people who care enough about you and who want to listen to and encourage you to help you level up to that place you know in your heart you want to be. It takes work and, in most cases, work is hard.

Ready? Set, here we go!

Don't be the girl who:

- ➢ Flirts with married men just to get attention.

- ➢ Flirts with engaged men to get attention.

- ➢ Flirts with men for attention.

- ➢ Flirts with men for approval.

- ➢ Enters into a man's room while he's sleeping—especially if you're engaged to be married … what are you thinking?!

- ➢ Makes sexual reference to a man's genitals when you're engaged to be married (she had no business naming Ike's private parts)

- ➢ Spends time alone with a man when you are either married, engaged to be married or in a committed relationship with another man;

- ➢ Touches a man's hands, neck, chest, and beyond. No, "To infinity and beyond!" in this case. Anything beyond an appropriate hug is not okay.

- ➢ Chest-bumps and makes references to "cute-sy" names from back in the day is not okay.

If you, like Maggie, are engaged to spend the rest of your life with that special someone, it's time to put an end to the flirting. Be intentional and honoring to your new man. Oh, the beautiful seeds that will be sown because of it. May your eyes and your heart only be for him, and may he know and never doubt in his mind, whether you have feelings for another. Now, back to Maggie, who—in the words of her bestie, "… just sort of spazzes out with excess flirtatious energy that (just) lands on anything male that moves." Yeah, don't be this girl. Especially when one of the ones you've been flirting with includes your best friend's husband. Not cool. Not cool at all.

Devouring death goddess

Engaged and preparing for her upcoming nuptials to Coach Bob, Maggie still doesn't know what—or who—she wants. All throughout the movie we see this so clearly in just about every scene of her interactions and engagement to Bob. She's shifty and he doesn't even see it.

From his visualization exercises reinforcing focus on Maggie and focus on Bob through both verbal and visual signs, to reminding her of the "penalty box," it is painful and embarrassing that he is publicly relating to her as a coach does to his players. This is NOT the way for a relationship to organically flourish. Between her need to be the center of attention with "the guys," and all this coaching, we see many red flags have been raised in regard to Maggie marrying Coach Bob. She wasn't ready. Not only that, but he also wasn't the one for her. Their relationship was all technique and coaching. They were not well-suited for each other.

Cyndi: Why is it that we, as women, will put up with a man's behavior—even if it makes us feel uncomfortable or childlike? I remember dating a guy, who was a great guy, in my very late 20s. He and I could not have been any more different from each other, except for the fact that we both loved God very much, ate extremely healthy, enjoyed long-distance jogging, and had powerful times of prayer together. Very early on in the relationship, I noted that there were many instances where I was constantly being gently scolded or reprimanded. He was not controlling, mean, or aggressive, but he was very opinionated about how I chose to handle my finances, for example, and would constantly try and teach me about the power of delayed gratification and those types of principles. Now, while this is actually a lesson that remained with me, I remember finally coming to a romantic halt in my heart when I realized that more than anything, I felt like I was continuously being fathered by him, realizing this was not a relationship I wanted to be in. I already had a father—and not just one, but two. My dad who raised me was my stepdad by marriage to my mom when I was five, but he was my dad. I also had a biological father, as well. I didn't need a third! The best way I could describe this relationship was that my size 10 foot was being crammed into a size 9-1/2 high heel shoe, while being on my period, having swollen feet due to salt and water retention. Not a good fit. It took me meeting and dating *another* guy to get me out of that relationship. So, although I knew my relationship with him was not a great fit, what I should not have done was jump right into the next, not giving myself time to learn and reflect, to not have to go through that again.

Maggie shouldn't have been in that relationship with Bob. A great-fit of a relationship shouldn't take that much work in the beginning. Notice we say in the beginning, because like everything we walk out in life, even the most romantic of relationships will take work. Anything worth fighting for will take work and it will be hard, but it shouldn't start out that way. If there are already sweat beads and you feel like a misplaced child with the man you are dating or marrying, he ain't the one. Stop trying to make it fit and see the obvious signs that everyone else (but you) is paying attention to.

If you find you're in a similar place emotionally or mentally, you are most likely not ready to tie the knot. Neither was Maggie. As she was struggling to stay put in her fourth engagement. While at odds with Ike, the movie's protagonist, she decides if he's going to do the true story about her and follow her around to prove she is every bit the "maneater," he wrote about in the paper, he needs to do the story right. Even though she's stumbled on his post-its of how he perceives her, "...she's not that beautiful," "SHOWS NO REMORSE," she agrees to allow him to follow her around town as she prepares to marry Bob. After laying out the guidelines—and the money it'll require her to give him her story, he agrees, and a new horizon has opened up to Maggie. Here's where—movie wise—the going gets good and the story begins to shift. Even though we know it's coming, you're thinking, "Oh no...this isn't good." Or is it?

One of the things that's so amazing in life is the unknown power of post-it notes. Between the Post-It notes and Maggie's conversation with Peggy, she has had both confrontation and "carefrontation," a word Cyndi strongly resonated with after reading an incredible book called, "Caring Enough to Confront." Through the words written on the Post-Its, and the firm-yet-gracious words she heard from Peggy, Maggie is now at a point where she can either ignore these truths she has heard about herself—and agrees with; or she can ignore, pretending she was never faced with the hard facts about how she behaves as a single woman looking for love (in all the wrong places). She "mans up," and is ready to take life—and love—head on, clearing her name of the reputation she's made for herself once only kept to her small town of Hale, but now known to the many readers of USA Today, thanks to Ike.

As she begins to close in on her wedding with Bob, with Ike feverishly taking notes at her side, he not only softens towards this woman he was out to destroy in following her every move, but he also begins to see inside the life of Maggie, putting the pieces together of who she is and why she is the way she is. Now, don't get us wrong—we know that not one person could ever know everything about why we behave the way we do, but his being with her for reporting and journalistic purposes caused him to see her in ways that even those closest to her did not get or understand. Not even Peggy. It's amazing what a fresh pair of eyes will see. She lets him into her life, and so he sees her as a person—and no longer as a journalistic conquest. He gently taunts her various previous engagement rings from Brian, Gill, and George, as well as her current one from Bob, learns of (and validates) her "Designs by Mag," fixtures. While she's trying on yet another dress for her latest wedding, he sees the treatment and the skepticism in the sales lady assisting with picking out her dress, encouraging Maggie to invest in one that's not so expensive, for fear of her wearing it only for "... ten minutes or so," before running out on groom #4. While we see her point, we celebrate Ike's advocacy for Maggie in that no matter what her past was and regardless of the cost of the dress, let the girl buy the dress she wants to wear for her wedding.

They begin befriending each other—one deep conversation after another about relationships, attraction, proposals, taking place in somewhat secluded or intimate settings between just the two of them. They are becoming more comfortable in each other's presence. Next thing you know, Maggie is moving her hair behind her ear while talking to Ike, while giving him a Miles Davis album. Beyond that, he sees her. He sees her pain when she's placing her drunk dad in her pick-up truck. There's a weight he realizes she's carrying with her dad as she also runs the store for her dad since her mom's passing. It wasn't until fiancé #3 sees that Ike is now drawn to her, "... like a moth to a flame," that he tells him, "... she got to you, too!" And voila, yet again, in asking Bob what kind of eggs she likes, he finds that she liked her eggs, "... poached," just like Bob. The girl does not *know* who she is or what she likes! Have you found out that you, like Maggie, are also wishy-washy in what you do and don't like? It might be a good indication you are not ready to be in a dating relationship with anyone just yet.

The funny thing is that when it comes to hearing and giving Ike post-divorce advice, Maggie is all-knowing and wise, which seems to be a tad off from her flighty character, but all the same, they're getting to know each other in the baring of their souls. And in taking her advice about talking to his ex-wife, they both get the closure needed. As the movie continues, it's clear that even though Maggie is just days away from her wedding to Bob, it's official. She has developed feelings for Ike. Big-time feelings. Furthermore, the feeling is mutual, and it's evident and he's pretty gutsy at the wedding luau where Ike comes behind her, standing way too close to her for comfort, and she does *nothing* to prevent or break that behavior up. Coming to her rescue at her wedding "roast," while she uncomfortably sits through the jokes, he defends her. Sidebar, ever heard the saying, "Sticks and stones may break my bones, but names/words can never hurt me..."? We couldn't disagree more. The words that were being spoken to Maggie hurt her. Names can hurt someone so deeply that that individual could continue to think that way about themselves. It's a tough pill to swallow, but even if it's just a joke, there is a likelihood that there is some truth in what you are saying, so please be kind with what you say to or about others. Out of the abundance of the heart, the mouth speaks, but before you go judging someone else, be sure to stop and remove the speck from your own eyes.

While we're on the topic of eyes, yes, Ike now has eyes for Maggie, and she has eyes for him. Not only could you feel it outside as they are fighting at the pre-wedding luau, but it comes to a climax at the wedding rehearsal. Still proving her point that she'd go through with the wedding, Coach puts Ike in the game as a stand-in for the groom, so he could coach her on walking down the aisle, as it was obvious she was having difficulty when Coach was the one standing at the altar. That is all she wrote, folks! Now seeing Ike—the man she really wanted—standing there, she not only walked down with her eyes fixed on him, but his were also locked on hers, as well. And just as Coach continues to role-play that he is the minister, declaring "...you may now kiss the bride," they kiss for not five, ten or even fifteen seconds. It's more like almost thirty and is interrupted by Peggy's very loud, "Noooooo!" Although Ike had written on his post-it notes that Maggie showed no remorse, they both would appear to have no remorse in that very intimate and long kiss that took place in front of her fiancé at *their* wedding rehearsal. Not the best time and not the best move. But since we are saying to *not* be this girl—for the coach's sake—we are glad it happened before the wedding. But girl, you literally went from kissing your fiancé earlier that day, to kissing another man that you're now professing to love.

What happens next shocked us even more. Still standing on the porch of the church, literally seconds after her ex-fiancée, Coach Bob, leaves the church hurt and angry, they decide that all wedding plans should remain intact, except for that now, she'll be marrying Ike, not Bob. Though we saw the relationship coming, we were shocked that Ike proposes to Maggie, who then decides that he is someone she can see herself marrying. While there is something to be said about her envisioning being married to him, her fiancé literally just left the building. Girl, can we just take *some* time to get to know Ike? Or how about taking at least an hour to grieve the loss of your ex-fiancée? Have a little respect. First-off, we submit that this isn't love, but lust. And a montage of fun, romantic scenes does not equate to getting to know someone long enough to solidify a lifetime commitment with them.

Have we completely forgotten that they have only known each other for maybe two weeks tops? She hasn't met his family. What about children? Will he be happy in this small town? Where would they live? These are the types of questions that take place early on when getting to know each other in the dating phase. We also see this type of foolish behavior in our chapter about *Fools Rush In*. He says he feels inspired that he can now write novels, but how long will that last for a New York City writer who has transplanted his city-life into that of a quaint small-town?

There was a point in the movie where Ike referred to Maggie as being lost. It was when they were arguing out in the field while her pre-wedding celebration luau with Bob was taking place in the barn. He was right. She was lost. So, for her to go from the arms of Bob right into the arms of Ike was not only unfair to Bob, but it was also unfair to Ike, and most importantly, to Maggie. However, as lust would have it, they proceeded to move forward with their plans to marry. What Maggie did next, surprised no one, except Ike. Almost making it to the altar, Maggie, at the last minute, bails on Ike in front of the press, Ike's friends, Coach Bob, and the whole town of Hale. Unabashedly unashamed of his proclaimed love for his future bride, Ike chased after her on foot until he could no longer see the back of her escape vehicle, a FedEx truck.

I once was lost but now I'm found

In the case of Maggie and Ike, all's well that ends well. What we see Maggie doing after she leaves him at the altar, is what EVERY girl should be doing—working on herself. She came to the realization that for every man who she attempted to marry, they had no idea who the "real her" was, and so it would have been a lie. And even though Ike was the only man who knew the real her, and the only man she truly oved, she finally knew she had no idea who *she* was. Before she could commit her life to him, she needed to at least find out who she was. 100%. She makes time for Maggie, getting clarity, doing many things including putting her lamp and light creations in a store in NYC, and testing eggs to see what eggs she really likes—Eggs Benedict. That's what she likes. That, and small weddings. Yes, girl! Find out who you are and don't rush the process. Do you need to meet with someone? A coach or a counselor? Do you need to pull out your Bible to remind yourself who you really are through what God's Word says? Do everything you need to do to work out your stuff. You'll be so glad you did, and so will those you love.

Now while we would rarely speak favorably of a woman proposing to a man, this is one instance where—on screen—we don't frown upon Maggie's actions of recompense for how she ditched Ike, the man she loved, at the altar. After taking time to identify areas in her life that needed work, Ike finds her in his apartment. Though not approving of her being there initially, she shares her heart and the process with which she needed to discover who she was to be with the man she loved. Surrendering her running shoes to him, he knew it was serious, and it was confirmed the moment she got down on her knee to propose to him. By this time, his heart is soft and their banter by this time on the screen is quite cute and comical. She finally recites to him the vows he shared with her when first getting to know each other. He gets up, puts on Miles Davis and the next scene, it's just the two of them getting married on a hilltop, they say, "I do," their friends run up the hill to celebrate and off they go into a sunset.

Goodness, gracious, how do you just go from being in love with one guy, to the next? Well, the reality is that some girls do, and many of us have. What we've learned from Maggie are the behavioral issues that needed to be worked out before committing to anyone, and that's not just relating to marriage. She said it best when telling Peggy that she was, "… PROFOUNDLY AND IRREVERSIBLY SCREWED UP." So many of us have had traumatic experiences happen to us, dating back to when we were children. What that means is, there is work to be done. There are people out there who can help. There are counselors, ministers, books, and organizations to help you walk through your stuff. Believe it or not, there are people who just genuinely care about your well-being. It's not anything to be ashamed of or about. Jesus came to break all that shame. We have both personally experienced that, and it is so freeing. Each of us has experienced shame for many of the things we did when we were younger, but God truly removed all guilt and all shame. You are no different and can (and should) experience the same.

"Do not be afraid; you will not be put to shame. Do not fear disgrace; you will not be humiliated. You will forget the shame of your youth and remember no more the reproach of your widowhood." (Isaiah 54:4, NIV)

Once you hand over your shame and any guilt from your past, you begin to realize you got some thangs to work out, we can see how we wouldn't want to be Maggie. The kind whose flirtation spills out on everything male that moves. Maggie presents so many variants of the girl not to be, and so although we listed these above, here comes the recap. Learn it and know it inside out.

Don't be the girl who:

- ➤ Dates a man because she's addicted to love.
- ➤ Is a serial dater, going from relationship to relationship.
- ➤ Accepts a proposal without knowing who she is.
- ➤ Is a maneater, or a "devouring death goddess".
- ➤ Flirts with married men just to get attention.
- ➤ Flirts with engaged men to get attention.
- ➤ Flirts with men for attention.
- ➤ Enters into a man's room while he's sleeping—especially if you're engaged to be married … What are you thinking?!
- ➤ Makes reference to a man's genitals when you're engaged to be married (she had no business naming his private parts).
- ➤ Spends a lot of alone time with a man when you are married, engaged to be married or in a committed relationship with another man.
- ➤ Touches a man's hands, neck, chest and beyond. No, "To infinity and beyond!" in this case. Anything beyond an appropriate hug is not okay.
- ➤ Chest-bumps and making references to "cute-sy" names from back in the day when you were dating. This is not okay.
- ➤ Leaves your fiancé at the altar—may you find out who you are long before this ever happens.

It's time to reflect and jot

Anything in Maggie's chapter that you relate to? Write it all out—so that you can see it with your own eyes. Take time in this chapter to write the things *you* really enjoy doing—the things that make you happy. Write it all down—everything from your gifts and talents to your desires and dreams, your music tastes, sense of fashion, the food, and flavors you like, activities you enjoy, places you like, and even a list of your friends (your friends should still be allowed to be your friends) when you start dating or getting to know someone.

Once you've finished writing everything that comes to mind, we want you to list any areas of unforgiveness you might be holding against yourself or others. Once you've made your list, we'd love for you to actually *do* something physical that represents the act of forgiveness and let it go.

> **Toss those rocks.** One of the gals interviewed in *She is Single. She is Strong*, had mentioned that in order for her to get rid of some of the issues or unforgiveness, she decided to write the issues on the rocks and when she was ready to truly let go and forgive, that's exactly what she did. Replicating the concept in an interior version of that, we had the ladies write the name of something that was so heavy they couldn't let go of it and then then dropping it into a vase filled with water. It was a powerful time and many of the women that had experienced something major were able to let go and never turn back to it.

> **Write it out.** Though this may sound similar to what we're recommending with writing it on the rocks before tossing them, this is more of a letter or something along the lines of you expressing all of your feelings and emotions before either tossing it, or you can also use something so powerful as writing it on "flash paper," paper with chemicals in it that cause it to vanish in flames once lit. There are other options of things you can do that are similar, producing the same emotional, mental and physical release.

> **Getting rid of the letter you've written as a sign of release or relinquishment.** This can be somewhat used as the previous way to let things go and forgive. Ever heard of a message in a bottle? It's the same concept, however, we recommend *not* doing it in an ocean, but rather somewhere that won't contaminate or harm the water animals. Get creative but please be considerate of innocent animals, and the environment.

> **Verbally saying (or yelling), "I FORGIVE YOU, _____!"** There is power in the words we speak. Tell them you forgive them, inserting their name at the end. When we say something—especially when it's repeated, it's likely that your body, heart, and mind will eventually follow.

> **Ask for forgiveness.** You may actually need to go and ask for forgiveness in person—this includes asking yourself to forgive yourself for something you've done or something you may feel guilty for allowing to happen. Even if Individual is gone or no longer around, this might be something you need to do with a letter, along with a meaningful act.

> Lastly, **don't look back.** You've moved on, and so all you should be focused on, it's what's ahead of you.

Though discovering who you are can be scary, it is a beautiful process. And if there's one thing I've heard about the process—we need to learn to trust it. This is where self-forgiveness, release, forgiving others takes place. It is a time of growth, and sometimes as we know, pain can be involved. What it will produce, as most growing pains do, is a beautiful transformation. For some it may even be a total metamorphosing time, and that's okay. Find out who you are, embrace the real you by yourself... and for crying out loud, PLEASE eat your eggs (and everything else), the way YOU like them. May the days of conforming to—and becoming the female version of—your beau, fiancé or even hubby, be over.

Playlist:

♫ *Don't Fence Me In* by Ella Fitzgerald

♫ *Addicted to Love* by Robert Palmer

♫ *Maneater* by Hall & Oates

♫ *Ready to Run* by The Dixie Chicks

♫ *You Can't Hurry Love* by The Supremes

"Most people don't know what it is they want until I show it to them."

Anna Brady,
Leap Year

Anna Brady, The Uptight Socialite Who Doesn't Like Surprises

Leap Year

In this fun Irish-holiday film centered around the Irish, we are introduced to Anna, a successful home-staging professional in Boston. She is a seemingly confident woman who takes charge of every part of her life, but between her career of staging things to look a certain way and having her eye on the prizes of life, we get the feeling that this ideology has spilled over into every area of who she is, which is a dangerous thing. Walking to the rhythm of her perfectly curated self, the girl is "put together." Her outfits are on point, with not a wrinkle in sight. Not one hair is out of place. From head to toe, everything appears perfect, and though we get that she likes order and control, things are a tad bit too calculated for our liking. Now, we realize that there are those who are so to the needle-and-thread measurement in every detail of their lives, but for most of us who are just trying to live life, a run to the tailor on the regular isn't quite the life we live. For some of us whose legs are a little shorter than most, you might find us visiting a seamstress for that once–a-year pantsuit or dress, but we get the feeling from the start that Anna is a little extra, and that she might actually believe the world she lives in not only revolves around her, but that she should be able to acquire the things she is striving for in life. She's got the coat, the bag, the shoes, the jewelry and everything else a girl would seemingly need or want, but there are two things she's after that she doesn't yet "have": residency in an apartment building—The Davenport—a place she has dreamed of and has her heart set on, as well as marriage to her live-in boyfriend, Jeremy. Though it is evident they work hard for their money, Anna comes across as Entitled (yes—the capital E was on purpose). Everything about this girl is entitled and extra, and now we enter into the "everything in place" world of Anna Brady, played by Amy Adams.

As you already know, we live in an imperfect world, and life is always subject to change. That in itself sets the tone that things are about to change for someone is an OCD-control freak, expecting their lives to be lived out exactly the way they have planned. At the start of the movie, you catch glimpses of the lives that her and her boyfriend, Jeremy live. They›re in fact being interviewed by a board to become residents of an elite apartment located in Boston—the right careers, the right couple, the right clothes, the right neighborhood. He›s a heart surgeon, she is in the real estate business. Outwardly, they have everything anyone trying to live the American dream would strive for. It›s sad to say that early on in the movie, even their love life seems very cold and calculated. Not calculated in the way where there are schemes, but calculated in the way that it they have to slot in time for everything, including time to love each other. You can tell she invests into her looks and wardrobe with her just-right makeup look showing she has makeup on, but it's not overly done. She›s not gaudy by any stretch of the imagination. She wears fine, couture apparel that is classic with clean lines, giving her a sleek, elegant, and professional appearance. Chanel, not Vivienne Westwood. Gucci, not Guess. Ever. From boho to chic, current and vintage, we love it all! Back to Anna. We're yawning already because there is nothing exciting about the romance between these two. It's scheduled and predictable. Where's the fire? Where are the sparks we saw between Isabel and Alex? In fact, is there romance at all with these two? Taking a photo of her in front of The Davenport she asks, "... don't you like us?" We're not huge fans of scheduled or slotted romance, so we'll answer that question for you. No.

Words like, "In sync," and "preparation," are what you hear her saying in reference to different areas of her life. It is our experience to say that relationships that are rehearsed and practiced feel forced, rarely allowing room for fun, organic spontaneity. "You know I don't like surprises," she tells Jeremy before they part ways. His response, "You'll like this one." Will she? Once the movie gets going, her friend lets her in on a secret—that Jeremy (played by Adam Scott) was coming out of a jewelry store with "a little red bag," which could only mean one thing—an engagement. Rehearsing staged reactions with her friend to appear surprised when he proposes at dinner that evening, it is evident that being genuine isn't at the top of her list. It's so embarrassing to watch. She'd rather play the part, which isn't the way you want to start a marriage, but that's Anna. We're watching thinking, "Really? You want to spend the rest of your life like *that*? With *him*?" We've seen more passion between two floating balloons bouncing off each other. This couple is dry and seemingly passionless, but are all about the looks, status, and appearance. Confessing to her friend she "dropped" a hint about proposing about six months before, she is hopeful about how dinner that night will unfold but checks in with her dad before doing so. Thrilled for his daughter who has "been with this guy for over four years," he proceeds to tell a story of her grandparents getting engaged over a leap year—a year where a girl can ask a man to marry her. She has been with her for quite some time, and now they are applying to live in her dream apartment in the city. However, there is still no ring on her finger, and she has been patiently waiting for that very moment.

One of the beauties of movies like this is getting a glimpse into childhood through a look at the parents. In this case, Anna's dad couldn't be more opposite from Anna. He's late, wrinkled, and appears to be a jolly old soul. She could definitely use a bit of all of those qualities in her dad, yet who knows, it could be the very thing she is trying to not be like. But he's friendly, likable, and we find that he proposed to her mom only one week after knowing her. Because of this, he doesn't grasp why it's taken Jeremy four years and they're still not married. Before ending their short time together, her dad shares a myth of Grandma Jane who proposed to her grandfather on leap year, February 29th in Dublin, to which she assures him that's something she won't need to resort to.

Bidding him farewell she heads to her date with Jeremy where she gets to act surprised by his proposal. The thing is, she doesn't have to act at all because she really is surprised when opening the little red box he gives her, and sees there is no ring in there, but instead—a pair of diamond earrings. She is surprised, and disappointed. Now don't get us wrong, the diamond earrings he bought for her were absolutely gorgeous (in fact, Cyndi is *still* waiting to own her first pair). From the angle the camera shot on Anna's earrings, there wasn't a single flaw in them. But what she had hoped for and wanted, wasn't a pair of diamond earrings, it was a diamond RING. "They're earrings ... for my ears," she says quietly at the dinner table. He doesn't even read her body language. Ladies, that is a RED FLAG for sure. If this guy is "the one," he should notice even the most subtle things about you because he knows you that well. This guy? Not s'much. Devastated and disappointed that the little box Jeremy gave her was not a ring, but, in fact, a beautiful pair of earrings, she was speechless. Though he does question her about trying them on, he's clueless. For once—and beyond her control—there wasn't much she could do as he announced mid dinner that he needed to head off to an Aorta surgery, and then he'd be off to Dublin for a cardiology conference. And thus, the story of her quest for love begins ...

He's dragging his feet and needs my help

May we remind you that men are hunters and need no help in getting what they want. Anna didn't seem to understand this notion and so felt it was her duty to assist him in getting this ring on her finger she had become so obsessed with. Confident and in control of every other area of her life, this can't possibly be what life is handing her after all these years of dating the man with the perfect career (yet, not so perfect, as we can see). Isn't it something how those of us can get so used to doing something for a work or career, that it carries over into our personal lives? Here we have a bright and talented young woman who stages homes for a living, making them look like the perfect place to live so that someone will buy it. And yet, even in the midst of something that cuts to the heart while watching it on-screen, we can see she's still in "staging mode." Anna is used to getting what she wants, and so while she may have all of the right toys, status, lifestyle and now these stunning diamond earrings, what she doesn't have is the engagement ring to Jeremy. Have you ever found yourself in a similar situation? Feeling like you had all of the right things in place, yet you perhaps didn't have the one thing you *really* wanted. And in most cases, you kind of already have an idea of what that thing might be. It might even be the thing that came to mind as you were reading just now. For some it might be landing that job, having that purse, living in a specific neighborhood, owning that house or car. Ever heard the saying, "... let patience have *its* perfect work, that you may be perfect and complete, lacking nothing...."? (James 1:4, NKJV) Newsflash! There will always be things in our lives that we want, but when we have them too prematurely, just as a premature baby being born will have its share of difficulties until strong enough to do what it's body would normally do at full-term. We've got to learn to ... wait for it ... wait for it ... yeah, actually wait for it. Wait until the right thing comes along. It's okay to wait. In fact, waiting is a good thing. We're just so used to everything being given to us now, instantly, overnight, or express, that we tend to get a little fidgety when it comes to waiting. But waiting is a normal part of life and truly we should practice it. And practice it again and again, for whether it's on a person, place, or thing, it's a part of life. Don't rush a thing before it's time. In a relationship, don't rush a person before they're ready.

Ivette: I'm sure most of us can relate to this in one way or another. When our friends are getting married and starting families, but we aren't, it's hard to be patient. I had said that I was perfectly happy being single for the rest of my days before I met my husband. I figured since I couldn't find the right guy that it would be better if I was single. Now I know that I wasn't ready, and neither was the man I was meant to be with. Timing was everything and knowing what I wanted in a man would make all the difference in how long I would wait.

So, Anna—who is almost always in control—has mastered the art of looking polished from head to toe. We're not even sure if she's in love with the guy, but it's most likely that it dawned on her that after having been together for four years, she still has no ring. So, what's a woman to do who is wanting a perfect life that doesn't exist anywhere? Yep, a perfect life exists nowhere here on earth. You might need to repeat that a couple of more times. In Anna's case, she does what no woman should ever do...ever. She becomes obsessed with getting engaged to her boyfriend. Convincing herself that she's not rushing into it since they've been dating for that length of time, she makes a hasty decision, boards a plane, and heads out to Ireland to propose to Jeremy, only things don't quite turn out as expected.

On her way to Dublin, the weather runs interference with her plans, causing her Dublin-bound flight to land in Wales, not Dublin. Even in the midst of all flights being canceled due to the storm, affecting every passenger—not just her—Anna begins making demands that airport staff has no control over, saying, "That's not gonna work for me ... I really need to be there today." At one point you see her thinking she should be the exception to what every other traveler had to accept, as her only goal was getting to Dublin. Resorting to a fisherman's boat which could only take her so far with the tumultuous waves tossing it around like ping-pong ball in the middle of a very good match. While we realize the captain of the boat had a choice, she definitely put all of their lives on the line because of her determination to get to her final destination and so she ended up in Dingle, the cutest little Irish port town with a stunning scenic backdrop. Rather than being thankful for not drowning in the horrific sea storm, we see she's extremely upset that she is nowhere near Jeremy, and it is here where she is determined to do everything in her power to get there. That is her only goal. She's got a man to propose to. For a woman in charge and in control, she's everything but. Determination is a good thing, but we shouldn't allow our hardheadedness to put others at risk. Being considerate of others is not her strongest suit. But it should be ours. Furthermore, her pretentious behavior once she arrives at the little café/bar/hotel is painfully embarrassing because of how entitled she is. We see Anna going through all this trouble to propose to a man who bought her earrings instead of a wedding ring, obviously he's not ready. He bought you what he could commit to–a pair of diamond earrings. Save your money, ladies! If your man is dragging his feet, don't use up your funds on forcing his hand to do what most men can already do on their own. Why not, instead, take yourself on a fabulous trip with your girlfriends? Anna obviously had the money and the time. She was just spending it on the wrong person when she could have been treating herself.

Even on a trip to another place around the world, Anna did not know how to treat those helping her with dignity and decency. Aside from being slightly curt to those outside her normal sphere of life (even in another country), we find Anna expecting the world—along with those in Dingle—to revolve around her. Girl, learn how to enjoy new people as people, not as the help or your servants. She had a few lessons to learn and if that weren't enough, she acted as though the things were all subject to her rulership and authority, as well. She couldn't get to her hotel room any faster, and when she did , she completely ignored that fact that her electrical chargers didn't match the outlets in the wall of her hotel room. She could care less. At that moment, you see the determination of her plugging in her Blackberry, to which in the process she knocked over bottles, and furniture, along with pulling down curtain rods, totally disrupting not only those in the hotel where she was staying, but also the immediate surrounding area of the town, as she blew out the entire electrical circuit. So, she's also a tad bit inconsiderate—how frustrating (and sad) for Declan and the town of Dingle. Needless to say, she gets off to a bad start with Declan, as he sees her for the uptight, controlling, and semi-snobby girl that she is. Nobody likes a snobby control-freak. Don't be this girl.

While we know this is a girl we don't want to be, can we pause here for a moment to ask ourselves some questions based on what we see Anna walking out so far?

1. Why is Anna so bent on getting to Dublin?

2. Should she be doing this? Why or why not?

3. What would you do if you found yourself in a similar situation—would you wait on him to pop the question (even if you felt you waited long enough), would you break up with him and pursue a long-term goal you've pushed aside, or keep things the way they've been for the las four years? Why would you do that?

4. What is it about her relationship with Jeremy that she is so obsessed with proposing to him (especially when she thought Leap Year proposals were "ridiculous"?

_____

_____

_____

5. Do you see happiness or peace in Anna—a privileged woman—who is wearing the right clothes, and dating a heart surgeon? Does it look like she's head over heels for Jeremy?

_____

_____

_____

6. Why do we—as women—sometimes stay in dating or boyfriend/ girlfriend relationships that we're not truly happy with?

_____

_____

_____

7. What are three things you can do for yourself, to keep from ever being in that type of hollow relationship again? If you can't list three, what is at least one thing you can do for you, so that you no longer find yourself in an empty relationship with a man just "going through the motions"?

_____

_____

_____

8. Who are the friends that speak into your life so that you aren't settling for a man merely out of security?

_____

_____

_____

9. If no such friends exist, make plans to carefully make some, writing down when you'll start to embark on this journey of inviting others with wisdom into your life plans and decisions.

In love with Louie

In life we'll find that there are some people who are more in love with their belongings and designer brands, more than they are with people. Labels will come and go, and some will remain, but what is most imperative is connecting with your people. In Anna's case, we clearly see that what is of high priority to her, is her Louis Vuitton luggage, which you know costs a pretty arm and a leg. Desperate to get to Dublin, she ends up hiring a young—and yet, somewhat bitter, rugged and crotchety—guy, Declan, who finds that he needs to drive her to Dublin, though It's the last place he wants to be. In a bit of a financial bind, they agree on a price and though they've already had a rough start, he's her only hope of reaching Jeremy by Leap Year (which she mistakenly called, "Leap Day"). She has no idea about its history or significance, but we find that is somewhat how she relates to anything outside of her life as she knows it. Having somehow created this artificial identity of who she is—which appears to be solely based exterior things like what designer she wears or owns, the Louis Vuitton luggage that she owns, where she lives, who she's dating and what she does for a living, we find a very empty Anna with an extremely hollow love-life, that she is now very focused on chasing after.

While it's true that some things can bring you temporary happiness, we want you to be honest with yourself. You get that new job, or buy that new car, yet, once those "things" have been around for a while, do you find it difficult to keep that happiness once tied specifically to it? And if so, what do you do to fill that void? You see, it's a cycle. You feel empty or alone or sad or upset, and so what do we do? We, in many cases, will go out and either purchase or do something that we wouldn't normally purchase or do, only to find afterwards that we now have regret or buyer's remorse. Why? Because once you're over that initial happiness of the new thing, it goes beyond that. Happiness is temporary, so getting that guy to ask you to marry him or buying that home—for example—only brings you happiness for a moment. Once that giddiness dies down, you realize your life actually hasn't changed one single bit. So, we have got to get out of the cycle of thinking that owning or achieving a certain amount of status is the answer or key to life. It's not. It's the reason why we can look at the lives of some of the rich and famous and find that there still isn't any peace or true joy—regardless of stature, achievements, or financial status. Even for the wealthiest person, there may still be that hole in your heart and if that's you, purchasing another Gucci or wearing the latest isn't going to fix or change that. In our case, only Jesus can do that. But in this case, Anna is bent on getting engaged, so she can live out that staged life, which by the looks of her precious dowdy dad, looks much different than how she was raised. And who knows, that could partially be what's fueling her—provision and being taken care of by a seemingly wealthy man, but whatever the reason, she is pursuing Jeremy. Hard. And in the process, she's got Louis Vuitton right by her side. Panes, buses, trains, and automobiles ... he's going with.

Cyndi: When I was in my 30's, I was obsessed with shopping at The Alley, a garment district in Los Angeles, that would sell purses and clothing from various semi-high-end designers. If you've never been, the atmosphere is actually a lot of fun as the alley is all about shopping— for clothes, shoes, purses, accessories, sunglasses, perfume, makeup... the list goes on and on. That, paired with extremely loud music, movement and people and various food scents all in one alley, it makes for a great two-to-three-hour trip in the heart of Downtown L.A. Aside from the busy atmosphere and the excitement of it all, I loved being able to purchase the knockoff labels like Prada, Gucci, Tiffany's and other designer labels. Very soon I learned that even though it had the quote UN quote label, the quality was just awful. I quickly got rid of the Tiffany's jewelry that turned my skin green, as well as the purses I had once purchased with glee, determining I'd only wear authentic from that point on. Why did I feel the need to have these fake designer bags? Coming to terms with realizing that for that moment, it made me feel a little better about myself, I decided, "If I can't afford to purchase an authentic label, then I just won't have it. My identity, value and worth are not based on what labels I wear." Now don't get me wrong, do I like nice things, as well as nice labels and brands? Yes, but I now shop for value and style, rather than only for the brand's sake. I love Tory Burch designs and styles, along with Diane Von Furstenberg, pieces from the Michael Kors collection and vintage designer clothes (I go wild for thrift shopping). Besides their designs, they are affordable for me. I've also come to realize what I love most is fashion and the styles—not the labels, though wearing a designer with a name, means you are investing in a piece or garment that will last.

When I was in grad school, I realized that wearing clothes from Banana Republic, outlasted pieces I would purchase from the little LA Boutiques, mainstream shops and Walmart. I learned the same about shoes. I would stock up the shoes from Payless, but realized why someone *would* want to pay more (than Payless). All this to say, we aren't what we wear, or who we wear. If you—like me—enjoy the fashion side of things, then great! But you aren't who or what you wear. And you're certainly not the brand of your luggage. Sorry Louis Vuitton. I do think the purses look fabulous and they smell amazing, but I'm not going to base my identity around that beautiful bag of leather. Will I ever own one? Who knows, but until then, I love the life I've been given. To date, I've owned only one authentic Gucci purse (which was stolen from me in high school), and so I have had my eye open for a modern-day version of that beautifully designed bag. Nice things are nice but should never mean more to us than people and we'd be foolish to establish our identity on that which is not.

Ivette: I would have to say that although I am not that designer or label-loving girl, I do love fashion and appreciate the quality of clothes and other accessories. My mom always had very nice things, but never had pieces from the designers we all love today, so I've never felt the need or want. This changed a bit one day while in the Las Vegas Forum shops. I walked into the Versace store and fell in love with the quality of a particular dress and told myself I would have it one day. That day hasn't come yet (it was $1200) but I'm okay with that. I couldn't justify spending that much when I didn't have an event to go to or somewhere nice to wear it. Recently Cyndi and I have been spoiled with getting to wear some of the Michael Kors collection pieces, and I do have my eyes on a few pieces. Spending money on my loved ones or things that I can leave them, is more my heart. It's hard to wrap my head around spending so much on something I may only wear once, but we should be willing to treat ourselves to something very special every now and then (if you've never walked into an actual Michael Kors store, you're missing out). Ultimately investing in love over materialism is what I would suggest.

En route to Dublin & sweet dreams

Once Declan finds out the reason why he's taking her to Dublin, he has no problem letting her know it's one of the stupidest things he's ever heard of—even if it is an Irish tradition. Once Anna hears this, she turns the brat button on, and does everything from tossing his sandwich and favorite cassette tape out the car, to accidentally pushes his car into a small lake, gets her Louis Vuitton of clothes stolen by robbers, is the reason Declan gets in a fight with thieves, she falls down a slippery hillside in the rain and misses the train to Dublin... all in one day.

It is at this time where Declan asks her what the one thing would be she would grab if she had 60 seconds to get out of her apartment in a fire. Neither of them expounds, but between the hike up the hill, and her rolling down it in an attempt to catch the Dublin-bound train, a small connection had been made, leading up to a greater connection about to take place that evening. Because of the train they missed, they ended up a little home owned by a local. Not only did this put them in one room that had only one bed, thinking Declan and Anna were married, the couple that owned the home asked the couples around the table, to kiss. While we could feel it coming, it was one of the most uncomfortable scenes in this film and in this flick, there are a lot. They kiss (gently, and for quite some time, we might add), go upstairs to share a bed, and can't stop thinking about each other. But wait...isn't she in love with Jeremy? We think not, and now... it kind of feels like another man is now in the picture, until she calls Jeremy the morning after and finds out they got their dream apartment in the city. Suddenly everything is back to normal (boring...we're yawning again)? Apparently, we forgot about the kiss that took your breath away last night, and the fact that you shared a bed. After that call, she's back on her only goal—to be in Dublin by Leap Year (day), the 29th. As if he read our thoughts, Declan chimes in, "Why is that again, darling?" We love this guy. Well, to answer your question— her plan is back in effect. She got that apartment, and now she needs the hubby to go with. However, a shift has taken place.

Throughout several continued challenges and obstacles, they have now become a Dublin-bound pair. Now while we are not in favor of her spending all this time with a man who is not her boyfriend, we are in favor of things not going her way, forcing her to come to terms with things that are unplanned and unpredictable. In fact, if you find yourself in this predicament, probably best to break up with your boyfriend—or at the very least go on a break, so that you can be fair to him, as well as really think things through where your heart is concerned. As for Anna—who's not big on adventure—it seems that nature does her good and that she's starting to roll with the punches. Literally. She rolled all the way down that hilltop, and we were grinning from cheek to cheek. This has been good for her. Her hair is down, flowing in the breeze, rather than in that perfect bun. She's smiling more and connecting with another human being for reasons that don't involve appearance. She even managed to drink so much at a wedding they crashed, that she threw up on his shoes— "classy," he says, picking her and carrying her in his arms. In these few days, she seems more at ease with the pub owner, than a cardiologist. That's a good thing. She was wound up way too tightly.

Awkward situations & weddings

As they get closer to Dublin, they also become closer to one another. Beside sharing that saucy kiss, she gets to know more about him, rather than assuming she knows how he is because of what she sees on the exterior. Assuming he knows nothing about love because of his behavior and mannerisms, he opens up a bit about the love that broke his heart. Shocked and enjoying the wedding they crashed after walking into the church while the wedding was taking place, she drinks way too much—not to mention she's mixing it all—Champagne,

Martini's, Vodka ... plus the two of them dancing together—she's let her hair down big time. It's in all the drinking we see the distress she's going through underneath that perfectly coiffed hair. She's coming undone before our very eyes. From puking on Declan's shoes to staring at him all starry-eyed, she's not the same woman we saw in the very beginning. By the time they arrive in Dublin, we see her semi-flirting with him, as if to fish for what might be that hasn't yet been verbalized. What is that they say about you could never be friends with the opposite sex? While we don't fully believe that theory, let's be real—you have to be one strong girl to not fall into what could be a horrible situation if you were already engaged or wanting to be engaged to someone you are dating, while spending so much time with a handsome chap like Declan.

Predictably, Declan brings her to her final destination, but we already know they both have feelings for each other. As he starts to leave, he turns around, but just as he calls her name, Jeremy walks in and ruins the moment ... for all of us. What do we do at that point? Do we interject and tell the truth? Do we stop him and run into Declan's arms? Anna did neither of the two. Paralyzed with fear or uncertainty, she's just standing there—as is Declan. Jeremy gets down on one knee, and asks her what she traveled through hell and highwater to ask him—will you marry me? Jeremy comes off more like a brother to Anna. Even the proposal is dry and dull. The proposal was more like going through the motions of it all yet lacking the passion. In fact, his response to her "yes" was just sad. Is that what you've been waiting all your life for? To be proposed to—like *this*?

Question – would you rather marry someone like a brother to you with whom you have no passion and excitement? Or would you be willing to wait for the one with whom you have chemistry, attraction, real-life conversations, and adventure? Now, we realize this is a movie we're talking about, but when we watch these films—especially the Romcoms, we should put ourselves in their shoes, challenging the status quo of just "accepting" what we see to be as doctrinal truths, and yet so many of us mirror these stories, that don't quite end up like the movies we cherish, because life and romance just doesn't turn out that way. In unscripted life, it turns out differently, because we are being paid to act out a script. We would rather never marry—although one of us already is—than going through the painful act of it all. And would we have let Declan go? If so, why? We saw a very different Anna with Declan when adventuring through the beautiful landscapes of Ireland—hair down, messy appearance, outfits dirtier, burping out loud—she was everything with Declan, that she couldn't be with Jeremy. He's the one person she was her true self with, and she looked so comfortable being in her own skin. Is there someone you have ever dated that were able to be 100% of yourself with?

Cyndi: In all of my years of dating, it's sad to say, there have only been four guys I've dated that I was truly myself with. Sadly, two of the four of those relationships were in high school. The third was while I was in grad school, living in Oklahoma, and the last was in my late 30's. So, I was 16, 17, 28 and then roughly 37. Now, granted, I was a teenager in those first two relationships, and so we can argue, what do you know about dating when you're in high school? And while I wouldn't seriously recommend dating when you're that young, I had so much fun in those two high school relationships, as well as when I was 28. There was so much ease, I remember having fun and most importantly, I was able to completely be me in the entirety of who I was. This is important to note. Because of the difficult and even toxic dating relationships I have been in in between, these are the three I now hold as the standards in what a dating relationship for me should look like. And so that is what I'm holding out for—being with someone who loves and accepts me as I am, and someone I can be myself with. That means he loves EVERYTHING about me—ethnicity, personality, my calling and career, my family, my quirks, my looks, my style...ME! This means he is not trying to change me and make me someone he wants me to be. This means he's not making me feel embarrassed or ashamed because of who I am — especially when it's who I am and things I cannot change. If the man you are dating is requiring you to change who you are, he's not the one. None of this conforming- to-his-wants and desires, losing yourself along the way. As women, we must stay true to our identity and to ourselves. That is where true happiness will exist–when you are able to just be you. For some, that may mean being single for a very long time. Be okay with that. You're worth it.

Ivette: I didn't even know who I really was meant to be until about 15 years ago. Whether it was my brother, my best friend, my boyfriends, my bosses, I floundered around being what someone else wanted me to be—it was never ending. It wasn't until I had received healing that was needed from childhood traumas that I could no longer be what someone else wanted, but I needed to be myself. If someone else liked or loved me then great, if not, then I guess it was goodbye. For me, this also included my family, friends and co-workers. To this day there has only been one person that I've dated, that I could be myself with, without prejudging of any type … and I married him.

Fire alarm tested and tried

Anna quickly forgot how easy it was to be who she really was when she was with Declan. Once she saw that beautiful diamond ring, even though there was conflict within her—and you could totally see it—she accepted Jeremy's proposal, telling him yes that she would marry him. Girl, you are so pitiful! It's all about the plan. She's gotta stick to that plan.

And even if there was still inner turmoil in her newfound relationship status—and we can guarantee you that there was, because we've both been there, done that—she quickly jumped back into her old routine in her new life in their new apartment, rocking her new engagement ring. As "perfect" as things seem, they are anything but. Really? Anna has everything she's ever wanted, right? So, it would seem, until she finds out at their house warming party—in front of all their friends— that he only proposed to her so they can get the apartment. We cringed as he continued to explain the "package deal," of getting the apartment to his friends, sharing how the board was a little old fashioned, preferring them to be married, to which he told Anna and her friends he thought, "Why the hell not?" He even went as far as to say, "I don't know where it came from," referring to telling the board they were hours of getting engaged. Um yeah, we're sorry, but this is where we have to draw the line. Where *is* that love so strong you can't wait to spend the rest of your life with this person kind-of-love? We could probably rant over this one for a while (and we most likely will on our podcast...yep... coming soon!). Anna-dear, please note, you'd be better off (and so much happier) living in a hotel room of a pub, married to an adventurous Irishman who makes one heck of a sandwich, than living in an upscale penthouse with someone who proposed to you as a package deal for status' sake. You see her standing in this beautiful, lush apartment, with people all around, and yet unseen. This is not "home." We love what happens next. She finally came to herself. The girl snapped to it, remembering a conversation she had with Declan about what you'd grab if there was a fire in your home and you only had 60 seconds to get what you can before escaping. Now a little more spontaneous, she does the unthinkable (good for her), and sets the fire alarm to see what Jeremy will grab first. He doesn't even look for her. At this point, we agreed that if this was really on fire, let it burn, get the heck out of there and don 't look back. This is not the man for you. Our hearts just dropped...one of us is even crying (he's such a jerk). It is heartbreaking to watch this as a woman who wants real love.

Ladies, it really is time for you to know love the way every woman should experience it. A love that is true, kind, thoughtful, patient, considerate, caring, putting his needs before yours. A love that adores you and would go to the ends of the earth for you. A love that will drive, walk, climb, bus and take you all the way to Dublin. A man like Declan—a little rough-looking on the outside, not as manicured as Jeremy, but every bit the man who will love you and stay by your side through thick and thin. He may not be a cardiologist, but he is hard working, respectful and is mad about you...or should we say, crazy about you. In those 60 seconds she realizes she had, "...everything I ever wanted, but nothing I really needed." Batta-bing...botta-bam! And it was this revelation that she had, causing her to take matters into her own hands. Atta girl!

Anna makes the best decision ever, and she makes it for her true self, not for status or appearance. She takes a trip back to Dingle, Ireland. There are so many things we love about who she is now. She's different. And since it's a movie, we will just assume that she has taken the time to do the work. She does look different, and we love the new her. She's more casual, but still classy. Her hair is down. She looks like a fresh breath of air whisked into Dingle from the States. This is who Anna is. It's who she always was. Showing up at Declan's now-hopping pub, Caragh's, she makes a proposal to him—not in the way of marriage, but becoming vulnerable, letting go of her "gotta have a plan," in saying, "...Declan O'Callaghan, and I should probably learn your middle name, here is my proposal. I propose we not make plans. I propose we give this thing a chance and let it work out how it works out. So, what do you say? Do you want to not make plans with me?" We're so proud of her for not only her willingness to change her ways, but to admit this to him, especially in public. We admire her boldness, and that she has come to her true self, being true to who she is.

Turning around and walking away, Declan leaves Anna standing there, and we are a bit baffled and even a little annoyed, but to be fair, he has feelings too and we respect that given the way things ended between him and Anna in Dublin, with Jeremy proposing to her. Upset in the assumption that he has rejected her, she leaves the pub and walks to the beautiful cliff to cry. There she goes assuming again. Ladies, we've got to stop assuming things. Talk it out. This is a sore spot for us both, as we don't get why people just "assume," without first taking the time to find out. It's Stephen Covey's Habit 5: *Seek First to Understand, Then to Be Understood*[11]. Rather than making an a*s out of you and me [assume], ask the questions. That's all it takes. You'd be surprised at what you learned if you applied to all of your situations whether at work, leadership, play, friendships, and love-life. *Why did you ...? Did you think this ...? Have you already done this...? Have you thought about...?* It's so much better than assuming someone has done none of those things you think you need to school them on—especially if they've already done it. Just sayin'.

We already know it's a happy ending and we're genuinely happy for Anna, as she took the steps to relationship recovery. We don't know how long the time frame was between the time she left Jeremy to the time she showed up in Ireland, but we are proud of her in her willingness to not settle. He rejects her proposal, proposing to her that he doesn't want to not make plans with her, but rather he *wants* to make plans with her. Yeah, between that proposal and that backdrop, that'd be hard to reject. It easily won our hearts over. Getting down on his knee, with the ocean behind her, he proposes with the ring she actually encouraged him to get back from the woman that last broke his heart, running off with his best. That's another story.

. . . .

11   The Seven Habits of Highly Effective People: "Habit 5: Seek First to Understand, Then to Be Understood®", franklincovey.com.

And please, don't be that girl, either. The proposal was actually moving, bringing tears to our eyes. She made the decision to be true to herself in life, happiness, and love. Because of that, she will most likely experience a beautiful life loving this man who she can grow with and who she is very comfortable with and he with her. And thank goodness she said yes, the kiss shared between the two was just lovely (we are still cringing over the stiff engagement kiss shared between her and Jeremy). They marry, it appears life for her will now be Ireland. What she'll do for work, we don't know, but we're certain that the planning Anna who likes to be in control, will figure it all out.

Ivette: When I met my now husband, he had broken up with his girlfriend a week or two before and I was newly single myself. We both had very challenging relationships, to say it nicely, so maybe that's why we felt better about meeting someone new. In my experience of three, four, and twelve-year on and off relationships, I never in my wildest dreams thought that I would meet somebody and within a few weeks, know he was the person I would marry. I had never felt this way about someone. I just wanted to grow with him. I trusted him, never feeling like I needed to check his phone for any reason. He never gave me a reason to cheat or try to get his attention like I had done in some of my past relationships. Though I didn't fully know what I was getting into (one never really does), I knew that he adored me, and I found out quickly that he would do anything for me and my family. We started dating in November. By January, I lost my job and my mom. There was so much family drama after her death, and there he was, standing right there beside me. From bringing food to the hospital for my family, supporting me emotionally, after losing my job at such a pivotal moment in life and being supportive and not engaging in fights with my brother about my mom's estate. I could see that he was and still is the person that I wanted in my corner. And so, we were married a year later. As we celebrate our 11th year together, we continue to work on our marriage and grow together in life.

At the end of the day, we should look to be with those who accept us as we are. Will we need to work on ourselves? Yes. Are there issues that we all have that we will need to work at changing? Yes. And that will always be the case. We should always strive to be the best version of who we already are. But that's the key period we need to be who we already are, not trying to be someone else, on behalf of someone else. We were not created to be a clone of someone else who already exists. And if the person you are romantically involved with or dating, wants you to be someone else, it's time to let that person go. You need to be fully embraced as you. Everything about the way you were created and made is intentional. In a recent film released, *Identity Crisis*, a film written and produced by a dear friend of Cyndi's, the message is clear—you have been fearfully and wonderfully made. Every detail about you had much thought given to it. This is why there are still differences even in identical twins.

They have their own DNA, fingerprints, their own personality, and other slightly differing characteristics.

What are the things that make you uniquely you? Even if there are characteristics or traits you don't like about yourself, write them down so you can learn to love them. Yes, every part of who you already are should be loved.

Write out some of the traits and characteristics that make you uniquely you? Please note, this is only a section to list the things that make you different from others, not noting whether you like them. That'll come after.

1. _____

2. _____

3. _____

4. _____

5. _____

6. _____
   _____
   _____
   _____

7. _____
   _____
   _____
   _____

Use this section below to address 1) What *others* have said or pointed out about those traits; and 2) *Your* personal thoughts about the above-listed unique traits about you. This is a time to write what you think about those characteristics.

1. _____
   _____
   _____
   _____

2. _____
   _____
   _____
   _____

3. _____
   _____
   _____
   _____

4. _____
   _____
   _____
   _____

5. _____

_____

_____

_____

6. _____

_____

_____

_____

7. _____

_____

_____

_____

Lastly, we want you to write out only the good points about those seven characteristics or traits—even if you've only believed the negative about them, there is a positive side to each of them, and this is what we want you to focus on—the good. **This is time to reflect deeply and to give yourself permission to be kind about the uniqueness of who you are.**

1. _____

_____

_____

_____

2. _____

_____

_____

_____

3. _____

_____

_____

_____

4. _____

_____

_____

_____

5. _____

_____

_____

_____

6. _____

_____

_____

_____

7. _____

_____

_____

_____

Anna's ending was redemptive and beautiful. It was refreshing to see her end with the guy that got her and the one with whom she was able to be herself with. More importantly, she needed to know and discover who she was. Luckily for her, she met someone who reminded her of that, bringing her back to life and back to reality. It was about the status, labels, and lamp fixtures, it was about being honest and present with someone for them. She needed someone to remind her who she was and really mattered to her. For her, that person was Declan. He called her out on her funky stuff, and helped bring her back to the woman she already was. She just couldn't see it because of how deeply she had buried her. As we conclude this chapter, let's take a look at some things that Anna needed to work on—even though some of these can be considered strengths, she was so bent on these to a fault, that things became very skewed. Don't be this girl.

Reasons to *not* be Anna:

> ➤ Feels the need to always be in control.

> ➤ She doesn't do well with change or surprises.

> ➤ Seems to be more in love with Jeremy's cardiologist title, than actually being in love with him for *him*. Don't be the girl that accepts a less-than-romantic relationship in the name of status, title or monetary gain.

> ➤ Life and days are planned to the exactness of the minute, leaving little to no room for flexibility or change.

> ➤ Wait for the timing to produce what is right and needed for you.

> ➤ Don't go off other people's timelines or expectations.

> ➤ Thinks the world revolves around her.

> ➤ Behaves rudely and acts very entitled to strangers and people she doesn't know.

> ➤ Shares a bed with another man. She shouldn't have even been sleeping in a room with an almost-stranger—even if she didn't have a boyfriend.

> ➤ She assumes things before knowing the facts.

If you still struggle with the truths that you are a beautiful person worthy and deserving of love, go back to chapters 1 or 2, where we tackle this in both, Iris, and Bridget. You need to know who you are. You need to stop believing the lie that you are deserving of being treated poorly and less than. No! That is not you and the only way for those lies to be destroyed, is to replace them with truth.

Ireland was lovely. Now, off to Kenya.

"... the point is, love is an adventure, Kenya. It's not a decision you make for others. It's a decision you make from your heart...".

Dr. McQueen,
Something New

Kenya McQueen, An OCD Narrow-Minded Perfectionist Chained to the List

Something New

Kenya is a career-driven woman who, while single, is married to making partner at her firm. A daughter from a fairly well-to-do family, she has uniquely high standards for many things in life, which is good and all, except when it comes to finding true love (or a love that will last). Pretty comfortable in her own skin as a single lady living in L.A. (we like this), we find Kenya as the oldest of two who seems to enjoy going for early-morning walks, working even after-hours, and doing dinner with her girls (all also single in the beginning of the movie).

As we dive into Kenya's character at the start of the movie, we like her. And what's not to like? She's smart, savvy, kind, and she knows what she wants, which up to now are good qualities to have, but there is one area in her life where we would love for Kenya to ease up a bit—in her personal and home life. Early on you see the condition of her backyard which really symbolizes the status of her life—it's dry and brittle and needs a lot of work. Actually, saying that it's dry is an understatement—the trees are brown with no leaves anywhere in sight. If even the smallest hint of heat or fire would come anywhere near her backyard, that whole thing would go up in flames because there is not one ounce of life in it. Even the jacuzzi in her backyard is empty with no water in it, filled with dust, dirt, and stains. Come on, girl … get it together! We know you're busy with your career, but that is so uncalled for—not only that, it's also very unkept and is quite contrary to what Kenya's life appears to be, which is very together from the outside looking in. But perhaps that sad, and apparently abandoned backyard is not only what her love-life looks like, but quite possibly representing the sad and lonely condition of her on the inside, as well? We shall see.

Kicking off the movie on Valentine's Day, we see Kenya's schedule with every hour slot filled for work meetings, but after work nothing is scheduled after 7:00 PM. Despite no apparent heated plans for the night, she starts her morning with coffee and nice brisk walk, taking in her L.A. surroundings and neighbors' lives before heading into the office where she is greeted by her frantic assistant, Leah, who is soon to be married, ending their conversation with, "We've got to get you married...who do we know for you? You can't let this job be your life. Brian... this is going to be perfect!" Leah's excitement for newly-single Brian is rained on as Kenya announces that she doesn't do blind dates—Red flag #1—to which Leah continues adding to the "official" list of the other things Kenya doesn't "do," which includes sushi, dogs, and kayaking, among other things. Red flag #2. When those closest to you add another thing to an official list you have, that is a problem.

Though she may not yet have Mr. Right in her life, she does have her girlfriends, which is how she ends her Valentine's Day—enjoying a Galantine's dinner with them—a trend that has proven itself to be a celebratory replacement when a girl's "other half" has not yet manifested in her life. It is quite enjoyable, by the way. Her girlfriends are fun, informed, "looking," and have a lot to say about Black single women. In this convo, one of Kenya's besties shares about how they were in the 42.4% of Black women that had never been married. And if you are wondering if it's a thing, it's a thing[12]. Kenya, however, refuses to be considered a "victim," and rightly so, stating, "...I just have to keep believing I'll find the one!" And with that, we introduce you to Kenya McQueen.

The list

Though Kenya is still riding that train of expectancy for Mr. Right, what we see is that she is already narrow-mindedly hemming her way in as she first states that the man she wants is a "good *brotha*." While we may have preferences, what this does is automatically puts anyone who isn't a Black male out of the picture. Red flag #3. If you want a good man, be open. Broaden your horizons outside the cultural norm. This is the 21st century, ladies. If you're

- - - - - - - - - -

12   "Black Marriage in America," *blackdemographics.com*

single and ready to mingle, it's time to toss out that same-race-only card. Look around and see the beauty in every other culture outside your own. Immerse yourself in a culture you're not familiar with. Many cities have cultural neighborhoods like Koreatown, Little Armenia, Little Ethiopia, or Heritage Districts like Little Tokyo, for example. Now granted, all of these places are in California, but this is where we both live, so you get the point. Do some research, do a search on Yelp, and visit somewhere outside of your culture, spending a good portion of your day there. Maybe visit a museum, shop, and eat food from that culture. People-watching is another great way to appreciate beautiful people from every culture. Take it in and embrace the beauty in not only the differences, but also the similarities you'll notice—the dancing eyes, the smiles, the joy, and laughter.

Okay, so Kenya—While we do appreciate her resignation to go out with a man who doesn't have to have a lot of money (as long as he has a J-O-B), her list continues. He needs to be taller than her, be educated (Cyndi feels you on that, Kenya), yada, yada, yada... but just when you think she's bringing it to a close, she continues, "No kids, good teeth (we both feel you on that one) ...", to which shortly after that, the girls are shaking their heads at her list—*the* list. They are quite aware that this is what Kenya does. One friend chimes in that when you stick to these regimented lists—like having an IBM (*Ideal Black Man*), you keep yourself out of being in the lineup of the universal abundance that is out there. We couldn't agree more. From this talk around the dinner table, they adopt a known saying, "We've got to let go, in order to let love flow," to which together they all toasted, "Let go, let flow."

Cyndi: During one of our *She is Single, She is Strong* webinars that we offered, I led the ladies in getting rid of their list, asking to listen to their hearts about what they truly believed and felt would be someone they'd want to spend the rest of their lives with. I did the same, as well. I got rid of my ever-growing list of twenty-five plus years and got honest with myself. Now there are definitely a few things on my list that are non-negotiables–for me, my man must love Jesus and be someone who will always point me to Him, but those were the only two that won't ever come off that list. As I quieted my mind, I began to write words—new words (besides the non-negotiables), that brought tears to my eyes.

> ➢ *Someone who is kind-hearted.*

> ➢ *Someone who is patient with me.*

> ➢ *Someone who is gentle with me.*

> ➢ *Someone who "gets" me—ALL of me.*

> ➢ *Someone who champions me, my gifts and calling.*

> ➢ *Someone I'm very attracted to–inside and out.*

> ➤ *Someone who is loving to others—including the unlovely.*

> ➤ *Someone with whom I can create with.*

> ➤ *He can tease me playfully, but not someone who is demeaning or makes fun.*

When I look at this, this leaves a lot of room for a beautiful man to sweep me off my feet. What was exciting to me about my new and improved list, is that it eradicated a previous list that was not only too unreasonable, but also unrealistic and too demanding. I wanted him to make a certain amount of money, have a specific level of post-educational degrees, work in a distinct industry, dress a certain way, have a desire to serve alongside me in my ministry, be fit, have a particular look, and truly, the list continued. It was too much and additionally, I realized that if I wanted someone who was fit, I should probably work a little at it on my end as well. Men are visual creatures after all.

One of my best friends has been happily married for twenty-five years. When she talks about him and how amazing he is, her lips almost immediately start quivering and without fail and with tears in her eyes, she says, "I can't believe I am so blessed to be married to him. He is everything the Lord knew I needed in every area of my life."

I think about another married-couple, friends of mine who have been married almost thirty years. I'll never forget the groom telling me that he always thought he'd marry someone who loved fine linen, enjoyed fine dining and classical music. He then went on to explain that his wife loved country music, eating at Taco Bell, and wore her hair in a ponytail, yet that she was exactly who and what God had for him to marry–they were more than just compatible—they complimented each other very, very well!

Ivette: So, here's the thing...ladies, if we have a list of our wants and expectations in meeting Mr. Right, there is a likelihood that we will need to get rid of it. What once was decent-sized, begins to grow, and the longer you're single, the more likely you'll end up adding to the list, which will not only end up growing, but which will also become a tad more difficult for any one man to be all those things.

In Kenya's singlehood, there are those in her life who'd love to see her settled. In fact, her assistant flat out told her she needed to get her married, saying, "...There is a man with your name stamped on his forehead." It was known that Kenya had a list, but one thing was for sure—setting her up was not on there.

A surprise set up

Thanks to Leah, Kenya has agreed to go on a blind date—good for you, girl ... we're proud of you! This was a huge move for someone who 1) likes things to be in controlled environments; and 2) doesn't "do" blind dates. Arriving at Starbucks to meet her blind date, Brian, she hides from someone she knows who she hopes won't recognize her. And what's sad as she's stopped by this one guy—and she's scoping out the others who are with him—there is not one single guy in that group who would fit the bill of what Kenya was holding out for in a man. They were Black and they were men, but that is pretty much where it all stopped—grabbing her hands, informing her that she was, "Looking all cute," he introduces her to his posse. They were all wrong for her for oh so many reasons ranging from maybe needing a B-size bra, to having a long pinky nail, to already being married. Not one of them said, "Kenya," on their foreheads, and the way they gawked at her from behind. Nope. Pass.

What *does* take Kenya by surprise is both genius and funny. Still looking for her date, who she is assuming is her Ideal Black Man, she is approached by Brian, who is not her IBM, but instead, is a White male. In disbelief she asks him not once, but twice, "Blind date, Brian (Kelly)?" Both times, he answers, and surprised that he is not at all what she was expecting, she awkwardly laughs. He chuckles back, knowing full well that she is shocked as all get out. He handles himself well. Here she was looking at the "brothas" to see who her date might be, and here he shows up white—and as adorable as ever. Not an IBM, and not at all what she was expecting. He's confident but not cocky. He is kind, but also strong, calling her out on the carpet right from the get-go. Why? What did she do? Well, she did what any uncomfortable girl would do, and started talking like she belonged to that Black community, trying to prove that while she fit in, he didn't. Brian saw right through what she was doing, asking her if she was uncomfortable, pointing out that she's talking to strangers, making sure everyone knows "she's down." YES! He's already front and center for Kenya in our book!

Ivette: You know, now-a-days this is not a thing. In fact, it's pretty normal to see different races dating, bi-racial couples married and having kids. But when you come from a family that pushes same-race unions, it can be hard to break that viewpoint. As far as her list goes, he is basically nothing from her list, but I love him already! We can thank her assistant for that.

Cyndi: He is a man. While there are many guys his age that are still toying with the idea of committing to one person, what I liked in Brian is that he calls it like it is. Kenya says she went on this blind date because she told her girlfriends she'd be open, to which he responds, "But not *this* open." Bingo! You are good, Brian. Kenya, loosen up a bit, put your IBM ideologies high up on the shelf so they don't interfere with this good thing and good man you got going. He seems to be into her, but she's too blind to see it. Please, don't be this girl.

I do remember dating someone in grad school who was not on the list that I had somehow created. He was kind, talented, fun, had a lot in common musically, including our faith. We had so much fun together and had great chemistry. However, even with all of that, I decided that the relationship couldn't progress because of certain career qualities I had on my list that he hadn't quite reached. I was so adamant about it, that once I made my decision, there was no going back. Though I know he wasn't the one for me as I still don't believe I've ever even met my soulmate yet, it is embarrassing as to how stubborn I was to not even consider someone who didn't have only one or two traits on my list. Wake up, ladies! If you have a list and you're still single, it might be time to put it through the shredder and start all over again. Spend some time in solitude and prayer, reflecting on what it is that really matters to you. I'm not saying to remove aspects such as, "Good looking," and "fit," but where are you on the list that *he* has? Maybe it can change to something like, "Good looking or attractive to me." And please, for goodness' sake DO add these two to the TOP of your list:

> ➢ UNmarried—he must not be married—not even separated.

> ➢ UNabusive—he must not ever touch or hit you—not even verbally.

These non-negotiables must be written down, otherwise you are asking for years of harm, trouble, heartache and if he's the latter of the two, possibly danger. Please don't that to you or your kids. No man is worth the risk. No matter how much you love him, you cannot stay in an abusive relationship. That is something needing to be worked on with a professional. Be alone and wait until someone who is single and kind, who truly sees you and gets you, comes along. Check. Check. Those are two traits that should be on everyone's list. And if you know Jesus, then ladies, there's your third non-negotiable right there—a God-fearing man. Take your time with this list—this is your life we're talking about. Give it some thought, and when you're ready, write it down. You'll find that your list isn't finicky or quite so long!

Kenya's web

The minute Kenya left Brian to finish his Starbucks coffee alone—and to fend for himself being the only White male in an all-Black coffeeshop—Brian knew it was more than she could handle, but fate would have them meet up again, and this time it would be at Leah's wedding shower. This is where Kenya discovered he was a landscaping architect. Oh my. With a slightly wounded ego, he acknowledges that they've met to Leah's mom, who Kenya was raving about her landscaping to, as Brian entered the conversation. He gave her his card and went on about his day. A sweet guy with a dog who is a hard worker, his landscaping work takes him in the L.A. area near Crenshaw, and from what we can tell, though single, he likes color—not only apparently women of color but his surroundings are colorful and lively. From his music to the color of his seemingly vintage cool open-top truck, he is a creative outdoorsy guy who enjoys taking in life, and what could be so wrong with that? Well, for Kenya, there is a lot wrong with that. Starting with the fact that she doesn't "do" dogs—that's another one that is on her list. It is uncomfortable to see a successful single woman wound up so tightly, and even though this is a movie, we realize that there are many who might be in this category. For Ivette, Kenya is "... my worst nightmare—anal-retentive, and an over-the-top control freak!"

Nobody saw this play out more in front of his own very eyes than Brian. Unimpressed with the way she left him, he reluctantly gave her his business card since she was falling out over the backyard landscaping design at the wedding shower of her assistant. Though she didn't think she could quite afford what needed to be done in her backyard, we applaud Kenya in contacting Brian to give her a quote on landscaping her backyard. As a viewer we were surprised that she reached out to him at all, but the embarrassing thing of it is not only how she greets him, but she makes it clear she doesn't want his dog—or dog hair anywhere near or in her house. She also points him to going around the back which as a single woman is probably a safe way to go about it, but we got the sense that it's because she was treating him more like "the help." Still confident in who he is, he agrees, doesn't get offended and accomplishes what he went there for to begin with. Feeling the soil and earth of the ground in her backyard, we see him operating in his natural gifting and it is a beautiful thing to behold. Brian is played by Simon Baker after all. Enough said. She begins to soften up a bit as he shares with her the lovely landscape ideas of what could be. Feeling a little more comfortable with him than the day they met on their date, he convinces her to go with him to a nearby nursery which ends in total disaster as Kenya walks into a spider web at the nursery—a hysterical moment, but Brian was still so full of compassion for her—even with the webs in her weave. "...Creepy crawly things...," was something else she doesn't *do*, by the way. Houston, we have a problem...," Kenya is single and wants a man, but she's making it really easy for any interested man to want to "pass" on that. Sound familiar? If so, now might be a really good time to get that journal out and write out some of the extremely high expectations you have on yourself and others. Of those things, what are some that you can loosen up on or let go of? We realize it seems harder and harder as we complete a full orbit around the Sun, but there are some things we just need to let go of. Now is the perfect time to do it. Kenya did manage to get in the truck with Brian's dog, Max, so we gotta give her that. But ladies, don't be this girl. Thanks to Brian's playful poking in sending her the book, "Charlotte's Web," crossing out Charlotte, handwriting in "Kenya," in its place, she comes to her senses. Kenya needed both that, and the trip to the nursery to start letting that uptight guard of hers down a bit. For at that moment, she made the decision to let someone in to work on the brittle, forsaken and run-down areas of her home …and heart.

When will your garden grow?

Girl, let the dog in for crying out loud. Still stressing about Max's presence in her home, vigorously wiping down things, and wound up so tight working from home on a Saturday in her weekday outfit of a scarf, and heels, the girl needs to Let. It. Down. Brian agrees by kindly suggesting to her, "You need to relax ... you know, it's Saturday ... you're wearing a suit." As he's working on her backyard, and they get to chatting, we find a man who already is a huge fan of Kenya, telling her confidently that she will make partner with her firm. This is a guy who is confident in who he is, and he has no problem verbally cheering her on. That's what we're talking about! C'mon, somebody! Finding him more attractive than she's let on, the more he landscapes her backyard, sharing with her about the world he knows and loves, the softer the soil of her heart becomes. Don't get us wrong, it's pretty hard and still needs some breaking down. Her dirt does need some tillin'—BIGTIME, but we enjoy seeing Kenya smiling every now and then.

Soon on in the film, we meet her brother, Nelson, who literally has a different girl on his arm every time we see him, along her parents, "Dr. and Mrs. McQueen," who are "academics," (as her mom very intentionally puts it). The dots are now connecting. She has been raised by a mom who is very much into titles and accomplishments, as well as keeping the external looks of the family, "together." Good*ness*, Kenya is so badly in need of a beautiful, relaxed nurseryman like Brian, and with each interaction between the two of them, you see her walls coming down. The thing is, he gets her—even more than she gets her. He's a professional caretaker of things that need some life and attention. What is more beautiful and needed for Kenya than *that?* Maybe a family who'll ease up, as well.

"What's with all the beige? You are gonna paint, right ... bring some color in? ... It's safe ... impersonal ... feels a little like a hotel," ending with, "... it doesn't reflect you." Which, it actually does, but he's so into her, he sees the potential of what's locked inside beautiful Kenya. He's also been married before. Whether she was Black, or a different race, we don't know, but we like Brian. A lot. He's bold and is very much comfortable in who he is while being in her presence, introducing his world to Kenya, which is so ironic, not only in that she is the woman of color, but the country of Kenya is known for its diversity, gorgeous safari, and scenic land, along with its beautiful culture. Brian has us cracking up. He's inquisitive of the obvious things in her life, but she doesn't mind him asking as he is very kind, and she sees it's coming from a place of care. She doesn't get offended. She answers his questions like thoughtful friends, but her reply more than reveals to us more about Kenya's iron-clad ways. "My mother thinks bright colors are for children and wh*res." Bam. And there it is, ladies and gentlemen. The beast behind why Kenya carries herself the way she does. It's her mom.

Family values, culture, and traditions are a wonderful thing, but when opinions so strong like that directly suppress or squash who we are—even as adults, it's a good time to evaluate and re-think. Maybe you've grown up in a racist or prejudiced home, or under the tight control of a parent similar to Kenya's mom. Know that as an adult, it is not dishonoring to let go of some of those harmful beliefs. All cultures and races are beautiful. There isn't one that is more supreme than the other. Look around you. Look at the various fields and mountains of influence. There is diversity there because intelligence has been handed to every person in every race. Ever see the movie, "Hidden Figures?" Great movie! If you've ever battled with racism, watch that movie. Challenge yourself to see others differently. The same goes for growing up hearing strong opinions like Kenya's mom.

We know it's a harsh statement her mom makes, but we included it to depict unhealthy misconceptions that people have about others. If you've grown up with strong opinions such as what Kenya grew up with, it's time to take off the lid of the box and go outside. Kenya, for example, should explore not only the life and beauty of color and all that it has to offer, but she really should take the time to think about why those opinions have strictly enforced her behavior even as an adult. When we begin to discover more of who we really are and the things we like, reflecting and finding out why we like them, we realize that we start living a beautiful life of harmony—not hatred, arrogance, and anger. When hatred, anger and the like are present, that's a pretty clear indication there are still issues that need to be worked on and worked out. There are so many places available to help with working on those issues bringing about those negative feelings and emotions. Make time investing in yourself, and get the help needed. Brian challenges her by asking, "What do *you* think? ... I don't think you take the time to know who you are ... you're always working." Atta boy, Brian, make her think about what she believes and why she believes or thinks that way.

Cyndi: Though I'm definitely not as stuffy as Kenya, there are so many things about this movie that I relate to. From the first time I saw it in the movie theater at The Grove back in 2006, there were *many* similarities that I saw in myself while watching Kenya walk out her single black girl issues on the screen, starting with "the list." I've already mentioned that I have one. The movie helped revolutionize and change the woman I had *become* into a single woman who desired something different than what I had ever had or experienced where love and relationships were concerned. It wasn't just therapeutic or entertaining, but it helped me let go of several things the way I had known or wanted them to be, pushing myself to get out of a box I had unsteadily built for now about 23 years (not sure if I've already mentioned that my first boyfriend was when I was in sixth grade).

But if I can be real, my first real boyfriend was when I was 16. I was a Junior in High School. If there is anything I should have learned, it would have been to remember the simplistic ease and the organic steps and ways our relationship progressed when we were teenagers. Our personalities were so different, but really it was a great fit. I would say the same about my boyfriend my senior year as well. If we think about some of those first-love-type relationships that worked well months before some of the drama kicked in, those *could* be some of the traits that are still great compliments to who we are when we're older. Sure, our life experiences do change us, but for the most part, the core of who we are remains quite similar. So, for me, what worked was someone who was kind, someone who listened, someone whose personality was not as spastic or quite as vibrant as mine, someone who enjoyed laughing with me, someone who I thought was cute as all get out, someone who respected me and listened to both, my "yes," as well as my "no's." Someone who I could totally be myself with. Both, my boyfriend in my junior, and my boyfriend in my senior year, were these kind of guys. Kind and caring. Don't ask why I needed to have a different boyfriend each year. This again, proves my point that as adolescents, teens, and even young adults, we don't fully know what we want, we are wishy-washy and continue to be fickle about not only who we think we are, and what it is we think we want, as well as our identity. I was too young to be in those relationships, but I do know this—the relationships and who they were as young men, should have remained to be the essence of the type of guys I dated in my later years. ALLLL this to say, keep a simple list. The man you desire should be one who complements and fits you well, one that makes you feel good about yourself, as much as someone who you can be 100% comfortable in your own skin with. Some of the other things can be icing on the cake.

"I take it you don't do white guys?"

Though she has expressed to Brian (on more than one occasion) her preference for dating Black men, there is a definite tension building between the two. Not only has she attempted to pet Max, but she orders them a late-night take-out at home after working hard on her backyard. Comfortable in her presence, Brian asks, "I take it you don't do White guys? To which Kenya replies, "I just happen to prefer Black men ... it's not a prejudice, it's a preference." "Sure, it's your preference to be prejudiced," he quietly fires back, later adding, "I take hard earth and make things bloom." BOOYAH. He wrapped up that scene by leaving. She's intrigued and finds herself thinking of and exploring what could be—beyond the landscaping project. Yeah, she's thinking of Brian. And then one day, he heads-or-tales her into hiking. She doesn't think she enjoys it, but finds that it is beautiful, until it rains, to which her hair becomes the focal point of that moment. Take it from me, when our hair is "did," there's only one thing that will "undid" it, and that is the rain. This is when we, as Black girls, run for cover, to keep that water from making a mess. They have a moment under the tree as he gently kisses her. She responds by kissing him back, but just when you think she is starting to see the light, she regresses in fear telling him, "Don't think this is going any further because it's not." Mmmhmmm how many times have you said that and still, things go further? Well, she did, and this was yet another victory in tearing down her walls. Before we know it, and through a few heated arguments, letting him go as her landscaper and her kicking him out, "This isn't going to work, I don't know what I was thinking...,"—which stemmed from her insecurity of being a Black female dating a White male—she works through it, and he is more-than-patient, especially in the timing of kicking him out and humiliating him. She is mess—"A piece of work," is what Brian called her, but mostly because she's working through the racial walls of the unknown and realizing she likes him a whole lot more than she thought she ever would or could. And why not, color has not only begun to be added to her life and home, but even more importantly, she has really begun falling for someone—her UWM (Unideal White Man).

We loved the scene where he was getting the rest of his landscaping tools from her backyard, but the moment she came to her senses and asked him not to go, he immediately conceded. This is a humble man who clearly sees the bigger picture—even at the risk of getting stomped on. If you generally tend to stomp on the hearts of those who care about you most, please don't be the girl that takes pleasure in humiliating and emasculating a man who truly loves, respects, and adores you. There are plenty of women out there who have a heart to strengthen and encourage a kind man, and if you're not the one who's going to do it in his life, and you're not married yet, be good to him and let him go so that he can be loved on in the right way, with kind words, not being publicly humiliated and scolded. Men were not created to be treated that way. Neither are we, for that matter. Kenya feels like she can be herself and she is starting to bloom as the real Kenya. This is thanks to Brian for seeing her for who she really is.

While we are extremely thankful for her friends in encouraging this, it is her family that continues to play negatively against her budding relationship with Brian. Still unsure how to come out in public with him, she definitely confides everything to her friends, and they couldn't be more thrilled, spurring her on to just enjoy and go with it. So, what does she do after talking with her girlfriends? She jumps back in, of course. Don't be this wishy-washy, girls. Unless he's abusing you, still married, or you don't sense that "inner peace", stay in it, stop the childish games, and give it a go!

Ivette: I wonder how many of us have made decisions in our lives because of what someone else said. For being such a control freak she sure does listen to everyone else's opinions for her own life. Sadly, I can relate to this—trying to become a former control freak, I was always checking in with my other single and not-so-happy friends about what I should or shouldn't do. Now I've learned to never take advice from someone who doesn't have or isn't excelling in the things that I want. It's been said, "Don't ask your broke friends for financial advice". And the same goes in our love lives.

Cyndi: This movie was good for me in so many ways. I too, had a very similar knee-jerk reaction to being a woman of color, dating a good-looking White guy. Believe it or not we actually met on Facebook or Myspace... that's how long ago it was. He lived in Northern California, I lived in LA. We decided to meet up in San Diego where we'd be joined by his brother and another friend from high school. We definitely had chemistry. Great chemistry! But as I've learned, chemistry isn't everything. Whether it was to be a long term or short-term relationship, I hadn't decided, but I was just going along with it and being open to what might be. We were enjoying brunch at a very yummy restaurant, but it all came to a screeching halt when a group of young, cute blonde girls sat at the table very nearby. Because of a traumatic situation I had experienced in my early 20s while dating another white guy, it pulled a trigger and I immediately shut down with him. I stopped being present, focusing on what I viewed as competition, sitting at the table next door. The sad thing is that he never even noticed them. The whole time, he was fully engaged and everything happening at our table, even so much so, to notice that my whole demeanor had changed. Something awful that had happened to me about 15 years before, was actually triggering the way I was responding to my current situation. No matter how much he kept prodding and asking what was wrong, I continued to lie, telling him nothing was wrong.

I never told him why I reacted the way I did that morning at brunch, but I totally get where Kenya was coming from. You like someone, you are attracted to them, but if there is a race card—and mine never even existed until I started dating somebody in my 20's who let me know that our dating was a racial issue for his parents. That coupled with a handful of not-so-nice things said about my look and about the color of my skin, it really damaged me, making me ashamed of who I was. For a short season, I wanted to be anything but the woman of color I was. I didn't realize how badly I was injured until it resurfaced its ugly head that one brunch in San Diego. It took time and the goodness of God to heal me from all of that. I'm good now and love the racial makeup of who I am. When you're comfortable in who you are, it attracts others to you.

Little by little, you see Kenya begin to let her hair down—literally. From getting rid of her weave to painting her house with color and allowing Max to come inside. Though she was making strides in some of these areas, the race card was somewhat of a hang-up for Kenya. Though he was patient and tried to understand, even when being the brunt of the biracial relationship jokes, it started to wear on him. Know this—if you are in any relationship, it will take work, regardless of racial differences or not. If you've made the decision to be a couple, then be a couple and take the hits together, encouraging and strengthening each other along the way. If you're not getting hit for racial and biracial reasons, there will be other reasons. *Trust.*

Unfortunately, in Kenya's case, she was still wavering and trying to do what made others happy, pleasing them instead, even though it was her relationship, and the one who really needed to be happy was her—not her family or friends. And where her girls are concerned, we didn't appreciate one referring to him as the gardener, when one of them was dating somebody who was legally separated…aka "married." Not the best friends to get advice from when they are dealing with their own apparent "stuff."

Cyndi: I can think of a time where my close friends, along with one of my sisters, were really speaking into a relationship I had no business being in. I've already given it more space in the book, so I won't go into it any further here, except to say when they were saying what I needed to hear (and not what I wanted to hear), I would have been wise to listen, instead of getting offended and ignoring their sound advice. It would have saved me heartache and pain. I wouldn't personally be taking any advice from some of Kenya's friends, except for maybe one—and I'd have to also say that if my mom were like Kenya's, I would at some point let my mom know that as much as I love her, this is a loving man who cares about me, who goes out of his way to make me happy. In my book, that is nothing to hide about. Furthermore, I rather like my new haircut and the color you see popping up in my life! The fact that her mother said her prior hairdo was "her shining glory," but it was a weave, says it all. I don't enjoy having someone I'm not interested in pushed on me—I don't care how "well-spoken" he is. I've seen some of the most polished men, who aren't necessarily the kindest men behind closed doors. Those days for me are over. They should be for you, as well!

Ivette: Kenya's mom is a piece of work, but so is Kenya, though she's working on it. I do, however, love her dad. Her mom is a complete nightmare—always trying to find a Black man with a title for Kenya. She doesn't even stop to think that maybe her daughter is already happy. This isn't about her mom, but let it be said we definitely don't want to be *that* woman either!

Every good story has the moment where something good (or something new) shifts, taking a turn for the worst, and so things implode. Because Kenya has been unhappy at work seeing how she is treated being a Black woman in her industry, she totally misreads into just one thing Brian asked for which was, "Can we just not talk about it tonight?" Every day she is bringing him the troubles and woes of being a Black woman in a White man's world, and though he is more than supportive and eager to give a listening ear, he just asked for a little break to which she completely went off the deep end. It was so uncalled for, and it was embarrassing. Even though you're watching it on screen, you just wish it would stop and that she would realize and hear what he was actually saying, which was not at all how she was interpreting it. Please don't be this girl. Listen, listen, listen to what he is saying. Needless to say, they end their relationship after arguing in the middle of a market. So, what does she do next? She's on a date with Mark, her brother's mentor, who was being pushed on her for some time now. NOOOO!!! What are you doing, Kenya? You were falling in love with Brian! (Who by the way comes to her door to apologize, admitting he should have just listened to her that day). It almost brings tears to our eyes how sweet and crazy in love this guy is for Kenya. And it's even a tad frustrating because he's almost even a little on the submissive side, which means he may need to work on his firmness with her. Though he is confident and not afraid to question her, she almost wears the pants in this relationship, and we just don't feel 100% comfortable with that. It should be 100% but her hand is a little stronger than his, and so we're trying to assess how we honestly feel about that. Granted this is a movie, however, for real life relationships and marriages where the woman has the stronger fist, problems do emerge. Because of it, not only has she wrongfully assumed Mark is "more her type," she tries to convince herself he is right for her because he is Black and relatable. Wrong. They are the same color and maybe even cut from the same type of cloth, but he couldn't be more wrong for her. Brian professes her love for her and what comes out of her mouth next is just embarrassing. Ivette's got something to say ...

Ivette: Mistake number one in my eyes was in giving room for Mark. Just because she gets into a heated conversation with Brian, she opens the door to another man. Does she really think that color matters that much? I get that this is a touchy subject, but for her to say that she isn't seeing anyone (when asked by Mark), so that the door opens wide—how dare she! This is half of the problem with women today—their loyalty to their man.

And, in telling Brian who comes to apologize, "Look, I met someone else...it just happened." Really!? I just want to shake this girl! Listen, it's bad enough that this Mark guy was so forward to call her his, "Mrs." when doing a walk-through on a property he was interested in. It was just weird. Okay, maybe kinda cute, but completely too forward. She doesn't even know this guy, but because he's Black, has a title and her brother thinks he's a great guy ... Wait, let's think about her brother for a moment—when did *he* become the expert? He has a new girl on his arm every other scene. Woah, this has got me heated! What a horrible way for her to respond to Brian when telling her he loved her. Now don't get me wrong, we all have our right to feel a certain way, and no one should ever respond to an, "I love you," saying the same, out of obligation if you don't feel it. But this girl is delusional.

Cyndi: You totally feel for Brian as he leaves her house pretty devastated, telling her he loves her, yet calling her out when finding out about her new relationship just two weeks after they were over. He's no dummy, except maybe in loving Kenya so doggone hard. Ladies, please don't throw away the right guy for the wrong one. So, Kenya and Mark golf together and work on their laptops side by side—*so what*! Kenya girl, he is not the one.

Mark didn't waste any time. Two weeks was all it took, but the thing of it is, even though Kenya had found her lifelong search of her *Ideal Black Man*, she's unhappy with him. Very unhappy. Now, she's just "going through the motions." Why is this? Because he wasn't hers to begin with. Any time you're dating the wrong person or maybe the right person, but in the wrong season, it just isn't right and there will be complications. Dating just to date will come to a head at some point. One will want something from the other that they aren't willing to give or the other will be hurt, having unmet desires and expectations. Maybe you've found yourself in a similar predicament or perhaps you're in it now. Best-selling author, Stephen Covey, breaks it down the best in book, *Seven Habits of Highly Effective People*, teaching that we should always "Start with the End in Mind."[13] Starting with the end in mind helps to eliminate doing this just for doing its sake, regardless of what it is—what is the desired result? You should know what you're heading towards. No one gets in a car just to get in it without any clue as to where they're going. If you've never done this or if you have never read the book, it's a great read and guess what? It's never too late to start something new. Forming new habits will help to produce different results than the ones you've been getting for all these years of your life. Now get to it…you got this.

Before we go any further, stop, and ask yourself the following questions, and answer honestly. It's just you journaling. The one who benefits from this, is you.

1. Have you ever been with a guy and gone "through the motions," just for the sake of being with someone?

----

13   Habit 2: Begin With the End in Mind, *franklincovey.com*

2. Why did you do it?

----

3. How did that make you feel?

----

4. How did that relationship end?

----

5. What did you learn from that?

----

6. Did you ever find yourself at a place where you did that again?

----

7. What guardrails, systems or people do you need to set in place to keep from repeating this damaging cycle?

Will the real Kenya please stand?

It's clear from what transpires next that Kenya is not into Mark. Her disinterest in him is heightened by Brian's attendance to Leah's wedding with his ex, Penelope. Totally getting her "in the goods," it gives her an anxiety attack and we are just cracking up at how silly she is. She calls it quits with Brian and jumps into the arms of the IBM "Kenya and Friends" have talked about, but now that she's in it and Brian is with Penelope, she isn't happy. "You always get in your own way!" one of her girls spouts off, as she herself isn't in the best situation. Either way—not the girl to be. This scene with her friends is hysterical because they're all a mess, hollering things like, "Go deal with those demons," to making statements about Mark being a catch, telling Kenya that if she doesn't get it together, she'll marry him to give him a load of "Black, ashy babies." What is happening here?!

Though it would "appear" that Mark is into her, he's kind of a jerk about who he'd like for her to be, and you get the feeling he's as shallow as her mom. It's why they get along so well. Not only that, but he also made our skin crawl as he announced to Kenya's family that he used, "finding a house and doing the numbers," as a ploy to get Kenya to go out with him. While Kenya's mom is practically planning their wedding, she completely overlooks what Mark just said. He lied to Kenya to get to know her better. Newsflash: Deception isn't the way to start off a strong, trusting foundational relationship. We aren't impressed. We don't care how good looking he is. We would also like to take the time to mention that her mom is a great representation of the external pressure that often comes from people who love us, simply because they want to see us see us in a relationship, no matter the cost. The problem with that is the cost generally only affects us—not them. When things don't work out and we are discouraged or depressed, everyone else's lives move on wonderfully, and we are the ones left to walk out the pain of the loss. So why not just avoid all of that to begin with and not be in a relationship we already know we are not 100% in?

Everything Kenya had been through, led up to this one—and final—moment between her and Mark. Already not "feeling it," during their time at her parents and clearly on their ride in the car on the way back, Mark's true colors come out. Here's the thing ladies, if you're going to commit to being with someone for the rest of your life, it better be the man who loves you and accepts you as YOU ALREADY ARE. We just about fell over when he leans over to kiss her telling her, "I like that picture of you with the long hair. Do you know which one? You should let it grow." This not only made our hearts sink for Kenya, but what we really wanted to do was to put our hands through the screen and shake Mark, who represents so many men not satisfied until the trophy that they are showcasing is groomed and primed to be the show pony he wants her to be for all the world to see. Good thing for Kenya, that's pretty much where the light went on, but we're pausing to address this. Here and now. Sister-girlfriends, we know that there is already so much in between the pages of this book, but it's because we want our lives to be different than what they've been. Stop running yourself ragged to look the way someone else wants you to look. Do you for you, and only you. The thing of it is, we fill and tuck, alter and add, shed, grow and change— all in the name of keeping a man interested, but we should only be doing that for US. There's nothing worse than being with someone who appears to be "Mr. Right," yet who wants you to look and be someone else other than who you already are. It's one of the dangers and we see more of it today than ever before. Tucking, clipping, filling, lifting, pulling, taping (that's for those of us who can't afford the prior). We're in a plastic-surgery craze; we've also noted that even with all the plastic surgery that happens, some men will make you feel like you need to go under the knife time and time again or will encourage you to eat next to nothing, so that you can be what they want you to be. That's actually abuse. And if your man encourages you to be this way, you need to think again. He's not the one for you.

After stopping him from kissing her once they've reached their destination (he's a little too forward and fast for our liking), she tells him she can't do it. And once they're standing facing each-other, her eyes say it all. He's not it. "You're a great guy. Perfect. But this just isn't right for me." Tell us what we don't already know? Here she was wanting her IBM—and though it would seem he's everything she's been holding out for, he's ... not ... the one. "I'm just looking for something else. I don't know what it is, but it's not here." We LOVE that she says that. While she's clearly upset at what she's done, she second-guesses herself—we've all done it. Running to her friend's place she admits, "...he was fine and smart but there was no fizzle, no magic." You had the courage to say what needed to be said. You had been feeling it, yet repressing that feeling all along, but knew that if you didn't, you'd have to face it again further down the road. Best to do it now. "What will everyone say?" you ask yourself. Why does it matter? Go with what you know your gut is saying. Her friend's consolation, "You gotta listen to your instincts ... you did a brave thing," is exactly what we're talkin' about. Don't just say what Kenya wants to hear. Say it, girl! Tell her what she needs to hear. Yes, there's an inner tension where the emotions and thoughts run wild, yet once you've made that decision, deep down inside, there is a peace, almost like a very heavy weight has been lifted right off our shoulders. That's the feeling indicating that this is right for *you*. By the way— Kenya drove to the friend's house that had a good head on her shoulders. These are the ones we need to go to—the ones with counsel that is sound and wise.

As with most romcoms, you can already fill in the blanks for how things end for Kenya and Brian, but what it took was some humbling (or 'umbling as some of us call it), a lot of vulnerability, and having an honest conversation that Kenya's dad needed to have with her, as well as the one she needed to have with Brian. Finally realizing that the color of his skin and hers had nothing to do with love, she leaves a cotillion she was attending, after receiving the best advice and story from her dad, which gave her the strength to go find Brian. This, all on the heels of having a bad attitude at the ball, ending in a meltdown in the bathroom. She finds him at the nursery and though he's struck by her natural beauty and the love he feels for her, you see the hurt in his eyes. If you think about it— she has been doing nothing but rejecting him, keeping him at arm's length and putting him through the racial ringer before that last and final blow. But she knows, if she's not honest with him here and now, she may lose him forever. She finally tells him that she loves him adding, "I've never had to be anyone but myself with you...". BOOM. There it is. It's a moving moment, for sure, and what he does next is just priceless and precious as he tosses on a Mariachi suit to show up with her at the end of the cotillion—silly. He would have been better off wearing what he was working in at the nursery, but it worked for comedic relief. She didn't care. She got her man back; she was happy, and she wasn't trying to hide a single thing. He would have given her his left arm if she'd asked him for it. But this is what we're talking about. Men know what they want and so if they're not coming after you and finding ways to get you in their presence, you don't mean or matter to them as much as you think you do. Stop calling him. Stop texting him and stop trying to chase *him* down. This was a White man who knew that he wanted this beautiful Black woman. He even took a bit of a beating to get it, but for him it was well worth it.

Next scene is their wedding day, and they couldn't look happier. Dad is happy, mom is happy, friends are accepting and it's a beautiful scene with Jill Scott lullabying us in the background. Her baby brother, Nelson? Yep, he is of course running off with a bridesmaid. But that's a wrap, folks! If you're going to be like Kenya, make sure it's once you've discovered who you really are and how the only guy for you is the one could be 100% be yourself with. Brian loved everything about her—curly hair, dark skin, being uptight and all. He loved Kenya and everything about her. May you, like Kenya, be found by someone who you could be 100% of yourself with ... and someone who loves you for all of who you are.

What Kenya Teaches Us:

> Don't base a book by the cover.
> When it comes to love, be open to consider characteristics—or a race different than what you have predetermined in your mind.
> Leave room to be flexible–there is enough uptightness in the world today.
> If you're going to work from home on the weekend, dress down and be comfortable.

➢ If you have a list, go over it again. It might be time to reevaluate and revise.

➢ Live your life based on your convictions. Don't let others pressure you to compromise or conform to who you are. They are not and you are not them. Do *you*.

P.S. Oh, and by the way, Kenya *did* make partner at her law firm, having stood firm on her position at work—even in a room full of White law firm partners and peers. How does this encourage *us*? We, too, need to know what we stand for and should therefore be bold about it. Not only that, but the girl also went on to request one weekend a month off, for herself. Boundaries. Now that's what *we're* talkin' about.

"You're everything I never knew I always wanted."

Alex Whitman,
Fools Rush In

Isabel Fuentes, The One Night Stand that Ends up Pregnant... and Married

Fools Rush In

So, fools rush in. And yes...they do. One of the things making this movie so appealing right out the gate is that we love seeing Salma Hayek (playing Isabel Fuentes), and the late Matthew Perry, playing love-interest, Alex Whitman, together on-screen. There's just something about a fiery, beautiful, exotic woman, paired with the charming looks and personality of "Chandler Bing," that sets the tone for a romcom we're ready to take on. *Friends* was in its prime when this movie was released in 1997, which was nominated by the Alma Awards as Outstanding Feature Film in '98. What's not to love? Not only was it a well-cast movie with Hollywood sweetheart–types pulling viewers to live vicariously through this perfect blend of cultural tension, and a great script with comedic timing, the writers made it very easy for us as women to romanticize about what our love lives could look like if we just ended up with a great an all-around clean-cut, committed guy with the wit of Chandler Bing. We introduce to you to *Fools Rush In*. The title is inspired by a great song, and while we're fans of Salma, her character in this film is still the girl we don't want to be.

One night stand

THREE RED FLAG WORDS: One. Night. Stand. So, this movie has Alex—a company exec who lives in New York City—meeting Isabel in Nevada, as he's been sent to open a nightclub in Vegas. They meet at a Mexican restaurant while he's tasting food for work, and the two meet by "fate" or chance. They flirt for about five minutes total (if even that), and next thing we see, Isabel is waking up at Alex's house the morning after, shamefully grabbing her clothes, and leaving his house as quickly and quietly as possible. Before we go any further, let's briefly pause here to address a couple of things: Firstly, please don't go off thinking after watching this movie that if you meet a clean-cut guy at a restaurant, that going home with him is the way to find true love. Because what it *really* is, is the way to find yourself with an STD, a heaping dose of regret, and a horrible way to wake up in the morning; 'cuz let's be real, ain't nobody like doin' the walk of shame—I don't care how liberated and uninhibited you think you are. Deep down inside, you know it's true.

So now, Isabel. She didn't find herself with an STD that we're aware of, but we do know this—she ended up pregnant, which is the other situation we would not want to find you in. Short-term prescribed meds can help with the first—depending on the type of STD, and as far as the second scenario goes, even once the walk of shame is over, his seed now remains. When women give themselves to men in this way, many already start to feel the need to cling to him, hear from him, maybe even see him again. He's on your brain. You're constantly looking at your phone to see if he has called you or texted you. When he hasn't, you make up the excuse that he's probably still asleep or didn't have time or the chance to reach out to you after getting up, getting ready for his day, and heading out the door. In reality—9 out of 10—you will never hear from or see this guy again. In Isabel's case, she did and was now carrying his child.

Before we go any further, can we just say how influential this Romcom was in planting the seed for people to look outside their culture in dating and even marriage (which we love). While we're both proponents of cross-cultural and interracial relationships, this movie highly romanticized the notion of a heroic knight-in-shining armor that would come to your rescue—even if it's dating someone outside your race. Now, while this idea was not new by any stretch—even in 1997—what it did was inspire some who may not have otherwise given dating outside their race a second thought. Fun fact: this movie directly influenced Cyndi's White brother-in-law (who was 16 or 17 at the time when he saw this film) to marry a Latina—her youngest sister, Suzie, at the age of 20. To this day he tells of the inspiration of Salma dancing in the kitchen. Don't tell *us* movies don't influence people to do things! All it took was for an impressionable young man to see a beautiful Latina dancing to Gloria

Estefan's, "Mi Tierra," and his decision was made. In fact—let's be real, it was pretty much the moment we all fell in love with Salma Hayek ... and salsa. That very song is, in fact, playing in the background as these words are being written. Movies influence us in more ways than we realize.

Now as for Isabel and Alex, two people couldn't be more opposite. From scene one with our beloved Alex in the hustle-and-bustle of NYC versus the quiet and relaxing scene where we find Isabel floating down a river in Mexico. Funny thing is that as we're writing this book, there is no place Ivette would rather be than in that river, while Cyndi is all about that concrete jungle. So, back to the girl in the story. It's been about 3 months since Alex has seen/slept with Isabel. And like many men with little care for their one-night-sex, his life went on. For those of you wondering where the term, "one-night stand" comes from, according to Wikipedia, "It draws its name from the common practice of a one-night stand, a single night performance by an entertainer at a venue."[14] Yikes. A single night performance? Yikes! Unless you're an actor or comedian, this is definitely not what we're after in finding the love of our life. Why do we, as women, think that this is all it takes to "land" the man of our dreams? Is that how it turns out? Do we ever think about the repercussions? Let us answer this question: No.

Three months later, Isabel shows up at Alex's house, announcing that she is pregnant! Whhaaaa!! Let's back up a minute ... remember when Isabel and Alex met at a restaurant? Isabel was on the phone talking to her girlfriend, rehearsing how to get out of the current relationship she was in. She wasn't sure if she wanted to marry Chuy, which her family thought was perfect for her. So, here again, we find a girl, not even closing the door on the one relationship she wants out of, before opening another. And now she's three-months pregnant with a man she doesn't even know. "We were only together one night ... and I used a condom," continuing in that Chandler Bing-like way, "...but that's it's job. Its job is to work...". We have to say, though this is a less than ideal situation, we love the comical relief that only Matthew Perry can bring. Imagine the thoughts going through Alex's mind that suddenly come to a screeching halt when he hears her tell him, "It's yours." Of course, he's in shock, and rightly so. Nothing was more painful to watch in that scene then his outwardly obvious relief as she explains, "There's really only one thing to do here...", thinking she was had made the decision to have an abortion, in relief he exclaims as he's almost falling on her, "Oh, thank God! ... I mean, I understand ... I respect your decision ... I've always believed in a woman's right to choose." Annoyed at the father of her child—a man she hasn't known for longer than a day, she interjects, "That's good, because I choose to keep this baby." Good for you, Isabel! Shocked, the only thing Alex could muster up was, "Oh." He shoulda thought

. . . .

14   "One-night stand," *en.wikipedia.org.*

about that before bringing her home to keep him warm at night. An extremely sensitive and controversial subject, but if your one-nighter is happy about you having an abortion, he is not the person for you, or for a child. And he shouldn't be the one you are basing your decision on.

Cyndi: Pregnant as a result of a one-night stand. This is nowhere any single girl should ever want to be. This is where I ended up. And as mentioned before, I was this girl at 19 when I found out I was pregnant. Talking with the father of my baby—who was an ex at the time—he made it very clear that he wanted me to abort the baby and so was doing and saying everything he could for that to be the case. I, on the other hand, wasn't sure what I was going to do, and I just needed sound wisdom. That was when my dad asked what _I_ wanted to do. I let him know that though it was not a scenario I had planned on, and though I no longer loved my ex, I felt like I wanted to keep the baby; having made my bed, I told him that I was going to lie in it. That was when he did what any brave and loving father would do. He looked at the father of the baby and helped me to vocalize the unimportance of _his_ desire for me and the baby, as he was the person who cared the least about me at that time in my life. That being the case, there'd be no reason for his opinion to take first place in my life when really, his opinion ranked last. It always amazes me how a woman will allow what a man says—though he doesn't really give a rip about her—to dictate what she does over what she wants. Why should his opinion and what he wants trump _your_ desires?

That being said—and it makes me cry even now—my dad's stance on me keeping the baby still means so very much to me to this day. He's gone now, but I will always remember how strong he made me feel in supporting my decision to keep the baby. I miscarried in my 4th month of pregnancy. In fact, as I'm writing this now, the 34th anniversary of losing my little girl was just a couple of days ago. It doesn't matter that all those years have gone by. I often wonder what my life would be like had I not miscarried her. I know I didn't take good care of myself during those early years of my pregnancy. I was 19 and felt like I was invincible. I hadn't planned on her coming into my world, and even though losing her, I'm still so glad she was mine for those four months. Whether you're a young adult, middle age or maybe like I was—19 years old—if you find yourself in my shoes (unmarried and pregnant), I challenge you to 1) Tune out the other voices and listen to the voice inside of you that is the stillest and quietest of them all. It might not be the popular choice, but it's the one that will bring you peace—even during the chaos; and 2) Don't ever let the man be the one you base your decision on. You have a brain and it's a darn good one (even though you are in this dilemma). He can't save you. I know we've been trained and taught that as "damsels in distress," our whole lives and well-being hang on being swooped up by our knight in shining armor. But that's the movies and what Disney taught us to believe. And because we've bought into that lie for all these years, we've made some pretty poor choices. You know what's so amazing about that? You can start making better ones RIGHT NOW. Even in the middle of what might seem to be the absolute worst circumstance, you can be the one to turn it around. Now if you have not yet found yourself in such a situation, be responsible and do whatever you can, to not be this girl.

By the way, a beautiful book that brought me such healing was a book called, "I'll Hold You in Heaven." If you've never read it, and you know you need to, do it. The comfort that comes from this book is indescribable, and thanks to Amazon, is just a click away.

Ivette: Well God knows what He is doing when He brings people into our lives, even years later. Cyndi and I have so many similarities although, in this experience, I had a slightly different story, and it was not a one-night stand. Let's see if I can explain this without confusing you all. Like Isabel, I was somewhat in between boyfriends when I found myself pregnant again. You see this was actually years after I had my son. Although I felt I had found myself and knew what I wanted in life, there was a time in between the one of my many, "I'm on a break," moments that I had started to date an old friend from high school. He was fun but not someone I saw myself with long term. And my ex at the time was the love of my life. However, we had some serious issues we needed to work through, so we took multiple breaks and were on and off for 12 crazy years. I really thought we would end up together but his continued toxic lifestyle and my becoming a Christian would make sure that never happened. So back to the real story here, I found myself in that same situation of being pregnant and not knowing who the father was. At this time in my life, I had some toxic friendships as well and the first thing my best friend did when she learned of my situation, was to take me to Planned Parenthood. I did the unthinkable, and when it was done, I put that decision in the very depth of my heart and mind and locked it up forever. In fact, it was only a few years ago that I talked about it for the first time since that happened as I was helping a girlfriend find healing about her abortion. It was then, and about 20 years later, that I forgave myself and received healing in my heart. Helping others has been a great way to heal myself from the craziness that was my life.

The plot to cover up the truth

"My father's gonna kill me," is what Isabel tells Alex as he's admitted to her that at this point, he doesn't know what to do. So, to help her out, he agrees to go with her to meet *la familia*. And this is where the lies begin. This is never a good thing. We're talking about a good scene as he meets her father, mother, and five brothers, plus aunts, uncles, cousins, and Chuy—

someone she's been in a relationship with—at a full-blown fiesta-style party. Together they scheme, building one lie on top of the other, so that one day when her family asks her who the father of her baby is, she'll remind them of the *gringo* she brought home to meet them all those months ago. Great idea, right? Wrong! And if you ever find yourself in a place or position where you don't think you can face your loved ones to tell them the truth, get out of that place. You can. They are your family for a reason. You are meant to go through life together in the good, bad and the ugly, and come out together on top. For whatever reason—fear most likely—Isabel didn't have the courage to tell her parents the truth. As scary as that would have been, that would have been the best thing for her to do then and there, and with Alex supporting her. Yes, her dad does come across a little scary, but at the end of the day, she was his only daughter, and he would have eventually come around with a change of heart towards Isabel, Alex, and the baby.

As the movie plot would have it, what started off as a simple little white lie, became anything and everything but. He's mingling with the family, eating, and enjoying not only the food, but the company and the vibe. Isabel sees how well Alex interacts with not only her family, but also—wait for it—how comfortably he looks holding a baby. Yes, it transitions into a slow-motion scene of him holding the baby just as Isabel walks out. Their eyes meet each other with a gaze that says it all: maybe this could work out for us after all. Well, of the many issues these two have, for one—they've just told her family a big fat lie. Correction—they just acted it out—pretending to be a couple; and secondly, they don't even know each other, so everything is based on what little things they've picked up about one another in the short amount of time. Yes, we, too, have heard of the love stories that actually lasted until the very end, but chances that most of those may not have included the baby factor. While it's also true their cultures couldn't be more different, that's not really the issue. The blending of two very different cultures can be a beautiful thing. You just need to take the time to get to know that person and their culture by immersion and a willingness to learn and love as much as you can about the culture you know nothing about. Now granted, that doesn't take into consideration how the parents feel about their child's love-interest. While we caught glimpses of this on TV show episodes like *Downtown Abbey* with the handsome Irish chauffeur who wasn't good enough for Sybil the daughter of elite English socialites, or *Ugly Betty* when dating Matt, the rich kid, who Betty's Hispanic, living-in-Brooklyn culture wasn't good enough for, in his mom's eyes; it's movies like *Guess Who's Coming to Dinner*, *Guess Who*, newer-released *What's Love Got to Do with It?* (2022) and even *Crazy Rich Asians*, that are classic depictions of on-screen couples being frowned upon by at least one of the parents for racial reasons. The couples themselves were willing, but their families? Not so much.

Here we have beautiful Isabel, introducing Alex to her very passionate and colorful family, which admittingly, was not anything he ever grew up knowing. So, by the time we get to this scene, emotions are running high, and as the evening ends, they couldn't resist the chemistry they had for each other, and so found themselves back in each other 's arms, kissing passionately in the backyard of her parents' home. Eventually pulling away, she walks away. Confused and unsure what to do, she's ready to say goodbye forever, but it's Alex who steps in, telling her that though he didn't quite know what he wanted before, he knew now that what he wanted was her, exclaiming, "Somewhere between the tuna melt and your aunt's tamales ... you're the one ... you are everything I never knew I always wanted." Well, what girl isn't going to gawk at that? One moment, he's walking away, and you're annoyed at him for doing it, because what kind of man does that? So easily walking away from his child just because the baby mama says you're done? We love the Chandler-esque Alex like most others do, but it's when he makes the dramatic gesture of love and pursuit by standing in front of her truck to stop her, that we're back in love with him, as well. Before you know it, she's smiling, for sure, but she still looks a little unsure... until he lets her know that even though he doesn't know exactly what that means, he believes it has to do with the rest of his life. What does he do next? He suggests they get married ... now. You've *got* to be kidding us. You have one hot night with a girl you picked up at a bar—or she picked you up, and now you're asking her to marry you? Oh dear.

That must have been some speech because it convinced her to marry him. But before we go there, you already know we're about to stop and look at a couple of red flags that every woman should look at before considering entering into a relationship with a man, even more so before marrying him. We get that chemistry plays a part in attraction, but really, come on, that is not the biggest factor needed between two people entering into a relationship or getting ready to tie the knot. We've said it before. Relationships should have a solid foundation of truth and honesty, as that breeds trust with one another, therefore, the relationship you are considering entering should never start off with a lie. It doesn't matter who you are, what you do for a living, or how much money you make. A sure key to love-gone-wrong is when there is deception or lying involved, which makes us wonder if it was real love to begin with. There is a wise statement in Proverbs 19:9 (NIRV), "A false witness shall be punished, and a liar shall be caught." There is another that is similar, but speaks to our point saying," A fortune made by people who tell lies amounts to nothing and leads to death. ... But the conduct of those who are not guilty is honest." (Proverbs 21:6 & 8, NIRV) No matter how you slice it, anything gained through deceit—whether it's a job, a friendship, a business, material things, a romantic relationship—a fortune of any kind acquired from a lie will ultimately end in death. Not necessarily physical death, but the demise of that relationship or thing, causing destruction and sometimes divorce.

Can we just take a moment here to be honest with ourselves? Throughout all our years as single women, including one of us who has been coaching both, single men and women for over thirteen years, we know *this*—here is nothing new under the sun. Nothing. We say this because you would be surprised at how many women say the same thing over and over. "But this guy is different," or "It's different this time." But the truth of the matter is, really, it's not. Different skin, same game. We don't care how good it feels, or how good he makes you feel. We don't care how convinced you are that this will be different from all your other relationships. We don't care what he says about his marriage that is now separated. We don't care what he buys for you, we don't care what he promises you ... we don't care! Why? Because at the end of the day, any time a relationship is based on lies and deceit, nothing good ever comes from it. Ever. All we've seen is heartbreak, heartache, devastation, damage, depression, destruction, divorce, and sometimes even death. It sounds extreme, but for those of us on the outside looking in, it's heartbreaking to see what comes out of what someone *thought* they wanted, only to not know or be aware of what was on the other side of that decision. We see it in the headlines and sometimes it's just gut-wrenching. Nothing is worth the pain that comes from loving the wrong person. We've said it before, but because we frequently need reminders, we will share it again.

"There is a way that seems right to a man, but its end is the way of death."

Proverbs 14:12 (NKJV)

"How do you know he's the wrong person for me?" Well, it may not always be crystal clear, and a lot of times you just take those steps of faith in the direction of romance, but when there are obvious red flags that pop up along the way, there are definite tall-tell signs that he's not the one for you.

We've taken the time to list them below in case you're still not sure of what those red flags might be.

- Someone who is dishonest, lying to you and others. If he lies to others without a flinch, he'll lie to you, too.
- Someone who is too busy to call and pursue you, so you're the one making all the effort.
- Dating someone who is already married—even if he is separated. He's still married.

168

- ➤ Dating someone who has a "baby" mama—even if he's single. If his baby is still a baby, it's too soon and smells like drama.

- ➤ Dating someone when you're already in a relationship. Make a decision. Or better yet, pull out of them both. You're not ready to be in one.

- ➤ Sleeping with someone who is already married—even if he's separated. He's still married.

- ➤ Lying to cover up or hide the relationship you're in. If you're needing to lie about the relationship you're in, he's not the one for you.

- ➤ Being with someone who is mean, disrespectful, and not honoring to his parents. How does he treat and talk to his mom? The way he treats his mom is a good indication of the way he will treat you.

- ➤ Staying with a man who has wandering eyes. That includes pornography. If he's got a wandering eye, he's got a wandering heart. You're so much better than that.

- ➤ Staying with a man who is cheating on you.

- ➤ Being with a man who forces you to do something you do not want to do.

- ➤ Staying with someone who abuses you—even if it's verbal. Verbal is often where and how it starts. Protect yourself and the ones you love. He needs professional help and dragging you by your hair while he works through it won't help him out one single bit. We don't care how sorry he is or how much he begs you, he needs help and possibly even healing and deliverance. That's not for you to fix. Please do whatever is needed for you (and your children, if you have kids) to be safe.

While there are so many more red flags we can list, these are the ones with precautionary warnings that scream, "Do not proceed." This is not only important for you and your protection, but also for those you love and care about. Taking time to get to know that person helps give you time to see what they are really all about and the stuff they are made of. In Isabel's case, the idea to lie to her family really was hers, so Alex should have been the one to proceed with caution to see if this was a habit of hers and something she did regularly. Nonetheless, marriage is on the table as Alex just professed his feelings to Isabel. What happens next? Vegas. And let's just say what happens in Vegas, doesn't always stay in Vegas. In fact, Alex didn't even *live* in Vegas. He lived in New York City. But seeing as how the most important thing was jumping into bed and getting her pregnant, that conversation didn't quite come up. Don't be this girl.

Viva Las Vegas

Alex and Isabel bypass all the marital ceremony and celebration, entering their matrimony with just the two of them, Elvis, Neiman Marcus lingerie and a high-rise hotel suite, still knowing nothing about one another. They enjoy their night as Mr. and Mrs. in honeymoon bliss, and Monday, they're right back to life as they knew it, living in the "divorce capital of the world." It all quickly comes to a halt as Isabel's dad shows up at Alex's job, fuming that her married her without a priest, without her close-knit family and not in a Catholic Church. Here is where things begin to surface from the mess of their all-too-quick marriage was built on. And now is where we'll begin to see why marrying someone you've known for literally not more than a total of two days isn't the best idea. Slow your roll. What is it with wanting to go from zero to 90 in three weeks, or in this case, three days?

We discussed the four stages of a relationship in a previous chapter, but we have got to have a handle on what is real. Now, we know that there is a lot we overlook in the first stage of euphoria[15], but let's add some guardrails to this thing called, "love." There is a progression that relationships should go through and these two have done the overnight delivery on the marriage so all of what is supposed to happen in that first stage is already out the window in terms of getting to know someone. Isabel isn't happy about her father's disowning of her, and what daughter in a close-knit Hispanic family would be? It isn't until she's complaining about it to her now-hubby, and her best friend, Lanie, that Alex mentions that they're only there for four months. Unsure of what he's referring to, Isabel probes him as to what happens after four months. She is shocked when he responds, "We open the club, and we go back to New York...," to which she asks, "You mean you don't *live* here?" We are cracking up at the looks that go between her bestie, Lanie and Alex's co-worker, Jeff, who is a bit of a jerk, by-the-way, and the kind of guy no girl should ever want to be with. But back to Alex explaining that he lives in Manhattan. Isabel, with her foot down, has no plans to leave Vegas. "Well, I live here, and I like it here. My family's here and my friends are here ... you can't raise a baby in that city ... my life is in Las Vegas." Furthermore, she argues that she just finished paying off her camera equipment for the book she wants to make about the desert. There is no desert in NYC. "This is the kind of conversation you have on a second date," Lanie chimes in. Precisely. In our lust or excitement, we often move way too fast, missing key conversations that could very well reveal deal-breakers. This conversation should have been had *before* they were married.

What's the rush, girls? We go out with a guy once, and already you're humming, "Here Comes the Bride," as if he's the boy you're going to marry. How about enjoying the process of getting

. . . .

15   Abrams, LCSW-R, "Navigating the 4 Stages of a Relationship," *verywellmind.com.*

170

to know him? Take your time. If there is one thing we can say, it's that while we realize no one is perfect, relationships have definitely evolved, looking so much differently than the previous generations. There are several reasons for this—for one, technology has certainly played a role that never existed prior to what it is now; whereas in previous generations it was either boy-meets-girl in real, non-superficial ways, or even possible parental matchmaking, that took place in person. No doubt, some of the dating apps and platforms today such as Tawkify, Match.com, Hinge or Tinder used to meet a romantic love-interest is different, giving quick and easy access solely based on someone's looks, but additionally, the older generations seemed to have a better handle on how to navigate through the "for better or for worse," than most modern-day relationships. In 1960, the divorce rate was only 2.2 per 1,000. The divorce rate in 2000 was 4.0 per 1,000, but as of 2021, that number has decreased to 2.5.[16] That's not to say marriages in the 60's didn't have their challenges as we suspect that some stayed together more for family's sake or even for appearance's sake, but the success rate at love, marriage and relationships looked different then, than what we see happening now. Marriage is a big deal. Dating someone and committing yourself to exclusively be with this one person is a big deal. Take your time. Get to know them. Does falling in love feel good? Heck yeah, but what doesn't is the breakup and ending of it all. Taking your time to fall in love with someone for the right reasons can help not only build a solid relationship, but it helps to keep from being in a rushed one, later leading to disillusion, heartbreak and failure.

Ivette: Yes, I agree 100%. Unfortunately, most of my relationships moved a little faster than they should. Listen ladies, I'm the first one to admit that I may know what's right, but I haven't always done things that way. Like Cyndi said before, we tend to think this one is different. After so many not-so-perfect or quick-to- jump-in relationships, I asked God to just let me be single. I couldn't handle one more heartbreak or disappointment. But just after that prayer, I met my now- husband, Kyle. And let me tell you that at 43 years old and now being someone that wanted that solid foundation and like-minded person, I had an arsenal of questions—make and break it's—if you will, that I shared with him the night we met. I was not about to waste one more second to fake talk or flirting aimlessly. Well, to my surprise he didn't run away. So that was a good sign of what was to come. Another important thing for me was to make sure that he and my son got along. My son did not like the guy that I was previously dating. He was right—the guy was a complete lie. Everything about him was a lie, and so I swore to never date someone that my son did not approve of ever again. Kyle and I continued to get to know each other, and we were both very honest with each other about what we would or would not accept in our lives. This made it so much easier to move forward. We say it all the time, communication is key in relationships of any kind.

. . . .

16   Ortiz-Ospina, Esteban and Roser, Max, "Marriages and Divorces," *ourworldindata.org*.

Isabel finally makes good with her family, and when they make up and resolve the hurt feelings, her family goes all in! From painting their house, to frequent visits, the music, the dog, and being thrown into a trip with the men in her family, Alex has a lot to learn about Isabel and her culture. One thing he could never seem to get used to is talking to each other while using the bathroom. Yes, these things matter. Though it would take some time for a man who is a bit more modest and old-fashioned to get used to, what he does learn to love almost immediately is Isabel's dancing to salsa. Isabel, on the other hand, is realizing that Alex is nothing like her. He isn't as open as she is, and in fact, although her dad initially disowned her for the shot-gun wedding, Alex didn't share his marriage with his parents *at all*. Anyone spot any red flags in him hiding this huge life event from his parents? This isn't a girlfriend we're talking about—this is his wife and the mother of his baby on the way. How would that make you feel if your relationship was being hidden from your spouse's family? Not only that, but he also forgot her name for a hot minute when introducing her to his parents. The gut-punch came when his parents mistook her for the "help." This is happening again! Kenya's family thought the same in *Something New*. The difference here is that Isabel was his wife, and he lied to her and her parents so that he could keep this a secret. Coward. Again, the lies. Red flags popping up all over on this one. Has that ever happened to you? How did that affect you and how did you respond to that?

Ivette: I think I briefly mentioned this before—when I started dating my son's biological father, his parents were very rude, disconnected and unwelcoming to me whenever I would go to his parents' that the reason was because he was still living with his girlfriend at their house, and I shouldn't have been in the picture in the first place. He had obviously not told them what was going on. He never really cared what they thought anyway. The problem with that is that his lying made me look like the other woman, which was so upsetting as I did not know he was in a relationship with someone else to begin with. This caused such an uncomfortable relationship between his parents and I, so much so that even after the baby came, they were being told lies from their son and so they had nothing to do with us for about 3 years. I'm happy to say that my mom had a conversation with them and confirmed the lies, giving us the opportunity to start a healthier relationship—one that has continued to this day.

The two families finally meet, spending time on the lake, which was quite comical. These two families couldn't have been more different, in every way. His family was Presbyterian, and hers was Catholic. It would have been a much-needed time for both families to become well-acquainted, but it was tense, and ended badly, especially for his family, who in a heated argument with her parents, announced, "In case you hadn't noticed, the white people are melting out here." Though it had its tense, awkward, and funny moments, this needed to happen. Now married and expecting a baby, it's imperative and helpful for the two families to know and learn about each other. Though it happened backwards, it needed to happen. It also needed to take place because it's causing Isabel and Alex to confront some important issues, as well; she wants to raise the baby Catholic, while he is leaning towards Presbyterian. "The faith I have in that crucifix and the faith that I have in us, it all comes from the same place inside of me ... you, on the other hand, you're not even a practicing Presbyterian." How a couple plans on raising a baby is so important—especially when it comes to faith. Yeah ... like we said, conversations that should have taken place on the dates they never had.

Now that the marriage has happened, and the two try to figure out their groove, tensions are a little high as Alex is feeling the pressure from work, which revolves around the club he's in Vegas to open. It's not as easy as that now that his wife—who he didn't have when he first was assigned to that city—also requires him being fully present through all her pregnancy months and moments. Though it would seem as though the honeymoon phase has ended, and there are definitely factors involved that would make it seem that way, you do see a couple who is really trying to navigate through their situation together. They continue to learn more about each other. This is key for every couple—married or not—to continue to do no matter how much you do or don't know about them the day you marry. Keep in mind, that even though you may think you know everything about that special person, you will forever be finding out about them for the rest of your life. As for Alex, we see his focus shift, and it's not just because he's committed to being a family man who provides for his wife and baby on the way. His boss has dangled the club he has had his eyes set on for quite some time, but with that, meant moving to New York three months earlier than he had anticipated. Up to that point, he and Isabel had not yet fully agreed on New York being their place of residence. Well, as movie plotting would have it, Isabel comes to learn this the night the club opens in Vegas. Did Alex have plenty of opportunity to bring this up to her? Yes. Had he brought it up to her? No. Again, and this is not even a boyfriend-girlfriend scenario, they are now husband and wife. Is it possible that he chose to withhold this information from her because of being used to all the hiding and secrecy that existed in their relationship from the beginning? Old habits are hard to break. Ya better make sure your man has good ones ... and that you do, too. The hard part for Isabel it that she's pregnant, and though they should be growing together, they were starting to grow apart in his deliberate actions of alienating her from these very important parts of his life.

Communication is part of a healthy relationship. We repeat, communication is part of a healthy relationship. It's needed and is a must. Not afraid of taking her stance as we see throughout the entire movie and being the independent woman that she is, she lets him know she has no problem raising the baby on her own—most likely a statement that would not have been made had they not conceived during a one-night stand. In fear, he retaliates, "I thought we were a family." Her response was so raw, honest, and sad. "You don't understand the concept of a family ... love is a gift, Alex, not an obligation." (Ivette is crying) Verbally it got ugly after that. He should have stopped and let her leave before spouting off at her about the "brass ring," and chance for him to be something to his boss and the company he worked for. "I'm not giving up because one night I put a $5 ring on your finger in front of Elvis as a witness!" Jerk. It is said that out of the abundance of the heart, the mouth speaks (Luke 6:45, NKJV) And boy, did his ever?! At first, he communicates *nothing* to her about the plans for New York in July and now his words are cutting like a knife. And the thing with words—once you've said them, there's no taking them back. They have done their damage when used in spiteful and painful ways. Unfortunately, for Isabel, his words broke her heart, sending her to the hospital, unbeknownst to him, as he didn't return home until the following morning. He rushes to the hospital as soon as he gets a call from Lanie, but when he gets there, Isabel, who just experienced a scare with their pregnancy tells him, "There is no baby." He's devastated and can't believe this. She's hurt and upset with what he said the night before. She's also upset with the way things have been going in their marriage, and so her choice rather than to deal with it, was to push him away and out of her life. With her back to him she tells him, "We're too different, Alex...and we will always be ... we're not meant to be together ... this is not gonna work." When he gently pushes back, the strong and courageous woman in her rises, yelling at him. "Get out," she yells. Dumbfounded, he is paralyzed with unbelief. "Get out," she yells again, before he turns around and leaves. She breaks down crying, broken, devastated, and still pregnant (*spoiler alert*, sorry!).

It's good to pause here because you see the conflict in her, and while we certainly are not proponents of lying to your husband, there were so many emotions flying, not to mention the fact that she was pregnant. How many of you who have been pregnant can attest that your emotions and even logic sometimes runs a little wild? But it is good to acknowledge that lying to your husband is not the way to go. It's never the way to go. Even though things are hard, you must be willing to lay it down, telling your spouse or the love of your life the truth, even when it's hurtful. And in so many cases because we are the ones that are hurt and crushed, we sometimes feel like we want to pay them back and hurt them as much as they've hurt us. This wasn't at all fair to Alex, but we get it. We understand and have both gone through similar situations ourselves, choosing to deal with it the Isabel way.

Cyndi: As mentioned in another chapter, I chose to handle it very similarly in the way that Isabel did. I wanted to hurt him so that he could feel the pain. Even though it humiliated him, I only ended up hurting myself more. Thankful for the epiphany of undoing the wrong I had done; he was gracious to forgive me when I fessed up to my mission and ploy to destroy. I'm still not proud of myself for doing what I did. If you've ever done anything similarly, start with forgiving yourself, and then be sure to follow-through in asking for forgiveness.

This is never the way to deal with someone you love. Let's be clear—covering up and lying is never okay. Even though we get why Isabel did what she did. She had the chance to resolve and to come clean with the truth. Did she? Nope. Instead, she flees to her beautiful place of solace—her *abuela's* peaceful home in Mexico. As for Alex, he comes to his senses and heads to the hospital, only to find she is no longer there. He reaches a dead-end, unable to get any answers from her family, and so finally relocates to New York, where he is served divorce papers, with six days to contest. We hate that this happens in front of his friend, Jeff, whose only two goals in life are to land women and be a success in their company. Ladies, there are many men who are like this, and so please don't be blind to that when you meet someone who is just like Jeff.

As most romcoms have it, the tide starts to turn in favor of the couple, and so for Isabel and Alex, this happens simultaneously, though they're now on opposite ends of the earth. Isabel's beautiful and wise grandma speaks truth, letting her know that it was fear that caused her to do what she did. If there was one thing we saw Isabel do since the very beginning of the movie, it was following signs. She was talking about signs when she was on the phone the moment she and Alex met. Throughout her prayer life at church with her mom, they'd talk about signs, and now signs pop up yet again. It reminds us of *Sleepless in Seattle* and *Serendipity*, movies also based on signs and fate. As Alex is processing his divorce and trying to move on with life, he begins to see signs he believes is pointing him back to Isabel. Simultaneously she and her *abuela* are having deep conversations and her grandma challenges her that though she thought she was doing Alex a favor in letting him off the hook, that what she was really doing was letting herself off the hook. And that is when we, the audience, visibly see that she is still pregnant.

The older generations who love us, see right through our foolish choices and shenanigans as many have walked difficult relational things, as well and are all the wiser for it. Thank the Lord they are still around to not only tell us about it, but to call us out when we're making immature decisions. In this case, Isabel took matters into her own hands, lying to her husband, and then filing for divorce. Her grandma is beautiful and bold, challenging Isabel, "You denied your heart and lied to the man you love. Why?" That was so unfair to Alex, but the truth came out. "Because I had to. If I didn't leave him, he would have left me ... I really don't think I could've handled that." She did what no woman should ever do on her own in a marriage. In fear, she made a decision affecting the entire family, including the baby on the way. Don't. Be. This. Girl. For the record, no one pulls off that beautiful red Huipil (Mexican Puebla dress), better than Salma. We are glad she was processing this with her grandmother, who so wisely replied, "You will never know love unless you surrender to it." And there it is—truth so beautifully dressed in authentic embroidery and lace.

All great stories have at least one antagonist, and though she doesn't make a whole lot of appearances in this film, she makes enough to let you know she will once again be an annoying little gnat as the plot thickens. Alex has been running from Kathy since they were young kids, and this woman has been hot in pursuit of him and is not shy or quiet about it. In fact, the reason Alex 's parents even showed up at his and Isabella 's house early on in their marriage was because Kathy called them, letting them know that they needed to check on him in Vegas once she had found out that he was married. She's a "butt-insky," someone who butts into other people's business—a snooty, jealous busy-body. Calling him just as he happens to be staring at the divorce papers he's contemplating signing; she invites him to join his parents who will be joining her family that upcoming weekend. We are yelling, "Don't do it, Alex!" It's so crazy how this girl knows where and how to find him. If you're anything like the very-forward Kathy, we also warn you, don't be *this* girl, either. With much prodding and persuasion, Alex, in his weakness and brokenness of his soon-to-be divorce, caves into Kathy—another reason why it's never good to keep forcing yourself on men. Just because they cave into your pressure and forwardness, doesn't mean they're into you. Alex was not at all into Kathy. Men know exactly what they want, and even if you're not it, they'll settle for the time being, and you will be the one who is hurt at the end of the day. Plus, give a man some time to grieve ... sheesh, Kathy!

Though Alex was not a huge proponent of signs, this is the point in the story where signs show up once he's made this decision to finalize the divorce and move on with his life. Everything from a man telling him that, "there are signs everywhere" as he is walking by Gray's Papaya, the iconic hole-in-the-wall hot dog joint where Isabel ordered Alex's favorite hot dogs, overnighting them to Nevada for his birthday, which they enjoyed together with a beautiful canyon as their backdrop, he sees many signs. The one we believe cut him to the heart, was the one he sees at the heliport--a precious little girl named, "Isabel," who runs after him just as he's about to board the helicopter. All signs point to Isabel. Kathy is disappointed, his dad looks perplexed, but his mom understands.

Manning up to go after his wife, he heads to Mexico in search of his love riding a truck filled with villagers, ending his journey to her grandma's house on a donkey, where, in Spanish, she says, "So you are Isabel's great love ... my dear, sweet boy," kissing him in that precious way grandparents do. His journey takes him to the Hoover Dam's Stateline of Arizona and Nevada, to wait for her after learning she was on her way back to Vegas. Almost running him over in the rain, he tries to convince her that they belong together, confessing, "I love you so much it hurts." Now he's fighting for her. We like that! And this is the part he learns that she is still pregnant, and they are, in fact, having a baby. In the middle of the two of them arguing at the Stateline, she confesses, "You lied to me, so I lied to you." That which a man sows, that he will also reap. This relationship that started with the lie of being a couple to cover up the truth to her family has swung from lying-branch to lying-branch, using familiar branches of deceit to get to the next thing, another lie.

So, you know the rest—even if you've never seen the movie. They have a beautiful baby girl which she delivers in the rain on the Hoover Dam with the help of the paramedics. Their divorce becomes finalized at midnight, and they remarry in front of all their family and friends, with a minister, and a gorgeous natural backdrop of the Grand Canyon as the landscape. There was no song more fitting than Elvis' "Fools Rush In," to end this tumultuous love story that predictably ends the way Hollywood prescribes—a happy ending. But let's be real, the song is perfect, because it is *truly* only a fool who rushes in.

Being hopeless romantics, we too, love a happy ending, however we realize that for some who've walked this out in real-life, things may have turned out a bit differently. Or maybe you've never experienced any of what Isabel went through. Regardless of where you stand, we have faith in you. We believe in you. This chapter was written so that you don't become the statistic—the one-night stand who gets pregnant and ends up alone, the one-night stand who gets pregnant and marries solely for that reason, and ends up divorced again, or the girl whose relationship started off with lies. All of these are real-life situations that happen. Because we've both personally walked out some of this through our poor choices as young women in search of true love, we can tell you this: If you're willing to set your heart out to seek truth and are willing to turn from those destructive habits, it doesn't matter which of those above-scenarios you are in—there is hope and you can have victory, even if it doesn't turn out the way you want. Maybe you won't end up with that man you have set your heart and eyes on, but if he is no good for you and your future, that is a good thing.

Please know this. Our desire is to see you victorious. You are stronger than you know. Say that out loud. "I am stronger than I know." Say, "I am stronger than I feel." Matthew 19:26 (NIV) says, "...with God all things are possible," and Philippians 4:13 says, "I can do all things through Christ who strengthens me." You are stronger than you know, and calling on the One who gives the strength will empower you to do things with a peace you've never known until you do those very things. The time to make a change is always now. It's never too late. So many underestimate the power of the Bible or the Word of God, mistaking it as just stories of old, but did you know there is life in His Word? It is a living well that also operates in "now time." If you knew you had access to something that was living and powerful that would forever change your life, wouldn't you want to know? And wouldn't you want to use it and go to it regularly? Our lives both look differently than they did when we were making mistakes in search of love, because God's Word became a river of living water to each of us, forever quenching our parched lives and souls. Our journeys were both as rocky as Isabel's but, for the grace of God, we are here to tell you we are now stronger than ever before—even in deep pain, we found hope. And even in yours, you will find it, as well and will have victory.

Here are some scriptures for you to declare (out loud), to journal and chew on that will strengthen you and give you the wisdom needed to navigate even the worst and direst of situations.

Verses for you to declare out loud:

- ➤ "...with God all things are possible." Matthew 19:26 (NIV)
- ➤ "I can do all things through Christ who strengthens me." Philippians 4:13 (NKJV)
- ➤ "And we know that in all things God works for the good of those who love him, who have been called according to his purpose." Romans 8:28 (NIV)
- ➤ "And He said to me, "My grace is sufficient for you, for My strength is made perfect in weakness." 2 Corinthians 12:9 (NKJV)
- ➤ "A wise woman builds her house, but a foolish woman tears hers down with her own hands." Prov. 14:1 (NKJV)
- ➤ "According to 2 Corinthians 12, My strength is made perfect in weakness. Therefore, I am not weak. I am strong and full of strength. I am a strong woman strengthened in God."
- ➤ "Based on Proverbs 14, I am a woman who has wisdom, and one who makes wise decisions."

Playlist:

- ♫ *Ain't that a Kick in the Head* by Dean Martin
- ♫ *Mi Tierra* by Gloria Estefan
- ♫ *It's Now or Never* by Elvis Presley
- ♫ *Why Do Fools Fall in Love* by Frankie Lymon & The Teenagers
- ♫ *Can't Help Falling in Love* by Elvis Presley

"You complete me."

Jerry Maguire,
Jerry Maguire

Dorothy Boyd, A Single Mom Desperate for a Man in Her Life

Jerry Maguire

It's frequently common for a single mom to want to find a man who will not only provide for her family, but who will also be a good father figure to her child. In some cases, this is more the factor in allowing a man into her life—even more than for love itself. But there are also those who desire both—finding love again, and a good man for her child. And for Dorothy Boyd, played by Renee Zellweger, it is clear this is her heart's desire. *This* movie. It is our belief that some of the reasons why many women—including us—have had warped expectations in relationships is because of some key phrases in this movie that've been forever embedded in our minds. Between "You had me at hello," and "You complete me," many-a-women have bought into the false notion of romance these words bring, reminiscing moments of an unrealistic scene created by writers. Even if you've never seen the movie, some of the strongest quotes from the film still live on today ... "SHOW ME THE MONEY," and, "YOU HAD ME AT HELLO." This is the world where we find Dorothy—a young, single mom working at a sports agency firm with Jerry Maguire (played by Tom Cruise), an engaged, charismatic, handsome, and successful sports agent. A very charming chap, we see that even though he's engaged to be married, there are many female coworkers who swoon over him, Dorothy included.

Though he's never really noticed Dorothy, they one day find themselves not only on the same airplane, but also at baggage claim where she's hollering for her son, Ray, who she can't seem to find. Jerry steps in to assist, quickly spotting her son and so they briefly chat it up for a bit while Ray takes the opportunity to swing while he's holding both of their hands. We already see what she's thinking. The look is in her eyes. Complimenting him on a very long memo that he drafted and sent to the whole company, she shows an already slightly obsessed side as she's clearly put Maguire on a pedestal, stroking his already-huge ego. Even when he's at the office, you see her eyes glued to his every move. And then, an interesting turn of events happens because of the said-memo Maguire wrote, challenging his company to embrace the one-on-one personal touch between agents and their clients. As a result, his company lets him go, and he is fired by his protégé (ouch). Realizing he's now on a clock in a fight against time so as not to lose his clients, he starts attempting to call each of them one by one, only to find out that this huge list has now shrunk down to only two. As Maguire is walking out of the office, he invites others to go with. At that moment, Dorothy makes a decision that will forever change her life. It's an impulsive one. With courageous-fear, she stands up— in front of her co-workers— saying, "I will go with you!" We're shocked. This is a single mom. We're thinking of her finances and her medical insurance, but it's too late. She's made the impromptu decision. Not only that, we're also seeing how irrational this is as Maguire appears to be having a breakdown; so now you're following an unstable leader. She must have known from the beginning that this would not go well, but she somehow talked herself into it. So, off they go to a new start——Maguire, the fish he took from the tank, and Dorothy. As they head into the elevator, they witness a deaf couple (also in the elevator) signing, "You complete me." Dorothy translates to Jerry the words exchanged by the couple, and thus, a new journey for Dorothy and Maguire begins.

Knowing the ropes of a sports agency, Dorothy's going with Maguire is a huge asset for him as long as lines and boundaries aren't crossed. Clinging to the two football player clients he has—Tidwell and Cushman—he jets out to meet the one who is on the fence in person. Because this kid is young and fresh, Jerry is sure to give him all the attention needed, so that he'd stay with Maguire, and not with the agency that let Maguire go. After dropping Jerry off at the airport, we see Dorothy's heartstrings being pulled as sees another family kissing and hugging goodbye. It is clear to see that she is in dreamland, which is not a wise place to be with your new boss—or better yet, with your boss. Period. If she can keep her eyes on why she is with Maguire to begin with—to work as his only employee—she'll be fine. But she doesn't. She has already let her thoughts and emotions get the best of her. Ladies, if you know someone isn't for you, why *go* there? To top it all off, Jerry loses Cushman—his best client— to his former agency, leaving him only with Tidwell. He now finds himself not only out of a job, and one player short, but he makes the decision to also call it quits with his fiancée, as well, telling her, "It's over."

Jerry is now a free agent (no pun intended) and so having no one else but Dorothy to lean on, she is the one he reaches out to. Yep, our dear, darling (and most likely starving-for-love) Dorothy. As far as she knows, he's still engaged, but that doesn't keep her from inviting him over. He's drunk, she's smitten ... boundaries will be crossed.

Give the man some time to heal

No matter where life takes us, it's so imperative to have a voice of reason in our lives. For Dorothy, it's her disapproving sister, Laurel, who warns her about the dangers of her boss' inability to be alone while riding this midlife crisis, "... he better not be good looking." We are cracking up at her response to him when she greets him at the door. "Hello ... you're just the way I pictured you." We love her candidness. Dorothy needs it. We all do, but Dorothy *really* does. She's a daydreamer who is a single mom. The moment he announces he broke up with his fiancée, she actually gets excited. Excited? Hello ... he *just* broke up...with his fiancée. Why the excitement, ladies? What is wrong with us? We see it on-screen, and though we're cringing at her behavior, this is us. And if it's not you personally, this is our culture. This is what we've become—desperate opportunists who aren't willing to wait for the best life has to offer. We'll take the sloppy seconds. And right now, he's super sloppy. If you think him running into your arms the *same* day he calls it quits with his fiancée is the best life has to offer you, think again. You can better. *So* much better. If you cave and comply, you are on dangerous, shaky ground. Clearly, Dorothy forgot her place. The only reason she was in his life at this point is because she is now working for him and is his employee. Some may defend her in her age saying, "Oh, she's young." It doesn't matter that she was only 26 at the time, it wouldn't have mattered if she were 19, either. She still should have known better. We know better. Don't you ever hear or sense that quiet little internal nudge? We need to pay attention to that a lot more than many of us have. It's when we don't pay attention to wisdom or sound advice, that we find ourselves in danger. Ignoring Laurel, her better sense of judgement, she runs to his to take care of him. Granted, she's a mom and so has a maternal nature, but we have a feeling it's a little more than just that. Getting him something to drink, as well as Aloe Vera for his cut, her sister scolds, "This guy would go home with a gardening tool right now if it showed interest." Here's something to note, girls. When coming out of a relationship or marriage, men don't like to be alone. It's not uncommon for him run into the arms of any available woman. A man who has been married, but who has become a widower after losing his wife, may look to remarry shortly, but if you're the woman he wants to remarry, give him about a good year to heal. If it's a man who has lost his wife to divorce, he'll need much longer than that—not only will he need healing, but he's got some things to work through before jumping back into another relationship again. Any woman jumping into a relationship the moment he has just broken up, separated or divorced his wife, is asking for trouble. You are the rebound woman and will most likely end up devasted and broken hearted by this man. That is a not just a red flag, it's an entire banner with flashing lights warning, "Don't go there."

Laurel sees the signs. He's hit rock bottom, lost his job, his best client and now, his girl. She continues, "You have always been very responsible with Ray...I don't think it's right for him to wake up and hear some strange man's voice in the house...". But hold up, Dorothy, again, this dude is also your boss. What in the world is going on in that mind of yours?! Justifying herself at sister's questioning, she defends herself asking, "...Do you know what other women my age are doing right now?" She continues that while most women her age are out at clubs trying to find and keep a man at clubs, she's trying to raise one. "I'm the oldest 26-year-old in the world," complaining to her that she's only had three lovers in four years. Girls, this is not how—or who—we want to be. Especially as a single mom. And wait just one minute—he's her boss. But now she's talking about lovers in the same sentence?! No. No. NO. Where did the common sense go? Why is she running to this guy in such an irresponsible way? And since when did casual sexual encounters become the norm? Well, we do have an answer for that. But we'll remain focused on Jerry Maguire, as our last chapter will deal with the sexual revolution in the 21st century. Ignoring Laurel and blindly desiring Jerry, she doctors him up, admitting, "I care about the job, but mostly, I just want to be inspired...I'm working with you because of that memo ... I loved that memo." Moved by her words, but mostly by the fact that he's drunk, he goes in for a kiss. This is horrible for two reasons, no three. 1) He's drunk; 2) He's her boss; and 3) He *just* broke up with his fiancée earlier that day. He shouldn't be making moves on his single-mom employee. And she should have listened to Laurel.

A single mother ... That's a sacred thing

There is something beautiful and resilient about single moms—about all moms—but there is something significantly strong about the ones who go it alone. Such is the case of Dorothy, who has been not one, but two parents to Ray. You can see she has somewhat proceeded withcaution up to this point, as all women should—even more so when you're the primary caretaker of your child. However, when it comes to Maguire, she is not using wisdom. And neither is he. Unable to be alone, he asks his employee out on a real date. Wasn't he just engaged up until about 48 hours ago? And already, he's asking a girl out? His only employee, no less. Because of being a single mom, this movie was a sure fit in the book for Ivette who was a single mom for many years. Because this topic is sometimes not addressed, we were thrilled to shed some light on the vulnerability of single moms. Though Dorothy does seem to be a brilliant woman, her heartstrings are definitely pulled where her son is concerned. So much so, that she doesn't really notice that initially, that Maguire doesn't want too much to do with her kid. Though Ray is drawn to Jerry, Maguire is awkward and somewhat standoffish where this kid is concerned. Completely overlooking his body language, she chooses to focus on Ray's affection towards Jerry, rather than Jerry's towards Ray. Single mommas, do not do this. Protect your child and pay attention to both sides. Be watchful of everything you see going on. Listen to your children. If you're a single mom, you are *all* your children have. She's strong, indeed, but when it comes to seeing Jerry hugging her son back, she's all soft in the heart and weak at the knees. Her heart is smiling, her sister and Ray's nanny don't approve. The sight of this gets Dorothy extremely emotional as she tells her sister, "That is the first time I have ever seen him kiss a man just like a dad. Wasn't that just thrilling? ... He must really have been needing that." In the words of her sister when Dorothy left with Maguire, we too, said, "Oh dear."

Ivette: Ray kisses Jerry and Dorothy loses it! I get it as a single mom, the only thing we want for our little one is to feel complete, to not feel different and to feel loved (in a perfect world, by both mother and father). But let's not forget, he is just getting out of a meaningless relationship based on career status over love. What exactly does Jerry—a now essentially unemployed player that doesn't have or know much about kids—have to offer?

As they say goodnight on the porch, he kisses her in a way that was pretty much meant for a "room." And that is exactly where they end up. The way he said "goodnight" to her on the porch was quite steamy. The girl needed to have run away from that as fast as she can. If that wasn't a red flag, I'm not sure you will ever know what is. She initiated it, he ran with it and what started as an evening date, turned into morning. Almost another Isabel and Alex situation except that Dorothy has a kid. It is in the morning that Laurel warns her of how men are different when living on the bottom, but Dorothy could care less about him hitting rock bottom. Even knowing that it's true, she's viewing it as an opportunity. She's hungry for love. She's been lonely and probably craves being with a man. Though there are several things to take into consideration, the biggest one of all, is that right now your ONLY responsibility is to take care of your son. If you're a single mom, you get it and you understand. If you've never been a single mom, it really is difficult to "get" why Dorothy would be dabbling with her boss at all.

Both sisters don't see eye-to-eye, and Dorothy has pretty much already made the decision that she has no intentions on letting him go, explaining how "...everything in my body says, 'This one is the one.'" We're literally gasping. Your body is speaking to you because it just woke up from being asleep all these years. It doesn't get any better. She goes on to explain that she also has newfound revelation of love for her boss, as she tells her sister that she loves him "I love him... I do. I love him, I love him!" And if that confession wasn't painful enough to hear, it keeps getting worse. "I love him for the man he wants to be, and I love him for the man that he almost is ... I love him ... I love him ... I love him!" You LOVE him?!? For the man he *almost* is?! Please stop. You were so hungry for a man who just gave you the best—or only—sex maybe within the year, and now you *love* him? Let's put it *this* way—any stale cracker will taste amazing to someone who hasn't eaten a single thing in the last year. You don't love him, Dorothy—you just happened to have really good sex. You've been lonely and starving for affection. You've mistaken good sex for love because you've blinded by 1) how he made you feel; and 2) how starved you've been for human intimacy and affection; and 3) you, as a woman, just experienced the act of becoming one with him, receiving into you, what he, as a depositor gave you. Remember we mentioned earlier on that men are depositors, they give, and we receive. The anatomy of a female is meant to receive from a man. This is why it is the *only* way to naturally get pregnant—it can only happen this way (without science). Something significant happens to a woman's body when she receives form a man, which is why it's not wisdom to just jump into bed with every man—especially one who has just broken up with the woman he was engaged to...YESTERDAY! Good thing her embarrassing confession of love (lust) about Jerry to her sister was interrupted by Ray greeting Jerry in the hallway. Yep, he was listening, and he had heard it all. Every. Single. Word.

Cyndi: Being raised by a single mom when I was a teenager through my adult years, I have to say that my mom was more than just a strong single mom, she was fierce. Not only did she remain single for the rest of her life, but year after year I'd see her working two, sometimes even three jobs just to make ends meet as she raised me and my two younger sisters by herself once my dad left us for good in my teens. She may have felt alone. I'm almost sure of it. However, she was so focused on providing a safe home for us, that I think I only saw her go on a date once, maybe twice, and neither of them went any further than that. Smart woman. Why? I know plenty of married women who feel alone. Feeling alone has nothing to do with your marital status. It's a state of being. You can be married and still feel alone; and you can be single, and not feel alone. My mom, though single, never felt alone. She is also a woman of great faith. As I grew older, I asked her if she ever got lonely or missed having a man in her life. Time and time again, she would tell me "No," because God was all she needed, and He was the one who gave her the strength to raise us on her own. Additionally, we (her girls) were her priority. She is one of the wisest, and strongest women I know. I believe it's what I see in her that gives me the strength to live life to its fullest as a single woman who has never been married. It's not to say I don't desire it, but even at 54, I'm willing to wait until the right man (for me) comes along.

Bouncing back from eavesdropping that morning, Maguire seems to be moving in the direction of dating Dorothy, which he understands is dangerous as there is a child in the picture. His only client, Rod Tidwell (Cuba Gooding, Jr.), scolds him in that he needs to be fair to her because she is a single mom. "A single mother ... man, that's a sacred thing," he continues to point out, "She loves you. If you don't love her, you've got to tell her." This little speech would do well for any single bachelor out there to take note of—and not just regarding single moms, but single women. Is it just us or does it seem as of late more and more men just start regressing back to acting as little boys, playing both, the field, *and* the women who are on out on the field? Tidwell continues on, letting him know that a real man wouldn't, "... shoplift the pooty from a single mother." Again, a little brash in what we're sharing, but we want you to see the hard facts of what many men say and think. This brother is straight on, but Maguire isn't man enough to ever do it. Nope, he'd rather do his thing his own way, damaging every person in harm's way. The sad thing of it all, is that *is* what many men do, ladies. Some of them *don't* tell you what they should, and yet, you go on believing a lie that he is crazy in love with you. That is dangerous ground to be on or around. And if you see the signs, you need to get off as quickly as possible.

Thinking of herself and what she needs to do for her and Ray, she makes a bold move and decides to take a job out in San Diego. This is what we like to see in women—courage and strength. As they are bidding their farewells, our stomachs are in knots at this situation, knowing full well that things can turn for the worst at any given moment. We're like, "Get in the van, Dorothy. Go, don't talk...just go!" It's also what her sister, Laurel, was saying to her as she was watching them from the kitchen window. Her sister by the way, is definitely her voice of reason. She herself, is walking through divorce recovery, along with her tribe of friends that meet every week to get each other through the loss of losing a spouse and divorce. She tells him she loves him first as she gets ready to leave—c'mon, don't do *that*. Don't go there, Dorothy—now's not the time. And let *him* be the one to say it first. Let the man take the lead. She's going about this all wrong and is still somewhat daydreaming about it. We know how it's going to end in the movie, but when we—as women—attempt to walk out our *real* love lives in a similar manner, it hardly ever ends the way it unravels in this film. She and Ray are packed and ready to move, but Maguire, in his desperation to not see her and her great kid leave, asks her to marry him. Will you *marry* me? What are you doing? She say "Yes," only through her tears (yeah, she actually didn't officially answer him), and not only that, was his proposal for real? The initial proposal was more like a, "...what if we got married," kinda-thing so she wouldn't leave him. NO! Please tell us you see this as a marriage relationship-hazard, as well?!

Ivette: This is not only the worst time for a proposal, it's a desperate time to accept it. I actually think I might have thrown up a little in my mouth at the sight of Jerry stumbling over what to do. Okay, not really, but you get the picture. And then the dreaded "Wait, wait a second." We all know what's next. But in a proposal the question is, "Will you marry me?" not "What if we got married?" And let me tell you, if I got married every time I heard a half-cocked proposal like that, I would have been married at least 3 times. Thankfully, even though I didn't always make great decisions in my love life, I knew better than to actually accept those "What ifs."

Well, Dorothy apparently didn't see his "what if" as a problem in any way, shape, or form, so they marry. The bad news? It was all over his face. He was not happy. They were interacting like strangers on their wedding day... it was so awkward. This isn't how a man should look on his wedding day, and yet, we can guarantee you that there are many men and women, who unfortunately experience this type of grief on their wedding day, and yet proceed with it anyway. We could barely watch the two of them. What woman wouldn't see this look of fear on her groom's face as she's walking down the aisle to him? This was too much for us to watch. May those who read this, never walk down the aisle to a man who isn't ecstatic, crying or grinning from cheek to cheek as he's about marrying his soulmate. For whatever reason— whether it's because they're too far into it to pull out, or have invested way too much money to call it quits, or just the sheer embarrassment of what people will think, too many couples marry when they aren't even fully convinced—and sometimes already knowing—this is the person they are *not* meant to spend the rest of their life with. Don't let this happen to you.

More-than-pleased with herself in her new upgraded relationship status—married, she can't see straight enough to notice that he is not in love with her the way she is with him. However, it's when she sees the wedding video, she sees what she never saw before—footage showing a man who didn't want to marry her at all. Nope, he didn't want to marry her, and the only reason he did, was because of her *loyalty*. Please tell me he didn't say that. But yes, he did. Seeing what the videographer captured of Jerry before she walks down the aisle to him should not be anything any groom should ever look like on his wedding day. He was sweating, frowning, stressing—all of this before she pledged her vows to this man. Have you ever committed yourself to a relationship verbally, but your heart was so removed or detached from him? Have you ever been with someone you really didn't care for or love, just for this simple sake of not being alone?

If you have ever done that, and if you are not in a relationship now, would you, while reading this book, determine that you will never do that again? Not only is it not fair to them, or any others in close proximity of your relationship, it's also not fair to *you*. It's time to be good to yourself. *Stop* settling for the crumbs. We've said it before, and we will say it again. Better to be alone and happy and content with who you are, than being in a relationship where you are miserable or not loved, in the name of companionship. One more very important thing to note: Hot sex does not equate to marriage happily ever after. Your relationship isn't the exception. We will keep saying this all day long, because you need to get that into your head. Stop thinking this is for someone else. It's not. This is for you.

When we look at the history of love and marriage, we actually find that many—if not most—arranged marriages did in fact, work, as they were based on honor and respect. One would marry someone based on being set up by friends and family and build an entire life together from that moment on. It's crazy to think how much time has changed where love and marriage is concerned, especially when it was the norm to marry someone you didn't love, solely out of an arranged marriage. Now granted this was well over one hundred years ago, though it still exists in some customs today. So that's not to say that their marriage couldn't or wouldn't last, but it isn't the reason most of us desire to marry today. To marry for loyalty *only*? No thank you, we're out. But for Jerry and Dorothy, it's too late now. They are Mr. and Mrs. Jerry Maguire. And so, they do as best as they can. He is trying to stay committed, and she is still trying to figure him out. Don't do this. Don't say "yes" to marrying a man you don't know, simply to no longer be single. Don't say "yes" based on how good he is in bed—that's overrated. Say "yes" because he truly loves you and wants to cherish, provide for, and love both you, and your child/children for the rest of your lives. We love history and are thankful to see how marriages were strong and successful for so many throughout the years—many which were founded on respect and honor, which *isn't* what we see happening with Jerry and Dorothy.

I thought I was in love

Coming to terms with the role she played in it all, she is the brave one who fesses up, but darling Dorothy, this conversation should have started with him. Why is the woman so often the one blaming herself for something they both did? "I thought I was in love ... enough for both of us...". While we love that she's come to terms with this and is being honest with herself, this is a conversation she needed to have with herself, as well as with Jerry, before they got married—not after. "I pretended that the proposal by the car was real ... I did this, and at least I can do something about it now ... let's just call this next road trip what it really is ... a nice, long break ... I've got this great guy, and he loves my kid ... and he sure does like me a lot ... I can't live like that." Well, yeah. We could have told you *that*. What a mess, but good for Dorothy, taking a break from Jerry. Good sex isn't a good enough reason to marry. Providing for you and your children isn't one either. It's obvious that one of the reasons Jerry has won Dorothy's heart, is because of how he loves her son, Ray. And though she's unfortunately put her son through the roller-coaster ringer in her desperation to be loved, she's made the choice. We both would agree that while divorce isn't the route they should take, in some cases taking a break—even from your spouse—can be a good thing when both are taking the time to work on whatever the issue is, so that it can be fixed, bringing the healed and stronger parts back into the marriage. You may find yourself in the "for worse," part of your married life. We respect that rather than just calling it "quits," Dorothy was willing to take a break and figure things out." Immediately after "They're breaking up.

Ivette: The first time I watched this movie, I was this girl. I was so in love with the thought of Jerry Maguire paying attention to her, meeting her son and being so good to him. That's everything I ever wanted when I was single mom—someone that would be there for my son and teach him the manly things that I couldn't. It's so crazy how we bypass so many things in the name of provision or what we think we need. I didn't really think about if that relationship would work or not. The most important thing at the time for me, was to make sure my son didn't feel different. I wanted so desperately for him to feel like we were a complete family. 28 years later I feel much stronger about being able to be everything he needs me to be. Having stayed in that relationship—though very unhealthy—for the sake of a father figure, was the toughest time of my life. Don't get me wrong, I loved my boyfriend at the time, but we were not a good fit for each other at that time in our lives. But I was blessed to have someone that would be good to my son and teaching him many things that have made him a wonderful and talented adult now.

Also, can we just pause to say how much we love Tidwell's relationship with his wife, as much as we love what he has with Jerry? He's a good friend and funny as all get out. Recovering from a football injury scare while playing a televised game, emotions are flying high. While Rod becomes very emotional, showing all his affection to his wife over the phone, we see a light go off in Maguire's head, realizing his need for love, and the wife he realizes he still. Tidwell has no shame in showing his love and adoration for his wife, and we love it. Jerry realizes that is what he had in Dorothy, though this is a movie, we just need to let it be said that is not always the case in real life. There are some men who will just never see it. Ever. And we should stop pretending that they will, as we lose time holding out for them thinking that they will.

You don't complete me

Finally relenting to joining her sisters' divorce recovery (and sometimes a bit men-bashing) group, she just finishes admitting that men are the enemy, but continues on in announcing that she still loves the enemy. Enters Jerry Maguire. The girls aren't having it. He, however, proceeds to tell Dorothy, who is still his wife—in front of her sister along with the others in the recovery group, that he's not letting her get rid of him. For the first time, her sister is actually moved by something he says. Telling her he misses his wife, and that he loves her, he concludes with "You complete me." Her response? It's the line we've jokingly said ever since this box-office hit was released, "Shut up...you had me at 'hello.'"

Cyndi: This saying has played the culprit in the minds and hearts of many women—and men, for that matter. One person can't ever "complete" you. Ever. You, friends, must be your own whole complete person ... on your own. If you're half a person, and you end up with a half person, that will lead to catastrophe. You must be complete in yourself, *for* yourself, *by* yourself. The person you marry should also be a whole person. Period. May the days be demolished where we think a man will complete us. If you go into a relationship with that notion, you'll be in for a rude awakening. You complete you. And if you're a person of faith like me, God completes me and in Him, I work on becoming a whole person. But to put all that pressure on someone else, isn't cool. No other human being will ever complete you. Period.

Ivette: No one can complete you. I didn't learn this until much later in life. I grew up thinking that a husband, children, and a house would complete me. We are made to live life with a partner, that's why God made Eve for Adam. But until you have found all the answers to some of the questions we've been asking, and you find out who you are, you may always have that void in your heart of feeling incomplete. Good news, if I could find myself in all the mess I grew up in and all the ridiculous situations I put myself through, you can do it as well. And I can promise that once you complete yourself, you will never find validation in a quote like that again. It did take a long time for me to find myself and feel comfortable being single or doing things on my own until that special person came into my life. Dorothy took a chance with Jerry, and I can appreciate that, but still, for me the most painful point in this movie was watching the video of the wedding. I don't know that I would be okay with that playing over and over in my mind. I can still remember the way my husband looked at me as my dad and son escorted me down the aisle and the tears of joy that we shared as he and my son hugged at the altar when he gave me away. Priceless!

The rest, as they say, is a happy ending, but there is so much here to revisit and reflect on. If you related to this character, we would love for you to re-read it, allowing some of the key nuggets to be reinforced in your heart until you let it seep in. Here is a recap of the most important nuggets of wisdom—even if you're not a single mom:

- If you are a single mom, your #1 priority is your children—not your sex life.
- If you are a single mom, protecting your children from harm, as well as neglect, should be your primary focus as their mom.
- If you are a single mom, your primary focus should not be finding a man to make or keep you happy, or from feeling lonely. Change your thinking and be present with your children, finding the beauty in who they are, and special things they do. Find ways to do fun activities that will plant memories in their hearts and minds to last a lifetime.
- Marrying or dating someone does not abolish loneliness. You can be married and still feel alone. Learning how to be comfortable as a single woman is sure to set you up for a strong romantic relationship or marriage.
- A man will never be able to complete you. That is a sappy made-up concept in this film, but it's not true. You can become complete and whole on your own. Another human person will never be able to complete you. End of story.

"You'll never find anyone who is as good for you as I am, to believe in you as much as I do or love you as much."

Katie Morosky,
The Way We Were

Katie Morosky, A Contentious Advocate Who is Desperate for Just One Man

The Way We Were

This love story features Jewish beauty, Katie Morosky, played by Barbra Streisand, and Hubbell Gardiner, played by Robert Redford. Katie is a brave, charismatic, intelligent college student very much committed to her socially charged causes that push against the majority. Headed for a successful future and very much the All-American Boy, we find a carefree Hubbell—a jock and the school's star athlete, whose neutral stance on politics drives Katie bananas. At odds with one another for the first few moments of the movie, they couldn't be more opposite, yet they find themselves equally intrigued with one another at various points of their lives. Though his behavior and that of his friends tend to remind us of high schoolers more than college students, Hubbell is drawn to Katie's political activism, as are we. He has his friends, and she has hers; he's the life (and the looks) of the party, she's all work and no play. Initially not impressed with either Hubbell or his friends, he begins to peak Katie's interest. Not only was he witty, but there was an innocence and insecurity about him, hiding behind that beautiful face accented by his boyish grin. Between his friendliness and charm, he becomes more appealing to Katie just about the time they're ready to graduate.

Even amidst their social, political, educational, and societal differences, their onscreen chemistry is undeniable. While it's clear to see there is a definite connection between the two, what's even more clear from the very beginning is that these two aren't meant to be. She comes across angry and even a little rude. Him–not so much. Applauding his writing, they chat a bit over a beer, he ties her shoelace, and they part ways...or so they think.

Now adults and in their careers, the two reconnect at a party where Katie spots a drunken Hubbell (red flag #1) as he's sitting up passed out at the bar (red flag #2). This is when Katie flashes back to their school dance, where we both see and feel the chemistry generated between the two. Giving her dance card to university-bestie Frankie, played by James Woods, the two are cuttin' up the rug and having great time. Dancing with another girl until someone cuts in, Hubbell turns around, spotting Katie slow dancing comfortably in the arms of her friend. You see a look of surprise come over Katie as Hubbell makes his way to her, now cutting in to dance with her. Guys know exactly what they want. He was laser-focused, making a bee line right to her. With a hint of nervousness, she accepts the invitation to dance, somewhat hesitant in responding to his lead. That only lasted for a few seconds. You could tell that a million things were going through her mind, and his. Can anyone relate? She finally locks eyes with him, his gaze never having left hers. Though she is nervous, she gains the confidence we have known her to have as he smiles at her in a way that only Robert Redford can do. (Beat.) Without any words, an entire conversation is had.

Enters Frankie. This was no time for him to cut in, but he knew exactly what he was doing. Only now, Katie is mesmerized, but not with Frankie. Somehow, Hubbell has come in and fully awakened the curiosity for him in her heart and now, though back in the arms of Frankie, she watches Hubbell's every move as he walks away disappearing into the crowd, seeing him no longer. Um, wait. Hold up. He just left? They literally just had the moment of a lifetime and without any second thought to it, he just disappears, and never turns back around to look at her (he's got some nerve). Not only did he just leave, but he left her and never looked back. Why was it so easy for him to just turn around and walk away after such an emotionally charged moment?

This is where we, as women, should be asking ourselves these same questions when we have similar experiences. Rather than realizing you just got served, you, instead, daydream about floating on the dancefloor with this beautiful man. Rather than coming to terms with the fact you—in a sense—were rejected, most of us choose to run off to Lala-land (not the movie), creating a story in our minds that probably does not even exist. We tend to want to make more of that moment, than what it was. A dance. Instead, we begin building something in our minds and hearts (let's be real), that could be more than what was really going on in his. For him, though the movie didn't quite allude to this, we believe this was just another dance. And we're fairly certain that in a real-life scenario, it would be the same. Unfortunately, this is one of the ways we set ourselves up for failure in our love lives—by conjuring up things in our mind based on a one-time exchange. Before we go any further, props to the cinematographer who so beautifully captured those unspoken moments between Katie and Hubbell as they danced. We could hear and feel everything they weren't verbally saying, leaving hopeless romantics wanting more.

Waiting to exhale

Now coming out of that flashback moment, Katie exhales at the sight of "Hubbell Gardiner," her former college-classmate, who is now passed out sitting at the bar of a night club. It's a classic case of girl-sees-boy who is all-too-thrilled about the delusion she conjured up in her mind years ago at their school dance. Why would she think that she could recreate or continue a moment forgotten on the dance floor by Hubbell all those many years ago? Had there been a connection? Yes, but apparently after they danced, that connection had ended. It was over the moment he turned around and walked away.

So often we find that, as women, we quickly return to a romantic scenario or memory that once gave us all the feels mustered up in this short-lived moment in time. "We clearly had a strong connection—anyone looking from the outside in, could see it. He had even made the first move. So why is it that I was ghosted by the guy that couldn't take his eyes off me?" So now here we are. He is standing right in front of us. We could do one of three things—1) Be cordial, and greet him, chat for a few, and move on; 2) Approach him, greet him and invite him over to your place for an after-dance drink; 3) Ignore him, acting as if he were invisible. He did walk away from you after all, never giving you another thought. In this case, Katie forgets that he ever ghosted her after that heated moment and wanting to rekindle a flame that had been out for quite some time, she hurriedly approaches him, paying no attention to his present state-of-being, as if to say, "Heyyy, Hubbell. It's me, Katie! Do you remember our last dance?" Have you ever been this girl?

Cyndi: That happened to me once in grad school. A guy I had a crush on, came to my work, pointed at me, made a bee line for me with his eyes never leaving mine, walked up to me, asked me out and then that was it. Our schedules never aligned, and yet I was still somehow replaying that scene over and over in my mind. For months. So much so, that I finally chased him down, finding his number even *after* we graduated. Had I known then what I know now, that wouldn't have happened. It turned out, there was nothing there. He had ghosted me for a reason. He wasn't into me. I vowed to never be that woman again. And yet, I found myself being that same girl several years later.

It would do us well to start a journal solely about the mistakes we have made that we *know* we never want to make again. This way, when we start dating a potential person, we can go back to that journal reminding ourselves of things we've done in the past that we never want to repeat in our lives.

Katie notices he's with a girl who is very much into him, but it doesn't seem to faze her. Katie's boss takes the girl for a spin on the dance floor, leaving Katie alone with Hubbell, whose eyes are still closed. She is smiling a bit too much for our liking—especially since he is still passed out drunk and has absolutely no idea that she's even there. So embarrassing. She reaches out to touch his beautiful locks of blonde hair. Unable to resist his boyish charm even while passed out, Katie makes the first move. We cringe. "Hubbell, Hubbell," she says. She's older, more sophisticated now with her hair done, makeup on and dressed very fashionably all the way down to her shoes. Inebriated, he slowly opens his eyes, and what happens after this is so sad to watch, but it's nothing new under the sun as it happens daily, time and time again, all over the world. "Hey," he replies almost a frat-boy-type chuckle, "What do ya know? Did I fall asleep?" Katie in a smitten-stupor replies— in what is meant to be a sexy voice, "I think so." You *think* so? Girl, he is passed out while sitting on a bar stool. Why are you smitten with him? He's passed out drunk. Wake up, Katie. Wake up, sisters! This is not attractive at all—it doesn't matter how blue his eyes are, how adorable his dimples are, or how he couldn't take his eyes off you that one time you danced years ago. Now is not the time to reignite what might have been but never was. And yet, she attempts to.

Eager to get him to her place, they get into a taxi with her boss until they are dropped off at her place and she runs up the stairs ahead of him to make sure all is well in her apartment (as if this guy will even remember where he is or if your place was acceptable). It's girl-talk time. Come on, would this be you? Would you—in your right mind—be running to make sure your place is on point for this man who is about to come on over? We hope you answer is "no," and that you'd have some wisdom in this situation. She has tossed any wisdom out the door, and he is on his way up. Finally making it to her floor, he enters the apartment with a look that says it all—if he doesn't find a bathroom, he's going to throw up all, which is exactly what he does. This is how drunk he is. What a total turn-off. And if it isn't, it should be! We have both been this drunk in our much younger years, and it was not pretty. Nothing about being drunk ever is. You have poor judgment, leading to making horrible decisions, you sometimes don't remember things, it is harmful, unsafe and you feel awful the morning after. So, while Hubbell is praying to the porcelain god, Katie's in dreamland getting a pot of tea (or coffee) ready for him in the kitchen. The coffee wouldn't have been such a bad idea except that when she came out, she sees his clothes on the floor, trailing to her bedroom. Any plans to drinking coffee ended right here. She had most likely been hoping this would be that moment where they'd reconnect over conversation, but it wasn't. Disappointed, yet curious about his state-of-being, she walks into the room where the trail of clothes led to—and pauses, cautiously, she looks over to her bed, and there he is—passed out and, might we add, seemingly naked beneath her sheets. So, what would be the first thing that you do if you found this dreamy man asleep (and drunk) in your bed? He's asleep … and snoring.

Asleep and unaware

So, where do we go from here? Do we just shut the door and go to sleep on the sofa? Do we go back into the room, checking on him to make sure he hasn't thrown up while he was asleep? (That does happen and sadly, there are some who have died this way). Do you stay beside him to keep an eye on him? Do you take advantage of this situation he won't remember in the morning? How do you respond to this situation?

Cyndi: I experienced something so very similar to this with my college sweetheart before we started dating, very similarly to Katie and Hubble. We had gone out on a Saturday night for a night of dancing at an Elks Lodge in the area. I already had a crush on him, but he was a player and attracted many women, so I kindly took myself out of that equation. While we were at the dance, he let me know that he had had probably half a bottle of Hennessy with one of the girls, a fellow classmate we went to college with who also had a thing for him. Before I knew it, I was taking care of her as she was throwing up in the bathroom, and when I came out, I found him in a horrific state. He was just sitting in a chair against the wall, getting sick right there on the dance floor. He looked awful and as drunk as he was, I knew he was not the one who would be driving us home. We got her home safe and sound, making it all the way back to my house, where he'd initially picked me up. Only 18 at the time, I knew my mom would not be happy. At all. Still very inebriated and throwing up out the window all the way to my house, we put him on a sofa, bringing our kitchen trash can right by his side. You know who else was right by his side? Me. It wasn't the girl he decided to mack-out (different than making out) and get drunk with, it was me. The *last* thing on my mind was to take advantage of him. In fact, the thought never even crossed my mind (shame on you, Katie). All I wanted to do was help him, and make sure he was well-supervised while throwing up in his sleep. It was awful. He finally recovered the morning after with the horrible hangover which was to be expected. But by that time, I cared about him even more than I had before he made that stupid, and very unwise decision to get drunk on Hennessy. Though I did like it prior to his all-night vomiting, to this day, I can't stand the smell of the cologne he was wearing that night. Sorry, Lagerfeld.

Any of those would have been the decent thing to do, but it's not what Katie did. What she proceeded to do is something that had us screaming "no," feeling sick to our stomachs. She chose to take advantage of a drunk man while he was unconscious in her bed. She decided it was best to exploit him for her own curiosity and pleasure, even in his inability to make decisions. This is beyond being an opportunist. This is criminal. Don't get us wrong, there is nothing we'd love more than sliding into a bed with 500-thread-count Egyptian cotton sheets, but *not* beside a drunk man who is passed out, who is oblivious to your presence, and who is *not* your husband. Can someone say #metoo …? Wow. This scene is all wrong for so many reasons. But not for Katie. Nope, she goes for it. She approaches the bed and starts to undress quietly. Finally sliding in bed, making her way beneath the covers to lay down, the girl is grinning from ear to ear, as if to say, "I've been dreaming about this moment all my life." Like literally, her face says it all. We are cringing. It's embarrassing to watch. If this had happened in real life, and if it were the other way around (and it has happened), this would be a lawsuit with time locked up in prison.

If you think what we just mentioned was awkward, it gets even more uncomfortable for those watching the scene—especially once she's passed the timid phase of, "Should I or shouldn't I?" Initially reluctant (too late for that now), she starts touching his hair and, as she does, it causes him to move a bit closer to her, but the guy is still passed out and snoring. He's been snoring all along, and he probably smells a little like vomit. She doesn't mind. At all. Still sleeping and almost instinctively, he turns towards her, then cozying up to her, until his face was buried into her neck. If she had thought about stopping before, she wasn't stopping it now, as her arm is now under his neck, encouraging this by stroking his hair, slightly waking him out of his sleep, but get this–his eyes are still closed. Why? Because he's still drunk. Initially looking unsure, it is now evident that she has decided she wants this to happen. What in the world?! *Please*, don't be this girl. With his eyes STILL SHUT, they start going through the motions of having sex. Insert heavy breathing. She is in heaven. And just as she thinks it's going to go where she is hoping, all movement (on his end) stops. "Hubbell, Hubbell … it's Katie," she says. By now, a tear is streaming down her face. "You didn't know it was Katie?" Are you even kidding?! For being such a smart girl, are you seriously *asking* that? She knew he was drunk and not coherent enough to know anything about what was going on. And now she's upset and crying? *He* should be the one upset and crying. She just took full advantage of him as he was completely passed out drunk in her bed, and *that's* what she's worried about— that he didn't know it was *her*? You ought to be thanking your lucky stars that he passed out before you committed a crime. That's what you should be more concerned with. No doubt, if the shoes were reversed, there'd be an uproar, but something about it being a woman doing it to a man seems to make it "okay," especially for the hopeful romantics. NOT. It shouldn't be this way. She did not have his permission. She should have let him sleep it off. Don't be this girl.

The next morning, she is ironing his uniform shirt and has made an array of food and coffee for him. We take it from the heavy, hearty breakfast she's made him, she doesn't know a thing about being hungover (which is a good thing, but we're laughing just the same). She mutters several silly things, and he looks at her so very perplexed. We are cracking up at how confused he is by the things she says. Clearly, he has never known or spent too much time with the likes of Katie. Making his way to the door after putting his uniform back on, he says he has to get going. Of *course* he does. Starting to say goodbye at the door, he puts his hand out to shake hers as if they were just friends—never mind he was on top of her the night before. He doesn't even know what happened between the two of them. Without even a flinch, she pulls out a note from her bust with her various phone numbers in case he can't find a hotel the next time he's in town (he is stationed in Washington). As he starts walking down the stairs she says, "About last night...," interjecting he says, "I'm sorry. I've been falling asleep all over lately." Falling asleep? Is that what you call it? It is when you don't have a clue that you were sexually violated. How sad for *him*. "I hope my snoring didn't keep you awake," to which she replies, "That's ok. I like snoring." We are rolling our eyes, and literally want to shake her to her senses, because right now, she has none. Firstly, she should not treat last night as something casual. She full-on took advantage of a man who apparently still has no idea what happened to him. Yes, to *him*. It's not okay that the gender is reversed, ladies. As far as we're concerned, it's still sexual assault. Just because he responded to her after she knowingly undressed herself and got into bed with him while she was nude—in his drunken state—does not make it less criminal. Not only that, girl, get your head out of the clouds! He's trying to leave and is not trying to spend any more time with you at your apartment. If he's leaving, get a clue. Read the signs of his body language. He's not interested and would rather be somewhere else. And that's exactly what he does. He leaves her ... once again. See a pattern here, ladies?

So, we see a few major issues here with Katie. We hope you see them, too...

➢ She is fantasizing about Hubbell.

➢ She takes advantage of a vulnerable moment of another human being.

➢ She attempts to have sex with him with the chance that he won't even remember but is hopeful that he will (spoiler alert: he doesn't).

- She has a note tucked in her bust with all her numbers on it for him to call if he ever needs a place to stay while in town.
- She realizes that he in fact did not remember.
- She comments about liking his snoring to keep the conversation going.

Embarrassing, right? Yeah, we think so, too. Don't be this girl. And now, the story unfolds…

The meal that changed it all

Hubbell does end up reaching out to Katie at work, looking for a place to stay. There are no hotels to be found, so he calls Katie to see if he could stay at her place for the night. With sheer glee, she eagerly welcomes him, telling him he can get the key from her property manager. She is so excited.

Originally heading out to meet with friends, she persuades him to stay and eat the dinner for the two of them as she just bought groceries. She begged him to stay, listing all the things she bought from the market to make them dinner. "You've got to stay for supper … that's all there is to it!" He concedes, they have deep conversation, she builds him up, and as they wrap up this intimate conversation about his work, those attractions are strong again. That was the supper that changed everything. This meal opened the door to a new relationship for Hubbell and Katie, his number one fan in just about everything he does, but what she loved most—aside from his good looks—was his writing. "Your style is absolutely gorgeous … It is … It is gorgeous." She may be different than the others, and a bit uptight, but this man melts at the confidence she has in him. If there is one thing we *can* learn from Katie, it's this—to be your man's biggest cheerleader and believe in him. People don't like to be torn down—especially if he's your person. For Hubbell, it was hearing Katie say he must write another novel, because he was too good a writer not to. One minute, he's reaching out to stay at her place with no intention of even hanging out with her (in fact, he was *leaving* her place when she came home with the bag full of groceries), the next minute, he's leaning in to kiss her. Knowing this was going to be a committed relationship he warns her, "…but you mustn't be too serious." Katie replies, "I won't be." Oh boy, here it goes.

This is probably the one part of the movie where we both gave Katie a thumbs up. Not because of how she pleaded with him to stay for dinner, but because she is confident in what she knows about writing and builds him up as a good writer, as well. As women, we know the value of feeding a man's stomach, but she didn't *just* do that—she fed his ego and his soul. You can see the strength she gives him when she constructively criticizes his writing. Not only does he receive it, but he trusts her and inquires of her, asking her to tell him more. She tells him truthfully—yet gently—what she sees in his writing, and he is smitten by it. Hubbell is now falling for Katie. She's been into him for much longer than that.

I don't think we're going to make it

There's nothing like new romance. And many of us are suckers for falling in love with someone we've obsessed over for quite some time. While the same is true for Katie, she still can't seem to wrap her mind around Hubbell's circle of friends. Let's be real, if you're going to be in a relationship with someone, you'll not only be in a relationship with his family, but also with his friends—whether you like 'em or not. It would be wonderful if everyone got along with both sides, but we don't live in a perfect world, so we know that's not always possible. But even if it's undoable, fighting with his friends is not the key to a romantic match made in heaven. Unfortunately, for Katie, she had to learn this the hard way. Hubbell didn't just care about Katie, he loved her. You could see it in the genuine affection he had towards her—how he included her in the most intimate parts of his life. As in love as they were, Hubbell knew she was more than just a political advocate, she was an activist set on changing the world as she knew it. He was just along for the ride, and that wasn't in the cards for him. Not if he had anything to do with it. And this is where some of the trouble in the writers' paradise began. Katie is wound up so tight, she's not only riled up, but she has also now graduated into a habit of holding shouting matches with his friends she's annoyed with at *their* parties. She frequently makes scenes at friends' gatherings as if it were her home. If this is you, it might be a good to evaluate what gets you goin', noting what it is about it that gets you so upset, and what are some things you can do to turn it off when you are a guest at someone *else's* house. Nobody wants that at a festive event—especially when it's surrounding politics. No one had the backbone to go up against her, except for Hubbell. But it was one time too many. She'd made what he once enjoyed about their relationship, difficult and unpleasant.

Have you ever been in a relationship that took so much work it became too difficult to enjoy? Every little conversation or action turned into an argument or a fight? As much as Hubbell loved Katie, he was over her ranting, raving and adult temper tantrums. It was too much for him. It was too much for us. Watching on-screen, we were trying to find something to hide under, saying, "Oh my goodness…make it stop. Please!" Don't be this girl. There was one more party, but this time, she pushed him over the edge, to the degree that after cooling off for a few days, he stopped by her job telling her, "I don't think we're gonna make it, Katie." Honest. Brutally honest, but it was what she needed to hear. We're cracking up that she responds telling him that everything's too easy for him. "You really think you're easy?

Compared to what? The hundred-years' war? You're so ready to fight, you don't have time to understand anything," he chides her before leaving, listing the many things that have made their relationship so difficult.

He decides they're done, and though she seems to—at the time—accept it, what happens later that night is so embarrassing. Taking charge of the situation—once again—she calls him, crying for him to come over because of how upset she was at their breakup. Begging him, she pleads, saying, "I have to talk to my best friend about someone we both know ... can you come over please?" This is all too much for us to handle and if you've ever been this way with a man who wasn't your husband, that's a huge no-no. Men don't enjoy the neediness, especially when it's the icing on a cake only made from only one ingredient—begging. Sure, their ego might like it, but that's about it. A good friend, Brian, chimed in on this conversation sharing, "Oftentimes, neediness can feel difficult to a guy. There is a point when it's too much. You're needy all the time...and always complaining ... always nagging." We'll just leave it right here. Being the good guy that Hubbell is, he brings her sleeping pills, to which she has the courage to ask, "It's because I'm not attractive enough, isn't it ... I'm not attractive in the right way ... I don't have the right style ... for you, do I?" What he says next is shocking. "No, you don't have the right style ...," to which she immediately interjects, "I'll change." NO! Don't you dare change your style for a man. Girls, if he doesn't like your style, too bad. Now we're not saying not to have style. You do need to have that, but it needs to be your own, so that *you* feel good about you—*not* so that *he* can feel good about you, while you don't feel good about yourself. You are not a trophy piece.

Ivette: How are we so strong in some areas of our lives, but when it comes to looking a certain way for someone else—namely a guy, we just fold? I had a friend that became a boyfriend for a short time. He once told me that he would rather that I dress casually, wear no makeup and was quite detailed that he wanted to see me in Uggs and sweats or jeans and a pair of Vans, rather than dressed up at all. At first, I thought, are you new? I'm Hispanic and although I have my tomboyish side, I live for all-things-bling and that includes making sure that I am showered, dressed, and pressed, ready for that unexpected guest that might stop by (my mom taught me that). But I did what he wanted anyway. Why? Maybe a moment of weakness. Friends, don't be this girl, be YOU! Do what makes you happy and the right man will love you just as you are. That's the man I have now, he doesn't like the bling, but he knows I do; therefore, he just lets me be me.

Hubbell didn't want her to change. We love that he didn't. He felt that she was her own person and should keep her style, Pouting, she responds, "But then I won't have you. Why can't I have you? Why?" Isn't interesting that a woman who is so seemingly strong in every other area, including her opinions, is so weak when it comes to this one man. She wanted him so badly. Have you ever wanted to be in a relationship so badly, that you were willing to succumb and settle into being someone else than the you you really were? What about wanting to be with someone so badly, you were willing to sacrifice everything, no matter what the cost? Your true joy, happiness, or your actual self? What Katie is proposing will cripple her and who she genuinely is. Obsession began peeking out from behind the curtain. Please, have some dignity, Katie and put that away so that you don't have to be with a man who you have to beg and convince to be with you. Well, she did beg, and it worked. She didn't have the right style. To him, she pushed too hard, but that didn't matter. He came back, and off they moved to a beach house for him to write in Hollywood— a place and subject that originally was a huge point of contention for her.

Deaf, dumb and blind

Now Mrs. Hubbell Gardiner, she has taken on a new role as wife, but she could stay quiet for only but a minute, before falling back to her old ways. Taking a stand for what was right, fighting against what people were calling communism at the time, she was very vocal about it. You can't change who you really are because at some point it will either want to surface, or you will fight so hard to keep it down, that you begin feeling oppressed and depressed–like a prisoner locked in a cage. Oh, please don't do that. We've both been there. You were not created to be locked in a cage.

Cyndi: I remember being in a relationship where I was fully not able to be myself. He had let me know early on that I was a little too loud and talked too much. When we were out in public or with others, he didn't hesitate to shush me. Because I really liked him, I started making deliberate choices to change the things about me he did not like. The problem with that was that little by little I began to work hard at not being the person I really was. If there's anything I've learned through all these years of living, is that I should be able to me—no matter who I'm with. Is there a time and a place for everything? Yes, of course. I'm not saying that if you love to dance on tables, to do that in the middle of a business meeting, but what I am saying is that you should be able to truly be yourself with that person. You should be able to laugh as loud as you normally would, eat the way you normally would, while eating the *things* you normally would—being free to be you. Don't change who you are to accommodate someone else's preferences. Don't sacrifice the freedom of being the real you. People-pressure is overrated. I know now—even in my 50s—that there is a person out there for me who will love and accept me the way I am. Furthermore, this is true of those in my inner circle, as well. I heard it best when interviewing a very dear filmmaking-producer friend of mine on my talk show who said, "I'm not for everybody." I loved that saying and it has stuck with me since. You may not be for everyone, in fact, you won't be. Get that into your mind now. But those you are meant *for* you, will love, and accept you just as you are.

Ivette: This takes me back to the relationship with my son's biological father (I keep using this reference, because we call "dad" someone else). Before I became a mom, which changed everything about who I was and how I would allow people to treat me. I had to be good with living his life. He was in a band and very popular with the women as you can imagine. It was all about his practice times, his gigs, his friends, even his choice to be a vegetarian (yes, I even did that for a time). When he wanted to be clean in his lifestyle, we would be clean, not drinking, etc. ... But if he wanted to do anything recreational, he would do it and not allow me to. Yes, I said "allow me to". We were living together when I was pregnant, and I had horrible all-day sickness (not just morning sickness). One night he had a gig, and our roommate was having a party. Although I wasn't going to go to the show, I was excited that I could at least have some interaction with other friends that were coming over. But I was wrong. He actually told me I had to stay in the room and to only come out to use the restroom if I needed to. I was not to interact with the party. Can you believe that? And guess what, for most of the night, I stayed in the room, afraid that his roommate might tell him that I didn't listen. I have no idea what was happening to me in this season, but I was letting him dictate my every move. Somehow, I felt like I was the lucky one, because I had what all the other girls wanted. But apparently, they were getting a little piece of him also, maybe the good side of him while I was home dealing with the side of him that had me completely broken and caused so much stress and depression during my pregnancy. Have you experienced something similar? If he's breaking you, best to let him go. Please don't let this happen to you, you are not someone's puppet or trophy. You are fearfully and wonderfully made, stand up for yourself and I'll say it again, know your worth.

We are all for being who you are, but we want to be sure to take note that there is a time and place for everything, and that's something that every person should learn in life early on. Should we advocate things we are passionate about? Absolutely. Should we repress our thoughts and opinions, not saying things that we should? No way. But Katie goes beyond that, and though it may have been tolerable for Hubble when they were dating, it's a whole different ball game when it directly impacts or negatively affects your spouse. One of the things so very difficult to watch was how hard she would push. We actually felt a little suffocated for Hubble. While we love Katie's passion, she kept on, and on, and on... almost like a continual dripping of a faucet that you just want to stop. What it reminded us of, was a proverb that says, "A continual dripping on a very rainy day, and a contentious woman are alike; Whoever restrains her restrains the wind, And grasps oil with his right hand." (Prov.

27: 15, 16, NKJV) But that's not all Proverbs tell us about a woman who is contentious. It also says that it is "Better to live on a corner of the roof than share a house with a quarrelsome wife." (Prov. 21:9, NIV)

Being vocal and fighting for your cause is one thing, but being a contentious woman about it is another. For Hubble, this was a problem, and it began to wear him down. Ladies, if this is one of your primary characteristics, it would behoove you to take some time to learn how to advocate, minus the contention. Be passionate but not quarrelsome. Be unrelenting, yet with grace. Katie had fire, but day after day, month after month, year and after, it wasn't so cute, and like many men might be pushed to do, Hubbell looked for peace and quiet elsewhere—in another woman. You already know how we both feel about infidelity, so we're not at all excusing what he did. They'd just worked so hard to be where they'd landed. No matter what Hubbell did—good or bad, he could do no wrong. She always saw him as a "...good, Gentile boy." Has that ever been you? Have you loved someone so much that you overlook the horrible things they are doing to you? If not, that is wonderful news, and we are so thankful that you have not yet had to experience that. If you have loved someone so much that you turn a blind eye to their behavior and the way they treat you, here is where we'd love for you to read the following questions, reflect, journal, and write.

Why is it that you do that? What is it about him that makes you stay in a relationship that treats you so poorly? Is it fear? Is it not knowing what others will say or think? Is it that it will leave you without financial security? What is it? We'd love for you to be at a place where this not your situation and what you are experiencing. No matter what your life has looked like up to this point—even in the most horrific of situations—there is a life and a love that is beautiful and pure. You are deserving of that life and love. If it's strength that you need to move forward, giving you the courage to finally say, "enough is enough," one of our favorite scriptures comes out of Joshua, and strengthens us in the midst of fear and intimidation. Again— even if you don't read the Bible, this verse is so empowering and is the reason we are sharing it.

"Be strong and courageous. Do not be afraid; do not be discouraged, for the Lord your God will be with you wherever you go." (Joshua 1:9, NKJV) So many times we don't move forward because we are paralyzed with fear. But this verse has time and time again given us both the strength to move out and move forward in the things we are afraid to do. If you've ever heard the phrase, "Do it afraid," that's exactly what it is. But we do it afraid with a confidence that we are not alone, and that God is with us, backing us up every step of the way. This is what has given us the courage to do the things we've been too afraid to do. Fear will always be a thing. What helps is when you can close your eyes and visualize you doing it.

There is something about visualization. It's powerful and when you do it, you'll find that your confidence increases. Why? Because you've seen yourself doing it. The more you visualize it, the more your faith will grow. You just have to determine whether or not you will let it have power and dominion over you. Our response to that? Another favorite that gives us strength, which says, "For God has not given us a spirit of fear, but of power and of love and of a sound mind." (2 Timothy 1:7, NKJV)

The conversations between the two of them was solid, yet heartbreaking. It made me wish that's what every man would do, instead of just keeping it quiet. This might even help to reduce or eliminate unfaithfulness and cheating. Had he just been up front with her from the get-go when he couldn't take it much longer, it may have helped, but who knows? She returns to the idea of behaving better so that things would be smoothed over so they could continue on as husband and wife. "When you love someone from Roosevelt to me, you go deaf, dumb and blind," Hubbell said to Katie. Here they were again—at this crossroad, except now, they're married ... and she's pregnant. The repression and holding back has surfaced. In need-to-have conversations, Hubbell finally comes clean, sharing that he never even wanted to finish his book, that's what she wanted him to do—among other things. For whatever reason, she pushed him too hard. Supporting your man is a good thing, but not to the point when you're pushing what you want for him, more than what *he* wants for himself. Sounds like she didn't know what he really wanted. Everything from writing his book, to them going to France, those were all the things she was driving to happen—her desires, not his. Guess it's hard to tell a strong woman with an unwavering opinion, "No." So here they are now—having a real heart-to-heart. Sad to hear the man you've loved obsessively after all these years tell you, "... it was *never* uncomplicated." How did she not see or know this? Maybe she saw it all along but refused to believe or accept it. If you sense something, it's always best to bring it up. Don't sweep it under the rug. This response it damaging and can also be dangerous. Because we love who they could be, we too, are despondent at where they've landed after working so hard on their relationship after all these years. But didn't he tell her that earlier on? Quick to blame it on the girl he ran to, he let her know, "Katie, what's wrong with us has nothing to do with another girl."

Agreeing to stay together until after she has the baby, this beautiful and messy relationship of love and tension ends. As romantics, we are heartbroken for them. But they were wrong from the start. Why he doesn't get to see their daughter, Rachel, on the regular, we never quite know. Maybe it was the era. As the movie ends, we see Hubbell and Katie running into each other in front of the Plaza one last time. Now with the new Mrs. Gardiner, he seems content and Katie is natural again—no longer straightening her hair with an iron. Hubbell seems to notice and tells her it's pretty. Receiving the compliment, she heads to her post, in opposition of the new war, and he does what any loving ex-husband would—he comes back for one final goodbye. Still very much for Hubbell, she tells him, "Your girl is lovely, Hubbell." They're looking into each other's eyes, taking it all in, saying what they verbally couldn't—the moment magnified by the song from the soundtrack, "Memories," and of course, the waterworks are in full effect. She watches him leave one last time. Oh, how we wish she would not have to see this once again from the same man who has done this to her time and time again—from that first dance they danced together in college, to him leaving her throughout their relationship, and for the last time in New York City.

Though this relationship was true love, after being tested and tried, it was clearly an incompatible one. Hubbell wasn't for Katie, and Katie wasn't for Hubbell. The attraction was strong, you could feel it coming off the screen, but with their water and oil combo, it could never be—no matter how hard they tried. Better to not force something you already know is not a good fit from the start, no matter how badly you want it.

Characteristics we don't need to inherit from Katie:

- Being wound so tight you always come across angry to almost everyone.
- Assuming the worst in people because of their behavior or because they don't have the same worldview, political or other views as you.
- Ruining someone else's party, arguing with the host, or speaking out of line at a party *you're* not hosting.
- Seeing people through your lens from the past.
- Don't say things just for shock value. Enjoy those around you—be present in the moment with no ulterior motive.
- Know your place. Making speeches at a party you're invited to by someone else is not the time or place to advocate your platform.
- Pick your battles. Not everything has to be one, and you don't have to be so right, that you're wronging the relationship.

The *One* Must-Have Song from this Movie: *The Way We Were* by Barbra Streisand

By the way, while we're positive there are other things she'd rather talk about, if we ever have the chance to meet or talk to Barbra, we'd love to know what it was like to kiss one of the most beautiful men on the planet. And can someone please tell us why she (as Katie) was smoking and drinking when she was *pregnant*!? Don't' be this girl.

"The most exciting, challenging and significant relationship of all is the one you have with yourself. And if you find someone to love the you you love, well, that's just fabulous."

– Carrie Bradshaw,
Sex and the City

Carrie Bradshaw, Samantha Jones, Miranda Hobbes & Charlotte York, Four Fabulous Girls in Search of Love They're Not Ready For

Sex and The City TV Series (1998 – 2004)

We wanted to save the biggest (and for many perhaps even the best) for last. We knew the final chapter couldn't be about any other than four gal pals centered in NYC— Carrie, her girls: Miranda, Samantha, and Charlotte—and a guy named, "Big." For a television series that debuted over 25 years ago, the footprints of *Sex and The City* remain in the hearts and lives of both women and men around the world, impacting many as the show about four friends explored love, friendship, fashion, and the given, sex. A significant force in pop culture, it is likely that none was more influential on single women in our decade than a TV show written about four girls navigating through single life, than Sex and The City (SATC). Watching the lives of NYC's "It Girl," and her three besties portrayed against the backdrop of glamour, fashion, and love in the Big Apple as they explored real-life topics through their diverse experiences ranging from, "Can you be friends with an ex?" to being "Frenemies," and everything in between, this show revolutionized the way women saw themselves, influencing many to see themselves in a whole new light. An extremely appealing show—thanks to the casting of SATC's leading ladies and the show's witty writing, if it only revolved around strong friendships, careers and personal style & fashion, empowering women to assert their independence, that'd be one thing; however, the reason why this show made significant waves for the six years it ran its course? Amidst all the fashion, beauty, and glamour this TV show had to offer, it glamorized cheating, having affairs with married men and casual sex hook-ups, impacting women in navigating relationships, dating and sex.

Now, before you get on the defense about a show that you may feel interpersonally connected with or impacted by, in a recent interview, "Why Sarah Jessica Parker Keeps Playing Carrie Bradshaw,"[17] in The New Yorker, Sarah Jessica Parker, herself, shares that she "... could never do any of that stuff in my life ... it would be immoral ... unprincipled ... ". Isn't that something—that the star playing the lead character has shared that in real life, she couldn't do much of what she portrayed on the show, mostly due to the immorality; and yet, her character makes it all look so appealing. So much so, that the doctrine of SATC lives on even decades since the show's last season. Our thoughts about being a girl looking for love? If it's true love your heart is desiring, the casual sex hook-up isn't the way to go about finding it. Thanks to SATC, the approach of many women has changed not only in the way we approach singlehood, marriage, their careers, and fashion, but also love. Because of the direct impact this series had in shaping those entertained by it, we couldn't agree more.

Keep it classy, ladies

Taking love, friendship, city life and fashion to levels we'd never seen on screen came through four girls known as Charlotte York, Miranda Hobbes, Samantha Jones, and Carrie Bradshaw. Back in the day we caught glimpses of this in the lives of Blanche, Rose, Dorothy, and Sophia in *The Golden Girls*, but *Sex and the City* took the single girls' nighttime city lifestyles to a whole new level, focusing on the intersecting lives of these four fashionable and close-knit friends, whose conversation and actions give the "boys locker room," a run for their money with talk that was crude and in some cases, even vulgar. It's not to say that women shouldn't be able to talk real talk—especially with their girlfriends—but if we're trying to keep it classy, mimicking their conversations and the content in their quest and search for love – that won't do. We couldn't think of another show in this century as notably influential in tackling real-life issues for single women yet exemplifying the blind leading the blind. Are they deeply committed to each-other as soul-sisters who love each other through thick and thin? Yes. But we realized early on that we wouldn't necessarily want the advice given, as

17   Syme, Rachel, "Why Sarah Jessica Parker Keeps Playing Carrie Bradshaw," *apple.news*, June 19, 2023.

they made some of the worst choices a single girl could ever make, that is—until they each started settling down. Prior to that, we witness heartbreak after heartbreak, sexual behavior that is sometimes demoralizing, men being treated horribly, vulgarity, and unfaithfulness ... just to name a few. Though not a Romcom, the show is a Dramedy (Drama-Comedy), and so we felt not only would this work within the confines of our subject matter, but we could think of no greater group of supportive gal-pals to shed some light on to help us clearly see characteristics we should not strive to emulate, giving us plenty of reasons why we wouldn't want to be these girls. If it's true love you're after, respect you're looking for, the casual sex hook-up isn't the way to go about finding it. As casual and destructive as it may be, these four ladies forever changed the way real-life women approached singlehood, men, marriage, their careers, fashion, and love—and in some ways, broke some taboos. But were they taboos needing to be broken? And with that, we take a closer look into the lives of Carrie, Samantha, Miranda, and Charlotte. We know there are four of 'em, but don't worry, we'll make it quick!

FASHION IN THE CITY
~ Carrie ~

Fashion-forward to the umpteenth degree, Carrie Bradshaw—SATC's central figure—quickly became an icon for many single women both, in the city and country, alike, as she narrates insights on love, dating and relationships. From the start we find Carrie not only searching for answers pertaining to love for her column, "Sex and the City," but we find that she herself—a hopeless romantic—appears to be on a quest for love herself, dating roughly 28 men for the entire span of the show. We love Carrie. What's not to like? She's a good friend with depth, compassion, wit, an incredibly high sense of fashion, talent and the list goes on and on. But even for our beloved girl, that's about 25 men too many in our book. She gives great advice in her column, but what we see play out in her own love-life isn't quite as composed. Do as I say, but don't say as I do. We find that through the course of those years, she is on a romantic rollercoaster that encompasses finding love, cheap sex, disappointment, big love, rejection, off again, new love, on again, infidelity, off again, older love, adventure, and big love. Though we understand this makes for great television, it would be detrimental—destructive even—for a single woman to romantically take on all that Carrie did.

Ivette: Beautiful, talented, fashionable—-however she is still filled with self-doubt and over analyzes everything which leads to so many bad decisions and heartache. Although I felt connection or relatable moments with each one of these women, I think that self-doubt and trying to analyze everything is why I related to Carrie most of all.

Similar to Ivette, there are many who could relate to Carrie because they've personally ridden romantic rollercoasters of their own. While her narration on the actual series makes for some great girls' night out convos in her reflective questions—in most cases providing insight based on what she or her girls have just experienced, or what they've gone through—it's not enough to merely ask the questions if some of what is being discussed isn't personally being applied to our own lives. She exemplifies that while single women can be successful in their careers, they could very well simultaneously, be floundering in their romantic relationships, finances, and other areas of the lives. So, the question is, is that truly success? We see this taking place in Carrie's life for six (episodic) years. And that's no way for a girl as fabulous as Carrie to be, and the reasons below are no way for a girl as incredible as you, to be either.

Settling for the crumbs: On-again, off-again with Big

Carrie has a pretty good head on her shoulders and while we applaud her charisma, incredible writing talent, smarts, generosity, and independence, it is her love-life that we frown on for a majority of the show's entirety. Sensible and regularly speaking into the lives of New Yorkers through her weekly column, one of the main areas we see Carrie struggling is in her quest for romance—especially when it comes to her on-again, off-again boyfriend, Big (played by Chris Noth). If there ever was a clear-cut case of being strung along for six L-O-N-G years, it was in Carrie's relationship with Big.

From the first season where their befriending turned into something a little more, it was evident that though she caught his attention, she was way more into him than he was into her. A prestigious man of wealth in New York City, he was no stranger to women in the Big Apple and had a bit of a reputation for it. Smells like drama. She is drawn to him like a moth to a flame, or a mosquito to a Zapper, embarrassing herself in more ways than Carrie would like to admit. From bringing her things over to his apartment, only to have him bring everything back to her in a bag, to running into him and his new gal, Natasha at The Hamptons when she thought he was in Paris, it is one bad sitch after the other. We would have already said, "adios," after, but did that stop Carrie? Nope. And why not? Because Big was her greatest weakness.

The party's over: Big's getting married...It's time to move on

There's nothing more painful to watch than someone tightly holding on to someone, refusing to let them go, while they intentionally slip right out of their hands. Such was the case with Carrie with regards to Big. We see the pain or rejection and the struggle she endures as she navigates the news— of Big and Natasha are engaged.

Cyndi: It was bad enough when Carrie had the nerve to confront Big outside his engagement party while his fiancée waited in the car, but the manner in which she continued on with him after the engagement was truly catastrophic. There's nothing worse than a woman unwilling to face the hard facts: He's marrying someone else, and that person isn't you. Yes, some of these principles we are pointing out are repetitive. And do you know why? Because even after reading just one example, some of you may find yourself in a place very similar to Carrie— asking, "Why wasn't it me?" to that someone you loved, but who has moved on, and is now marrying someone else. If you, like Carrie, are the one being left behind, we are not saying that it's easy, we are not saying that we don't sympathize with the pain you may be feeling and experiencing. But if he has moved on, then girl ... get a grip and do *whatever* it is you need to do to get that beautiful heart of yours healed and whole so that you can move on. Stop the replaying. Stop looking at photos. Stop smelling his clothes. Get off his social media handle. Stop texting him. Stop texting her. If any of these sound like you, then we are gently letting you know, you should meet on the regular with a counselor or someone who can objectively listen and give you the help that is needed. This person shouldn't be your besties or your tribe. You should be meeting with someone who can help you heal and move on. And hopefully— prayerfully—you will receive everything you need to keep moving forward, not ever looking back. One of my life-verses (already shared earlier in the book) that has helped me: "I know that I still have a long way to go. But there is one thing I do: I forget what is in the past and try as hard as I can to reach the goal before me." (Philippians 3:13, ERV)

Cheating on her boyfriend, Aidan Shaw

We loved her when she was with Aidan. He was a good guy with a big heart. Although Carrie cheated on him while having an affair with Big while *he* was married to Natasha, we're singling this one out. We're singling out her cheating on Aidan (played by John Corbett) because aside from the fact that Big was already a married man, she was cheating on the one *she* was with. If you are in a relationship with someone and decide to see another person, then you are not being faithful. You are cheating. While some of the societal norms have changed stating that infidelity is okay if you're not married, it is not. It is never okay. Lying to your person is deceptive and wrong. A hot mess will come of it—take our words. That person deserves to know the truth. You already know we like the Book of Proverbs because of the mega-wisdom written in it. This particular verse says, "But a man who commits adultery has no sense; whoever does so destroys himself. Blows and disgrace are his lot, and his shame will never be wiped away." (Proverbs 6:32-33 NIV)

Listen, if you think it's exciting to cheat or you justify why you should be with someone else when you're already married or in a relationship, you've got it wrong and are gravely mistaken. It's interesting when talking with someone who feels justified to cheat; yet when the shoe is on the other foot, they're upset and devastated. The Golden Rule (also known as Luke 6:31, NIV) is simple: "Do to others as you would have them do to you." Have you made a vow to be loyal and faithful to someone? Best to stick to that vow and do everything you can to adhere to it. *No* grass is greener on the other side. Grass is grass, even if it's on a different lawn. Keep what is yours and let what belongs to someone else stay with them. Carrie needed to let Big work out his own issues with Natasha—no matter what he said (or did) to Carrie. If you have to do it behind closed doors or "in the dark," 9 out of 10, it's not something you should be doing. That doesn't just apply to cheating or having an affair. The same goes for everything else you may be hiding. Anything that must be done "in secret" probably shouldn't be something you're doing in the first place. Their illicit affair didn't just affect them, it destroyed Big's marriage to Natasha, and left Aidan devastated. No one wins when cheating and adultery exist. And when there are children involved, it's even more detrimental. Please don't be this girl.

The thing about on-screen romance, is that in many cases, the writers do such a great job in pulling the viewer into the characters, it sometimes has us rooting for the wrong thing. When everything came crashing down for Big and Carrie again, is it just us or were some viewers rooting for things to still work out between them?

Cyndi: I actually couldn't stand that Carrie and Big were together while he was married to Natasha, and she was with Aidan. It was so unfair and unkind to them both. My heart when out to Natasha—especially when she caught them. She was the one who doubly suffered, ending up injured, as well while she was the one who was innocent. I was so ticked. Think about this—if the person you're cheating with is cheating behind his wife or person's back, will he one day do the same to you? Do not be fooled, we reap what we sow. So, sow the stuff you want to see harvested and reaping in your life. We've said it before, and we'll say it again. Now is always a good time to change. It's never too late and you're not too far gone.

Spending so much on designer shoes that she had no money for a down payment on an apartment

Now that Carrie and Aidan were no longer a thing, he was moving out and she now needed to either buy her apartment or move. Buying her apartment was what she wanted to do, but she had no money for the down payment. She had a steady job that paid her bills and bought her the most fabulous fashion money could buy, but she didn't have any funds to buy her apartment. Confessing to Miranda that she spent roughly about $400 on each pair of shoes, Miranda pointed out to Carrie that she'd spent so much on shoes, it would have been the equivalent of a down payment on a place to live. "100 times 400, there's your down payment." Carrie's reply was priceless (no pun intended). "I spent $40,000 on shoes, and I have no place to live?" Here's where our shoes come off. Don't be the girl who owns 100+ designer shoes at roughly $400 each, that you have no money to purchase something you actually *need*...like a car or a home. It pays to save. If you can do both, great! But if you must pick only one and you love fashion, be intentional about saving, and shop that clearance rack.

Carrie Bradshaw is a trendsetter and quite possibly the most influential girl on-screen in this century when it comes to love and fashion, but the trends we most certainly do not want to follow is in her willingness to be strung along for six years, being the other woman, cheating on her boyfriend, and being financially irresponsible.

SEX IN THE CITY
~ Samantha ~

The most controversial of the four, Samantha Jones, is a force to be reckoned with, and any man within the same vicinity of her would frequently find himself caught in her seducing web, leading to one thing: sex. It is no surprise that when you hear the TV show title, *Sex and the City*, to many the sex *is* Samantha. Samantha *is* the sex. Now granted, all four friends dabbled in it and with various partners, but for Samantha (played by Kim Cattrall), it was the essence of who she was. Though successful in her career, her lack of vulnerability—coupled with her voracious appetite for sex—interfered with finding true love, but also landed her a reputation that in some cases, negatively affected her career, as well. Don't be this girl.

Turning to sex and running away from love

An extremely promiscuous character, Samantha spends a good portion of the entire series jumping from one bed to the next. While there were two men that captured her heart and one who we know of earlier on who broke it, Samantha is the only one of the girls, who consistently pretends to not have feelings or care about how she is being treated—which is primarily as a sex object. Because of this, she is treated poorly by every love or romantic interest, except for the one she used as a plot to get back at Richard Wright, and that was Smith Jerrod.

As the girl who had no shame in her sex game, clearly Samantha was the epitome of a woman waving her 1990's (and beyond) sexual liberation flag all around town, challenging even the ideals of the very girls she did life with—Carrie, Charlotte, and Miranda. As every player can tell you, in every game someone's gotta lose; and for Samantha, those losses included Dominic, a former love who'd played her prior to his coming back into her life. She swore she wouldn't fall for him again...until she did; And then there was the hotel tycoon, Richard Wright, the one man she couldn't seem to have, or keep—the one man who used her and had no problem cheating on her before moving on. It crushed her, and eventually, there was one with whom she allowed herself to be vulnerable with—even when she was fighting cancer, and that was Smith, the hot and much younger) actor. It started out as another one of her escapades, but different than the men who behaved like children, Smith was mature for his age, caring, easy-going and forgiving. True to her persona, she resisted Smith, intentionally cheating on him with Richard in an attempt to sabotage the best thing that happened to her on the show—a committed, monogamous relationship with Smith. We hated that she did that to him. It was probably one of her lowest moments on the show—and trust us when we say, there were several low-points to choose from. Ladies, if you're trying to hurt someone for whatever your reason may be, can you stop for a moment and think about what you're doing and why you're doing it? This is one of the times as you're reading, we're asking you to be honest with yourself. Why are you doing it? That is the question you need answered. Keep digging through and peeling that onion on the "why" until you get to the very core and very bottom. Once you've determined the why, that is what needs to be healed. Behaving in a certain way to just to hurt someone is toxic and shouldn't be what we're trying to do. Cyndi already shared in a previous chapter the reason behind her actions in getting revenge on every guy she dated after losing her baby at four months pregnant when she was in her early 20s. She had to be honest with herself as she realized there was hurt festering that needed to be uprooted and healed. We want the same for you and believe that when it comes down to it, you desire the same. Forgiveness, healing, and peace. Going about it Samantha's way won't bring you any of these.

Ivette: Successful, outspoken and uber confident—even I was attracted to those qualities about Samantha. Watching this as a young single woman in the late 90s, I fell in love with the thought of being so confident and successful. However, I was already a mother at the time this show aired and although still single, I was entering that Dorothy Boyd mode of trying to find that perfect man to partner with. So being like Samantha—when it came to her conquests—wasn't what I was striving for.

While there are many who'd shout, "Hip, hip hooray," or "Just do you, boo!" for Samantha's sexual escapades, when we think of Samantha Jones, unfortunately the word, "broken," or "empty" comes to mind. Of the four leading ladies on the show, she is the one seeking out sexual encounters, verbalizing how much she enjoys it. Uninhibited in this area, she is very candid about it, talking about it every chance she gets—even at the expense of the discomfort of others—including her gal pals, who constantly call her out on several inappropriate sexual endeavors.

If you're single and looking to mingle, this is not the girl we want to be. She's constantly got sex on the brain, and yet no matter how much she indulges, she's never satisfied. Why is that? She's still looking for love...in all the wrong ways and in all the wrong places. Let's be real. For most women, sex for sex's sake still leaves you feeling empty and alone. Have you ever felt that way while attempting to live a life of sexual freedom? How do you feel when you leave his place or when he leaves yours? What are the thoughts that have gone through your mind the morning after while doing that walk of shame? That's the part they don't address in movies or television shows, and they're not there to pick up the pieces when women decide that they, too, want the exciting and extravagant life lived out by a character like Samantha. What happens when you wake up and feel used, cheap, or unworthy? Who from the show's production is there to walk you through the aftermath? Only you are, and the sad thing is there's no glamour in it. It doesn't feel great and if this is what we're doing as a cure to loneliness, we as women find that we're still lonely. Once you've been sexually involved with a man, you've left a part and piece of you with him that you can never get back. For a man who isn't committed to you after this has happened, there is pain from the rejection. "I wonder what he's up to this morning ... why hasn't he called?" Some may say, "Oh, that doesn't bother me at all," but at the end of the day, your head's a little lower and your heart feels a little more broken than the day before. A bite has been taken from that forbidden fruit of the tree of life, and now we're stuck with the consequences—be it a broken heart, low self-esteem, an STD, or pregnancy.

We're not trying to be Debbie Downers, but we do want to empower you with honesty and truth. You already know that while we are of the camp that sex should be reserved for the act of marriage. Although we strongly believe that there are reasons for this, we have both experienced the downside of having sex outside of marriage. We both ended up pregnant and unmarried. If you are reading this chapter before the previous chapters, be sure to read the others, so that you're up to speed on how things turned out for the both of us.

Cyndi: Many might say of Samantha, that she owns her sexuality and walks in freedom, but can we be honest here? I don't agree with that. I'd even be so bold as to say that even with all the female empowerment and sexual liberation a woman may "claim" to have, when we take the time to be honest with what we're feeling deep down inside when no one else is around, there is most likely a loneliness that still exists at the core of who you are. I did share earlier on in the book, of how the pain of my miscarriage at the age of 19 caused me to view men as conquests. I wasn't nice about it, either. While some would say that it was sexual freedom, I was out to get revenge, but I'm pretty sure the only person I ended up hurting, was myself. I don't believe women are to carry on in this manner, but when you're broken or hurting, sometimes you're just doing what you can to fill a void or emptiness that can never be filled by what you're seeking out to do. For me, there is only One who could heal me. It was the One who is near the brokenhearted. "He heals the brokenhearted and binds up their wounds." (Psalm 147:3 NIV) I already share how it wasn't until I called out to God to heal the hole in my heart, that I literally felt a peace, warmth, comfort, and healing that I knew was Him. It was too miraculous and supernatural to not be Him. Pain that had been there well over a couple of years, was gone in an instant.

I was recently reading an excerpt from the late Matthew Perry who shared a similar experience in his book, "Friends, Lovers, and the Big Terrible Thing."

> "God, please help me,' I whispered. 'Show me that you are here. God, please help me.' ... As I knelt, the light slowly began to get bigger, and bigger, until it was so big that it encompassed the entire room ... What was happening? And why was I starting to feel better? ... The light engendered a feeling more perfect than the most perfect quantity of drugs I had ever taken ... I must have sat there for five, six, seven minutes, filled with it .... And for the first time in my life, I was in the presence of love and acceptance and filled with an overwhelming feeling that everything was going to be okay ... I started to cry. I mean, I really started to cry – that shoulder-shaking kind of uncontrollable weeping. I wasn't crying because I was sad. I was crying because for the first time in my life, I felt OK. I felt safe, taken care of. Decades of struggling with God, and wrestling with life, and sadness, all was being washed away, like a river

of pain gone into oblivion ... I had been in the presence of God. I was
certain of it. And this time I had prayed for the right thing: help."[18]

We have a God who has the power to heal every wound. He's that loving, kind and that big.
If you, like Samantha, have ventured on many sexual escapades and experiences in the name
of liberation, but still have that ache in your heart when no one else is around, we've got
great news for you. It can change today. Maybe you've already applied some of what we've
worked through from the previous chapters. It will require an honesty and vulnerability that
may not feel easy, but it doesn't matter what you've done, who you've done it with, or how
many times you've done it, if you call out for help, He helps, comforts, forgives and heals
any wounds, brokenness, and shame from our past. Let today be your day of freedom and
newness of life.

WORK IN THE CITY
~ Miranda ~

The girls were all successful women, but none worked harder than Miranda Hobbes—
a lawyer—whose sole goal was to make partner at her firm, and no man was going to get in
the way of her doing that. Unwilling to be taken off her course to success, we find that of all
the characters, she is extremely rigid. Rigid is good, especially for those who are goal-driven,
but where it can be a bit of an issue is when it comes to finding love. For Miranda (played
by Cynthia Nixon), this rang true. All work and little play, this practical thinker among the
four is constant to vocalize logic, sometimes creating conflict when the girls just wanna have
fun (*great* move with Sarah Jessica Parker, by the way). Having a no-nonsense approach to
life, her pragmatic and often dogmatic ways often proved it difficult to allowing herself to
find love, which she eventually does with Steve Brady (played by David Eigenberg), a local
bartender who after somewhat stringing him along (and having his child), falls in love with
him, and makes the compromises necessary to truly share life with your person.

Ivette: Ambitious and direct—these are the only traits that I can relate to with this character.
There is always that one character from a show that doesn't do it for us. And Miranda was
that one for me. Understanding why she was a perfect addition to this cast of characters; I still
could have done without her. Don't get me wrong, Cynthia Nixon did an exceptional job at
bringing Miranda to life, but again, I just wasn't that into her—pun intended.

. . . .
18   Perry, Matthew, "Friends, Lovers, and the Big Terrible Thing: A Memoir," (New York, Flatiron Books, 2022);
Kindle, pages 158 – 159.

Cyndi: Her career is her top priority, and her girls were right up there with it. For Miranda, it was mostly about her career, and her girls. And though I'd love to say I relate most to Carrie for the fashionable creative that she is, I very much connect with parts of Miranda's life in her work ethic and in her approach to love. Extremely dedicated to her work, I can recall several seasons in my professional life where that was all I did. It's not that I was all work, and no play, but I'd work until work was done for the day, and sometimes that meant 2 or 3 in the morning. My most recent experience with this type of lifestyle lasted for a little over three years. I'm embarrassed to say that for those three+ years, I'd regularly put in anywhere from a ten – twenty-hour workday, making for extremely long work weeks. I don't know how I was able to work like that for the length of time that I did. Sometimes I'd still be working when the sun would come up. It was insane and was definitely a grace I'd been given to do what needed to be done (the list is way too long to include here), but I wouldn't recommend working like this. Not only was it taxing on me physically and even emotionally, but there are times I wonder if that work lifestyle was detrimental on the love-life I still don't have. What it did do was put a strain on my best relationships with family and friends, who felt like work was my priority—and it was. Even while on vacation, I didn't quite know how to disconnect. I remember flying out to be with my dad when he was fighting cancer. Although I was working remotely while helping to take him to his various appointments and procedures, when he passed, I remember telling my sister how I wished I would have just used that time as vacation rather working remotely. I could never get that time back with him. That was our last week together. The next time I flew out to see him, he was incoherent and quickly fading. He passed away two days later.

Work will always be there. But those you love won't always be. It's funny how I never realized how similar to Miranda I was when watching the show almost twenty years ago, but in revisiting her character and seeing how married she was to her job, I'm now identifying that is not the character I want to be. Yes, I want to be a hard worker. Working hard is good and necessary. We should take whatever work comes our way, and do it with all our might, heart, and ability, but not at the expense of losing time, moments, and life with those you love. If it's after hours, turn it off. Shut it down. It'll be there tomorrow.

With regards to romance, I definitely identify with Miranda in how frivolous romantic relationships can seem or be. When I was in my 40s and single, I was constantly being asked if I wanted to be in a committed relationship or if I ever wanted to be married. Now in my 50s and still single, I get that question now more than ever. I think I may have mentioned earlier on that when it comes to romance, I have had a properly built—and extremely strong wall around me. Even in all the dating that took place in my life as a preteen into my late 30s, I was the one who set the boundaries on how close I would allow a man to get to me and my heart. This was because of the broken relationships I've already talked in-depth about.

If you, like me, find that you enjoy the feelings of romance, while still keeping those you're dating at arms' length, now might be a good time to find out *why*. For me it initially was fear of vulnerability, and being hurt again and being cheated on as I saw first-hand what that did to my mom, but also as I got older, I'd say two things were added to that: 1) I never wanted a man to be the reason I didn't achieve all the things that were in my heart to do; and 2) The guys for whom the walls never came down, I can honestly admit that I never felt that any were worth them coming down for. I had chosen to guard my heart, but I didn't realize at that time that's what I was doing. Proverbs 4:23 (LSB) says to, "Guard your heart with all diligence, for from it *flow* the springs of life." That being said, I think I was wise to keep the walls up, guarding and protecting my heart. But I will say this, I know now that I am ready for love. And so should the right one finally come along, the walls will willingly come down as Miranda's did, for Steve, who eventually became her "baby daddy."

As for Miranda's life, Steve gets her pregnant, and though she is far from ecstatic about her new state of being, Miranda accepts her pregnancy, deciding she'll power through it as a single mom attorney. We love this decision. Eventually she caves into Steve, who loves her dearly and she asks him to marry her. A "no" in our book, but for the woman who constantly rejected him—possibly even emasculating him in some cases—we will nod to Miranda's proposal to Steve. We see her vulnerability with him coming around. She's evolving, and she eventually finds a way makes room for both, Steve, and work. Complex as all get out, they meet each other halfway in compromises to make it work. This is one of the many things needed—compromise. If you're not willing to meet your person in the middle, you may not be ready for the relationship you think you are. You shouldn't be the one making all the decisions and calling all the shots. If you are still in this mode, there is still work to be done. Don't bring a nice, innocent guy into your mess. Will we ever be perfect? No. But we can at least bring our best to whatever romance life is bringing your way. Make time for some solitude to know where you're at and to understand what you need to do wherever it is you know you need to be. Revisit the chapters while at the park, the beach, or the mountains. Invest in you, making this time special. You are such an amazing woman. We want you to know that. Other people see it even if you don't. And if others around you tell you differently, there is One who will always see you as the apple of His eye. To you He says, "I have called you by name; you are mine. (Isaiah 43:1, NCV) He sees you, knows you and loves you. King David said in Psalm 139:3, NKJV, "You have searched me and known *me*. You know my sitting down and my rising up; You understand my thought afar off. You comprehend my path and my lying down and are acquainted with all my ways." You *are* seen. *You* are seen. You are *seen*. He sees you.

Steve saw Miranda for who she really was. When you are ready to let your walls down, may it be for someone who sees you for who you really are.

One last thing to mention here, why is it that Miranda is the only one who contracted an STD? The way each were provocatively living their lives, it is beyond unrealistic to think that the only one STD—Chlamydia—was contracted. Although Samantha did get tested for HIV, unprotected sexual activity taking place with multiple partners in real life is a recipe for sexually transmitted diseases and disasters. If the writers were going to show the carelessness of their sexual escapades, it would do our impressionable women well to show a little more responsibility and restrain. It is possible.

Cyndi: It's been more than fifteen years since I've been with a man in this way. People may ask if it's difficult. I'd say what's the most difficult about it is just missing the intimacy and something as simple as being held in the arms of a man. I definitely miss that. But I also have no desire to subject myself to sexually becoming one with a man again unless and until it is the one who I believe God has for me. Has it been easy? No, not always. But I am a firm believer that whatever I lack, God has it all to give to me. In my weakness, His strength is made perfect; and not only that, His joy is truly my strength, so it's not a painful thing I'm struggling or heavy-hearted with. It's like anything else that takes work or discipline–I just continue to strengthen that singleness muscle, while enjoying all the beauty in my family, friends and the life I get to live. There is so much joy and contentment in who I am. I've been able to pursue the dreams in my heart and have had some pretty incredible and amazing opportunities. I've been able to travel around the world and be a part of amazing communities, meeting new people and making beautiful friends along the way. The only thing I can attribute it to, is the Lord who has healed my brokenness, who has placed in me a joy, peace, and freedom I've never known. I love the life I am now living. Do I have a past? Yep, we all do. But there is no shame for my past—I'm no longer identified by it. He already paid the price for it, making me new. He wants to do the same for you if you let Him. How do I know? His word says, "...if anyone *is* in Christ, *he is* a new creation; old things have passed away; behold, all things have become new." (2 Corinthians 5:17 NKJV) That's not to say I'm denying that any of these things ever happened, in fact as you've well-read, I am well-aware of what my life once looked like; but what it *does* say is that because I've stepped into receiving what Christ did for me—receiving that by faith—I'm brand new. It's a brand-new Cyndi. I know who I was and what I once did, but that's not who I *am*. If you've never experienced that, you can experience it right now.

"For our sake he made him to be sin who knew no sin, so that in him we might become the righteousness of God." (2 Corinthians 5:21, ESV)

This isn't an altar call, but what it is, is an invitation to a new way of life—from the One who gives it ... from the One who gives life. "I have come that they may have life, and that they may have *it* more abundantly." (John 10:10, NKJV) We're inviting you to experience new levels of joy, peace, freedom, forgiveness, and love from One whose love will never hurt or harm you. It's a love that not only empowers, strengthens, and heals, but it redeems, and knows no end. We pray that as you embark in this journey with us, you personally come to find and know this love. This love is is patient and kind. "It does not envy, it does not boast, it is not proud. It does not dishonor others, it is not self-seeking, it is not easily angered, it keeps no record of wrongs. Love does not delight in evil but rejoices with the truth. It always protects, always trusts, always hopes, always perseveres. It never fails...". (1 Corinthians 13:3-8, NIV) Now, *that's* the kind of love we're after.

Before attaching yourself to another person, it is imperative for you to love *you* for who you are. We know—we've already said this in previous chapters, but it is so worthy to be said again. When you are single, it really is the only time you get to learn about who you are, to embrace all the beautiful and wonderful qualities of who you are, and in most cases, this is done when you are single and by yourself. Sometimes as women we're so busy looking for love, we have not yet taken the time to discover who we are. When we don't know who we are, do we really know what we're looking for in love, or are we just so bent on being in a relationship that we'll take the first thing that comes along? For some, the search for love is painful, experiencing rejection after rejection. For others, things just seem to fall into place. We suggest that this is an example of two fairly whole individuals coming together. And for others who may be true romantics who haven't done the work, it may require a painful journey of trial and error before a true discovery of who you really area manifests in every area of your life. Such is the story of the show's hopeful romantic, Charlotte York.

LOVE IN THE CITY
~ Charlotte ~

If there ever was an on-screen who put all her faith in the one love basket, it was Charlotte York. In love with love, Charlotte (played by Kristin Davis) is an idealist who sets out to find her very own fairy-tale love story playing by the rules as she knew them to be. Characterized by her traditional values, she dreams of finding true love and isn't afraid to say it. Unfortunately for her, in the process of meeting her perfect prince, she kissed (and slept with) one too many toads to find him.

A hopeful romantic (we believe she is more hopeful than hopeless) and one sees the glass as half-full, her biggest obstacle is that she is in constant pursuit of marriage, wondering if almost every guy she dates is "the one." Though she would be depicted as the one who is most conservative, in search of finding her one true love, she too, experiences many romantic highs and lows—with more of the latter than the former. We see her extremely frustrated and at times, at odds with Samantha, as well as the others any time they step outside her self-made lines of what it means to be "prim and proper." With marriage seeming to be her main goal, she was the first of the four to marry on the show, walking down the aisle to Trey MacDougal (played by Kyle MacLachlan)—only to realize it was not at all what she had dreamt or hoped for. Leaving her devastated, the façade came to end as both the interior and beautiful exterior of their marriage ended. For Charlotte who strove for a perfect image to those in their social circles, to those in New York City and to those closest to her, this was devastating and embarrassing. Because of her character's journey of singlehood, vulnerability, heartbreak, divorce, and loss while living on Park Avenue, she is relatable to the girl who is seeking not just any man, but true love with her Prince Charming and man of her dreams. Our heart went out to Charlotte for trying to do it right though things ended horribly in divorce.

Very similar to Kenya, Charlotte, too had her ideal of who she thought she'd spend the rest of her life with. She also had to upkeep her image. Because we've spent a great amount of time on reasons we shouldn't try to endeavor finding love the way our heroines have gone about it, as far as likeable Charlotte goes, while we appreciate her desire to find true love, we have to say we're unimpressed with the Park Ave. home she acquired in her divorce as a result of her very short marriage to Trey. But, as this Dramedy would have it, not only did she get to keep the home, but in the process of fighting for what she believed she deserved from her divorce, she also found love— true love, which *could* have passed her by had she continued on *as* this girl.

I'm way out of your league: Do you know how lucky you are?!

As idealistic as she is romantic, it's no surprised that Charlotte, the socialite who'd kept her eyes on the Prince Charming prize, eventually found true love. However true it may have been, there were several mindsets that needed to change in Charlotte's heart and mind before ending up with the man of her dreams. While he was anything but who or what she thought she would end up with, most would agree that he was "the one" was meant for Charlotte. Let's be clear, we're not talking about settling. We're talking about being open to the best thing that could happen to you, though the package may look slightly different than how you'd envisioned or imagined.

This couldn't have been more obvious than in the case of Charlotte meeting her handsome divorce lawyer, Harry Goldenblatt (played by Evan Handler). Not that we're comparing, but Trey was the epitome of what Charlotte liked appearance-wise. Harry was not. Trey was tall, handsome and had great style. Harry was much shorter, bald and was a profuse sweat-er... yes, as in a man who would constantly sweat. Feeling like she deserved better appearance-wise, she overlooked the simple fact that he was everything she needed (sounds a little like Alex's profession to Isabel in *Fools Rush In*). He was crazy about her, he was kind to her and when she converted to Judaism (he was Jewish), he was over the moon. But the tension of her idealistic man finally got the best of her, and our hearts sank as she asked him (as they were arguing), "Do you know how lucky you are to have me?! ... Do you know what people out there think when they see us together?!?" Oooof. Painful words that she could never take back. What he said, cut right to the heart. "Yeah, I know what people are thinking ... I just didn't think you were one of them." Bam. And just like that, he was gone. Please, don't be this girl.

He had already bought the ring and had planned on asking her to marry him. And for the time they were apart, she was miserable. Sometimes fleshing things out this way is necessary. It gave her clarity about what mattered most and how much she truly loved Harry, regardless of his external appearance. Let it be said that Harry was not a bad-looking guy. In our opinion, he was top notch, just like Charlotte, but he wasn't physically who or what she thought she'd spend the rest of her life with. We are thankful she finally opened herself up to love. Hoping to run into him at a Jewish mixer, it turned out be the best night of her life. He was there. Walking up to him, he tells her, "Out of all the synagogues in all of the cities, you had to walk into mine." The way he looked at her said it all. He's eyes and demeanor are so very gentle with her. He still loved her. Even though she wounded him with what she said to him? Of course. He loved her. He truly did. And she loved him. He was moved by her speech to him about how she was the one who was lucky—we agree! And before you knew it, right there in front of everyone at the mixer, he got down on one knee, and proposed to her, asking her to marry him. She says yes, and so it goes that Charlotte found her Prince Charming after all. Though it took her a hot minute to realize he was the one for her, she found and married her true love, and the man who was meant for her, and she for him. We are proud of Charlotte for opening up her heart and finding the love of her life ... Mazel Tov!

What's the "Big" deal

Okay, so now what? What happens now that we've shared how not be the girl who cheats, has too high of idealistic standards, has affairs, has casual sex with multiple partners, or one works so hard that she makes no time for love. What we aren't saying here, is to be boring and not have a life. We both love life, and all the beauty and complexities it brings, and might even enjoy it more than many. We love life, and as women, we are anything but boring. But there is something to be said here of the overarching theme of how this party of fashionable friends lived their carefree lives as singles in the city. Flawed, they give us wonderful glimpses of girls with fabulous lives from the outside looking in, fumbling, and failing in love and relationships as single girls.

Here are a few questions to think about, and honestly answer.

1. Have you ever hooked up with a guy for just one night?

2. Of that one-night stand, did that evolve into the relationship you'd hoped for?

3. Have you been so desperately in search of love, that you were willing to compromise who you were?

4. Have you ever been scared to fall in love because of the vulnerability it required on your part?

5. Have you ever resisted true love with a man because it didn't look like what you thought he should look like?

6. Looking back (but not for too long), would you have done things differently? Why or why not?

    _____

    _____

7. What are your thoughts about where you are in terms of finding love now? Why do you feel you are or are not ready?

    _____

    _____

8. What needs to happen and what are the changes you know (deep down in your knower) you need to make to be open to true love?

    _____

    _____

9. What will you focus or work on while you continue to remain single?

    _____

    _____

These questions aren't meant to shame you, but our hope is that in answering them, the eyes of your understanding will start to be open and enlightened as to the why so that the relational patterns of destruction can be broken once and for you, helping you find true love for you as an individual, and perhaps love, with another. Although the show revolutionized the way many women saw and conducted themselves, we are firm on the notion that if women seek to find love according to the likes and lives of Carrie, Samantha, Miranda, and Charlotte, there is sure to be heartbreak and quite possibly no love to be found at all, but if it's fashion or friendships you're after, they may be your go-to girls after all.

"

Listen to advice and accept discipline, and at the end you will be counted among the wise.

Proverbs 19:20 (NIV)

In Conclusion

We get that life imitates art, but movies produced by Hollywood aren't reason enough for us to attempt in becoming some of those romcom characters we idolize. We long for—and search for romantic love—but most of what we see on-screen depict clear examples of role models on how *not* to be. We've been influenced by them, and in many cases have made a plethora of mistakes and poor choices in the name of living out these fantasized, romanticized, and idolized character we have identified with on screen. Movies have screenwriters. And as many can attest (and as you've read just some of our personal stories), in real life it almost never turns out the way we've watched things happen on-screen.

So, what now? We take heed, hopefully learning from some of the lessons learned and toxic thought-processes shared in the pages of this book. For those who've caught it, we are thankful and continue to stand with you in your beautiful journey. For those whose hearts have been broken and shredded in search of love, we pray that what we've shared will help to strengthen and encourage you to knowing that healing is readily-available to you for wholeness and peace.

No matter how long the process may take, stay true to you. Don't be in such a hurry to please a man, to win *his* approval while compromising *your* identity. That's identity theft. Don't let your identity be taken from you. That's what happened to Tess, in *27 Dresses*, or even Sandy's very flawed character in *Grease* (which we didn't feature in our book). Drop the need to conform to someone else's desires or expectations in the name of external acceptance and validation. If it's love you're waiting for, then you need to be willing to walk out some of the sacrifices required in finding a love that will last. What does that look like? We'll break it down for you:

- ➢ This means loving and respecting yourself.

- ➢ This means dating someone who respects you.

- ➢ This means patience when you don't want to be.

- ➢ This means having trustworthy people you can be accountable to.

- ➢ This means an unwillingness to be "strung along," in the name of loneliness.

- ➢ This means letting go of something (or someone) that doesn't belong to you.

- ➢ This means becoming whole and secure in yourself for yourself, by yourself.

- ➢ This means doing the work and getting healed in the broken places in your heart.

- ➢ This means waiting for someone worthy of receiving all the love you have to give.

- ➢ This means being true to you, so that you don't conform to how he wants you to be.

- ➢ This means practicing self-control and restraint to protect your heart, mind, soul and body.

Because so many of us idolize and romanticize over several Rom-Com films, and we can think of at least 50 that we both love, we're going to wrap up this book with a fun little exercise. This is the part in the chapter we would love to have *you* list some of *your* favorite Romcom movies or TV shows.

List *your* top ten Romcom Movies or shows. In one to two sentences, write why you love each movie and their leading protagonist. If they have flaws you can identify, be sure to include how you can be different to finding love while *not* being that girl.

1. _____

2. _____

3. _____

4. _____

5. _____

6. _____

7. _____

8. _____

9. _____

10. _____

Beautiful, strong & amazing

What is it that you enjoy about each film? Go back to your list, writing what it is about that you like. What are some of the strong traits of the characters you've listed? Of those characteristics, are there some you'd like to possess but don't see operating in your life? If not, are you willing to try to process that in this season? Also, because self-reflection for change is important to process with at least one safe person, do you have this type of person? If there is hurt or trauma you carry due to any form of abuse, we strongly recommend meeting with a professional. You may already know of someone. We also have a list of handpicked counselors, coaches and courses listed at the end of the book.

In our book we talked about the power of declaring and how for Cyndi, singing the declaration to "set me free," brought her a miraculous and supernatural healing to a relationship that had a whole lotta stringing-her-along going on. Here is our final declaration playlist for you as you move forward in victory. Turn up the volume, sing them loud, dance, cry, clap... do it all, for today is your day. It's your moment of breaking through the stuff that has tied you down and held you back. We have prayed for this moment for you and are right there celebrating with you!

Victory Playlist

- ♫ *I Will Survive* by Gloria Gaynor
- ♫ *You Keep Me Hangin' On* by The Supremes
- ♫ *Ain't No Stoppin' Us Now*
- ♫ *Moving Forward* by Israel Houghton
- ♫ *Victory* by Yolanda Adams
- ♫ *I'm Coming Out* by Diana Ross
- ♫ *Ain't No Stoppin' Us Now* by McFadden & Whitehead
- ♫ *New Season* by Martha Munizzi
- ♫ *In Jesus Name* by Israel Houghton

Proverbs says, "Faithful are the wounds of a friend." And so, as friends who care, we are being honest to bring to light some of the things we may already know but act as though it doesn't apply to us. While some of what we've shared and broken down may feel a bit abrasive or harsh, we hope you hear our hearts behind the words, having shared in a way that was honest, yet somewhat light-hearted. We hope that the stories will get you thinking, reflecting and being honest with yourself and those you love. In all our years of coaching women crying in a car, on the couch, or at the table, it was time. It was time for us to address how we, as women can stop making the mistakes over and over again. If we want different results, we must do things differently. We can't keep doing what we already know does not work. Just because we've seen it play out on-screen, it most certainly doesn't mean that is how things will end up for you.

We love reading and we love books, so this was our joy to write and share our thoughts and stories with you. Our hope is that this gets planted in your heart and in the deepest part of who you are, that this sticks and is more than just a fad or a trend, but a movement. A movement where women of all ages realize their beauty and worth apart from a man. A movement inviting others into *Don't Be This Girl* book clubs, empowering women around the world, to do what we've known to do all along. A movement on behalf of every woman, regardless of how she feels about herself, says, "Though I've allowed myself to be in horrible and disrespecting relationships, I can no longer be this girl. And for that to change, I will have to see myself differently. I need to know that I am of value and worth, regardless of what's been done to me in the past, regardless of what others have said about me, and even regardless of how I have seen myself or what I've done. I am not that person and don't have to live as if I am. I am of worth and value, and I refuse to be in any relationships that treat me less than who I am—a beautiful, strong, talented, amazing, woman."

That is who you truly are.

Meet The Authors

CYNDI GALLEY

A dynamic communicator with a zeal to strengthen people to being their best version of themselves, Cyndi's energetic style is one that brings hope, strength and vision to the human heart and soul, through her contagious joy, passion for life and people! Desiring to see people empowered, healed, and whole, walking in true freedom, Cyndi is on a mission to share truths found in God's word, keeping it real, compelling, and fun! An avid reader ever since she can remember, Cyndi is the Founder and Editor-in- Chief of *Teen Fashioned* and *Fashioned*™ Magazines, publications reaching pre-teens and young women through fashion, faith, and fashion shows; and more recently published her first book, *A Tale of a Praying Princess*, a children's book for little girls.

Single and never married, Cyndi understands the plight that singleness sometimes accompanies. Coaching women of all ages, she

can be found encouraging and strengthening women to maximizing living their best lives now through speaking on podcasts, at conferences, events, retreats, as well as on her talk show, *A New Thing LIVE*, which can be seen on her YouTube Channel. Co-Producer and Director of a Documentary-Drama, she is the voice of *She is Single, She is Strong*,™ a movement encouraging single women to be strong in a society that may say otherwise. Believing the best in everyone she meets, Cyndi cheerleads individuals from all walks of life to fulfill their dreams using their God-given gifts and talents.

Receiving her bachelor's degree from Azusa Pacific University in Azusa, CA and her Master of Divinity Degree from Oral Roberts University in Tulsa, OK, Cyndi is an ordained minister with the Foursquare Denomination and has been in ministry for over 24 years. An advocate for higher education, she has also served as an Adjunct Professor at LIFE Pacific University. Fun facts: Cyndi co-wrote a song, *Now More Than Ever*, used in a short film, *What I See*. Cyndi was 14 when she found herself in a recording studio, later launching her first cassette album, "He's So Good," produced by Kuka Records, a label owned by her biological father. Cassettes of this album are still floating about the world today.

For more information about Cyndi, upcoming projects, and her organization, visit newgalglobal.com.

IVETTE P. OSBORNE

Ivette is a remarkable woman whose life journey has been nothing short of extraordinary. As a single mother, part time actress, CEO of a nonprofit organization, wife, grandmother and a passionate advocate for health and wellness, Ivette's story is one of resilience, ambition, and unwavering determination.

As a young mother, she found herself navigating the demanding world of single parenthood, a role that would shape her character and instill in her the values of perseverance and responsibility. Trapped in the party life, her love for her child was the driving force behind a complete lifestyle-change and unwavering commitment to create a legacy for him and generations to come.

Her love of the arts and music led her to pursue 14 years of backup singing and was featured on an album, called, "A Thankful People" a live album, recorded in Orange County, CA. Once her son had flown the nest, she propelled herself into a career in acting and modeling. Ivette's desire to make a positive impact on the world didn't stop in the arts. As a strong believer and a sense of social responsibility, she transitioned into the nonprofit sector, after serving in her community for many years. As the CEO of "From A Friend" she is dedicated to help her community and beyond, by acting with gifts and services of love. Ivette's commitment to health and wellness is more than just a personal interest; it is a way of life. She made it a mission to inspire others to live healthier and happier lives. She's committed her time to teaching and enjoys speaking on health at various events for organizations.

She is currently working on two book projects that will come out soon after this book is released. Stay tuned!

Resources

COACHING + COUNSELING

Finding Love For Today® Women's Organization
Dr. Shanda Y. Smith, Founder, PhD., LMFT
Website: flftwo.org
Email: info@flftwo.org

Mayra Bedolla-Lopez, LMFT
Website: newbeginningscounseling.net
Email: Mayra@newbeginningscounseling.net

Robia Scott
Success Coach, Author, Speaker, Actress
Website: rrobiascott.com
Email: contact@robiascott.com

Debbie Campbell, Certified Life Coach
M.A., Christian Counseling, Mental Health Counselor
Specializing in general counseling + crisis-counseling
Email: deecee@deeceelifestreams.com

Katrina Yniguez
Success Coach, Author, Speaker, Trainer
Website: YKatrina.life
Email: connect@ykatrina.life

COURSE + COMMUNITY

She is Single, She is Strong ™ e-Course & Community
Website: sheissinglesheisstrong.org
Email: sheissinglesheisstrong@gmail.com
IG: @sheissinglesheisstrong

Movie Bibliography

Chapter One: *The Holiday*
The Holiday, Directed by Nancy Meyers, Columbia Pictures, 2006.

Chapter Two: *Bridget Jones's Diary*
Bridget Jones's Diary, Directed by Sharon Maguire, Miramax, 2001.

Chapter Three: *Sabrina (1995)*
Sabrina, Directed by Sydney Pollack, Constellation Entertainment, 1995.

Chapter Four: *27 Dresses*
27 Dresses, Directed by Anne Fletcher, Fox Pictures, 2008.

Chapter Five: *My Best Friend's Wedding*
My Best Friend's Wedding, Directed by P.J. Hogan, TriStar Pictures, 1997.

Chapter Six: *Runaway Bride*
Runaway Bride, Directed by Gary Marshall, Paramount Pictures. 1999.

Chapter Seven: *Leap Year*
Identity Crisis, Directed by Shari Rigby, The Boylan Sisters, 2023.
Leap Year, Directed by Anand Tucker, Universal Pictures, 2010.

Chapter Eight: *Something New*
Something New, Directed by Sanaa Hamri, Gramercy Pictures, 2006.

Chapter Nine: *Fools Rush In*
Fools Rush In, Directed by Andy Tennant, Columbia Pictures, 1997.

Chapter Ten: *Jerry Maguire*
Jerry Maguire, Directed by Cameron Crowe, TriStar Pictures, 1996.

Chapter Eleven: *The Way We Were*
The Way We Were, Directed by Sydney Pollack, 1973.

Chapter Twelve: *Sex and the City*
Sex and the City, TV Show Created by Darren Star, Darren Star Productions, distributed by HBO, 1998 – 2004.

Recommended Reads

- *Boundaries* by Dr. Henry Cloud & John Townsend

- *Break Up with What Broke You* by Christian Bevere

- *Counterfeit Comforts: Freedom from the Imposters that Keep You From True Peace, Purpose and Passion* by Robia Scott

- *Do It Afraid* by Joyce Meyer

- *Do You Want to Be Perfect?: A Perfectionist's Journey to Perfect* by Rachel Caban

- *How Could You Do That?* by Dr. Laura Schlessinger

- *I'll Hold You in Heaven* by Jack Hayford

- *Kingdom Singles* by Dr. Tony Evans

- *Motivated by the Impossible: Recognizing Your Invisible Mentors* by Ceitci Demirkova

- *Prodigal Daughter: A Journey Home to Identity* by Cynthia Garrett

- *PROOF: Obedience Over Fear: Life Outside the Comfort Zone* by Katrina Yniguez

- *Seven Habits of Highly Effective People* by Stephen Covey

- *Ten Stupid Things Women Do to Mess Up Their Lives* by Dr. Laura Schlessinger

- *The True Measure of a Woman: You Are More Than What You See* by Lisa Bevere

- *The Five Love Languages* by Gary Chapman

- *A Tale of a Praying Princess* by Cyndi Galley

"A good woman is hard to find, and worth far more than diamonds…".

Proverbs 31:10 (MSG)

Made in United States
Troutdale, OR
12/04/2023

15316198R10142